Labor & Industry In Iran
1850–1941

by
WILLEM FLOOR

MAGE
PUBLISHERS

Copyright © 2009 Willem Floor

All rights reserved.
No part of this book may be reproduced
or retransmitted in any manner whatsoever,
except in the form of a review, without the
written permission of the publisher.

Library of Congress Cataloging-in-Publication Data

Floor, Willem M.
 Labor & industry in Iran, 1850-1941 / by Willem Floor.
    p. cm.
 Includes bibliographical references and index.
 ISBN 978-1-933823-28-7 (soft cover : alk. paper)
 1. Industries--Iran--History. 2. Labor--Iran--History. I. Title. II. Title: Labor
and industry in Iran, 1850-1941.
 HC473.F57 2009
 388.095509'034--dc22
                                                    2008050186

Printed and Manufactured in the United States

Mage books are available at bookstores,
through the internet, or directly from the publisher:
Mage Publishers, 1032 29th Street, NW, Washington, DC 20007
202-342-1642 • as@mage.com • 800-962-0922
visit Mage Publishers online at
www.mage.com

CONTENTS

PREFACE XI

CHAPTER ONE 1

  TRADITIONAL CRAFTS AND THE RISE OF MODERN FACTORIES 1
    Introduction 1
    The Decline of Traditional Crafts 3
    The Recovery of Many Traditional Crafts 6
    The Rise of Modern Industry 9
    The Impact of Modern Industry 19
    Reasons For Failure of Modern Industry 25

  CONCLUSION 28

CHAPTER TWO 29

  LABOR UNIONS, LAW AND CONDITIONS IN IRAN (1900–1941) 29

    PART 1. LABOR UNIONS 29
      Introduction 29
      The Beginnings of The Labor Movement (1906–1911) 31
      The Golden Age (1918–1925) 39
        The Situation in Tehran 39
        The Situation in Gilan 50
        The Situation in Tabriz 52
        The Situation in Mashhad 53
        The Situation Elsewhere 54
        The Situation in the APOC Area 54
      Guild Unions 58

The Reign Of Reza Shah (1925–1941) 59
Introduction 59
The Situation in Tehran 60
The Situation in Gilan 63
The Situation in Mashhad 65
The Situation in Tabriz 66
The Situation in the APOC Area 66
The 1929 Strike at Abadan 67
The Vatan Strike at Isfahan 75
The Suppression of the Unions 79
The Reasons for the Failure of Unions in Iran 79

Part II. Labor Law 84
Introduction 84
First Legislative Attempts (1900-1914) 85
Proposed Reform By Ziya Al-Din's Cabinet (1921) . . . 86
The First Debate In The Majles (1923) 87
Regulations For The Carpet Industry 87
The First Social And Labor Laws (1931–1941) 93
The Factory Act 95

Part III. Labor Conditions 96
Introduction 96
Working Hours 97
Occupational Safety and Health 98
Wages and Purchasing Power 100
A Royal Misstep 102
Social Conditions 107

CHAPTER THREE 113

INDUSTRIALIZATION IN IRAN 1900-1941 113
Introduction 113
The Labor Force Prior to 1914 114
Introduction 114
Traditional Industrial Activities 1900–1925 117
Pressure For Industrialization, 1922–1940 122
The Big Leap Forward (1930–40) 127
The Iron works 139
Conclusion 140

CHAPTER FOUR 143

FINANCE AND FOREIGN EXCHANGE FOR INDUSTRIALIZATION
IN IRAN. 1310–1319 (1931/2-1940/1), BY PATRICK CLAWSON & WILLEM FLOOR . 143

 INTRODUCTION 143
  Industrial Development And Its Financing 144
  Acquiring Foreign Exchange For Development 149
   The Pattern And Direction Of Exports And Finance 151
   Inducing Business To Export And Economize On Imports 158
  Conclusion 161

 APPENDICES
  A: *List of Existing Factories in Iran (1311/1932)* 163
  B: *List of Factories in Iran in 1940* 169
  C: *Official Note that Foreigners Need to Get Permission to Establish a Factory* 176
  D: *Program of the Ranjbaran (Workmen's) Party of Persia* 177
   Object 177
   Organization and Principle 177
   Fundamental 178
   Organization of the Government 178
   Military 179
   Justice 179

BIBLIOGRAPHY 181

INDEX 191

TABLES, APPENDICES & FIGURES

TABLES

1.1: Main Exports of Iran (in percent) 9
1.2: New Factories Built in Iran (Type, Location, Year, Investor) 13
1.3: European Type Factories in Iran and their Number of Workers 20
1.4: Composition of the Urban Labor Force in Iran (Around 1910) 22
1.5: Capital Investment in some Modern Factories in Iran (1850-70) 23
1.6: Direct Foreign Investment in Modern Industry in Iran (1890s) 23

2.1: Trade Unions and their Membership in Tehran 41
2.2 Trade Unions Represented on the Central Council in 1922 42
2.3: APOC Staff and Labor in Iran 1910-32 67
2.4: Growth of Large-Scale Factories and their Labor Force 1930–40 80
2.5: Workers in the Cotton Industry, by Sex 81
2.6: Wages for Day-laborers for 10 hour Working-day (1935-1937) 102
2.7: Average Wages in Riyals in the Isfahan Textile Mills 103
2.8: Daily Expenditure of a Family of Four in Khuzestan 1931 104
2.9: Prices of Necessities of Life Consumed by the Lower Classes in Isfahan . . 104
2.10: Typical Dietary Pattern in Urban Iran/Fars Province 1962-68 105
2.11: Prices of Articles Of Prime Necessity in Tabriz 106
2.12: Houses Built by the APOC at Abadan 109
2.13 Iranian and Foreign Workers Employed by the APOC at Abadan 110

3.1: The Population of Iran and Its Urban-Rural Distribution 115
3.2: Changes, by Branch of Activity, in The Structure of The Active Population in Developing Countries with Market Economies, 1900–1950 115
3.3: Employment in Selected Urban Economic Activities in Iran (Circa 1910) . . 116
3.4: Number Of Factories And Their Labor Force In Tabriz (1922) 118
3.5: Large-Scale Factories in Iran and their Labor Force 119
3.6: Employment in Tehran in The Traditional Industrial Sector (1925) 121
3.7: Number of Masters in The Traditional Industrial Sector of Isfahan (1924) . . 122
3.8: Employment in Selected Urban Economic Activities in Iran, 1940 133

3.9: Composition of The Industrial Labor Force in Iran 1940 (Military) Estimate . . .133

3.10: Employment in Selected Urban Industrial Activities (1940) 134

3.11: Growth of The Labor Force in Modern Industry Per Sector 1914-1939 . . .135

3.12: Number of Looms in The Carpet Industry (Urban And Rural) 1940 137

3.13: Budget Allocation per Sector. 138

3.14: Iran General and Industrial Companies Registered 139

4.1: Iran: Railroad Construction Finances, 1925-39 145

4.2: Iran: Budget for Investment by Government in Industry, 1310–1319 147

4.3: Iran: Increase in Share Capital in Private Industrial Firms, 1314–19 148

4.4: Iran: Balance Sheet of Major Banks, 1933 149

4.5: Iran: Composition of Imports, 1310–19 (1) 150

4.6: Iran: Balance of Payments, 1307 (1928/29) 152

4.7: Iran: Balance of Payments, 1310–19 (1931/32–1940/41) 154

4.8: Iran: Direction of Exports, 1310-19 (1). 154

4.9: Iran: Foreign Trade in 1310–19 (1931/32–1940/41) 156

4.10: Iran: Import Duties, 1310–19 (1931/32 - 1940/41) (1) 159

4.11: Iran: Exchange Rates, 1310-19 (1931/32 – 1940/41) 161

APPENDICES

A: List of Existing Factories in Iran (1311/1932). 163

B: List of Factories in Iran in 1940. 169

C: Official Note That Foreigners Need To Get Permission To Establish A Factory. . .176

D: Programme of the Ranjbaran (Workmen's) Party of Persia. 177

FIGURES

1.1: Woodworking machines in the Alleman, Mossig & Schünemann factory
in Tabriz (1910), from Walther Kuss, *Handelsratgeber für Persien* (Berlin, 1911). . 24

1.2: The interior of a modern spinning factory in Tabriz (1912), from Eberhard-
Joachim Graf von Westarp, *Unter Halbmond und Sonne* (Berlin, 1913). . . . 24

1.3: One of the new factories built in 1935, in this case the exterior
of a cotton mill in Isfahan. 112

1.4: The cotton spinning machinery inside the Isfahan mill 112

PREFACE

In this volume I have brought together a number of my publications that deal with: (1) the decline of many of traditional crafts and the first Iranian effort to become an industrializing country during the nineteenth century; (2) the development and unionization efforts of its labor class, the first attempts to enact labor laws as well as the working and living conditions of the factory workers; (3) the second and more successful implementation of an industrialization program during the third decade of the twentieth century, and (4) how Iran mainly financed this large-scale industrialization development from its own national resources, thus pulling itself up by its bootstraps.

Chapter one has been previously published in the *Zeitschrift der Morgenländische Gesellschaft* (ZDMG) and I thank the editor of the journal for having given me permission to republish them in this volume.[1] Chapters two, three and four have been previously published in the Occasional Paper Series of the Centre for Middle Eastern and Islamic Studies of the University of Durham (UK)[2] and they appear here with the permission of the director of the said Centre. The article in chapter four was co-authored with Patrick Clawson.

I have made no changes in the text, although here and there an editorial correction may have been made. The only new item that has been added is appendix four which reproduces the program of the Workmen's Party of Mashhad.

I hope that this publication will stimulate further study and research of the labor class and industrial development in Iran.

---

1. Floor 1991; it was earlier republished as chapter one in Floor 2003 b.
2. Floor 1984; Floor 1985 a; and Floor-Clawson 1986.

CHAPTER ONE

TRADITIONAL CRAFTS AND THE RISE OF MODERN FACTORIES

"In Persia there are no statistics, nevertheless the economic phenomena are by no means uninstructive."

J. Rabino

In this chapter an overview is given of the nature and structure of traditional crafts in Qajar Iran, how they were impacted by foreign imports. Although many declined in importance others grew into prominence. Also, government policy to counter foreign influence and imports is discussed, in particular the decision to import European technology, the impact of public sector intervention and that of direct foreign investment on industrial activity, as well as the reasons for failure of that policy and these investments.

INTRODUCTION

The dominant sector of the economy in Qajar Iran was agriculture. This was not only reflected in the distribution of the population, but also in the way the labor force was gainfully employed. Although exact data are not available it is estimated that around 1800 about 90% of the population lived in the rural areas. Probably all of them were engaged in agricultural activities as well as in non-agricultural production for part of their time. Around the 1860s it was estimated that at least 85% of the total labor force was engaged in agricultural production, whilst the remaining 15% was employed in non-agricultural urban activities, viz. handicrafts and services. In 1908 the Persian government estimated that only 70% of the labor force was engaged in agricultural production, so that during the period under study the agricultural force had decreased by some 20%.[1] Conversely, the other sectors in the economy, mainly industry and services, had increased in importance; at least where the size of the labor force is concerned.

---

1. Gilbar 1976, 125-156.

One may not, however, conclude from this alleged increase in the share of industry in the total labor force as an increase of the industrialization of Iran. Nor may it be concluded from the decline of traditional handicrafts that Iran was experiencing a process of de-industrialization. Although there is no doubt that traditional industries suffered ruin and decline as a result of penetration of the Persian market by European machine-made goods, one may not conclude from this that, for example, Iran became increasingly agricultural in nature. However, we lack the statistical data to argue such a contention, let alone to prove it. Nevertheless it is possible to show some insight in the economic processes that took place in 19th century Iran, and whether 'industry', declined. It may never be possible to ascertain the extent of [de-] industrialization that Persian industry experienced, but that there was some decline during part of the 19th century appears to be likely. It is this question to which we will address ourselves.

In what follows there is a discussion of (a) the decline of traditional crafts between 1830-1860, including the possible reasons for this decline as well as what measures the government of Iran took to reverse this trend as well as of (b) the introduction of modern European manufacturing technology and its impact on the economy. Although foreign imports caused the ruin of many Persian crafts, foreign capital was partly responsible for the recovery as well as for the coming into being of some new crafts. In particular, the spectacular rise of carpet manufacturing is discussed. The government of Iran's countervailing measures against the influx of foreign imports included trade protection and an action for 'buy Persian made goods,' and the introduction of modern European manufacturing technology. All these policy and technical interventions failed to have the desired objective of stopping the tide of European imports. It may be said that Iran experienced three periods of attempts to introduce European technology into Iran during the period 1800-1914. Each of these periods shows an increased intensification of these efforts, both qualitatively and quantitatively speaking. These periods also show a direct relationship with the degree and nature of European expansion in Iran and the increased contacts between Iran and European states.

The first period ran from 1800 to 1848, the second from 1848 to 1870, and the third from 1870 to 1914. These periods, of course, overlap with one another, but they have sufficient different characteristics, which make it appropriate to mark them off from one another. Roughly one may characterize these three periods as follows: in the first one it was tried to introduce technology to modernize the army to withstand the European (especially Russian) penetration. In the second period the main thrust of modernization was aimed at import substitution and self-reliance, while in the third period direct European investment on a considerable scale took place.

Finally, the impact of modern industry and the reasons for the failure of Iran's modern industry to take off are discussed. Despite the considerable investments that took place in the modern industrial sector there was little effect in terms of industrial output, trade, or employment. Iran's modern industry suffered from lack of effective protection, bad site and project planning and bad project implementation, which factors compounded infrastructural shortcomings (energy, roads, skills, labor) of the Persian economy. As a result, it were the traditional crafts rather than modern industry that continued to provide employment to the growing urban and peri-urban labor force.

THE DECLINE OF TRADITIONAL CRAFTS

In describing the economy of Qajar Iran practically all commentators, be they Persian or foreigner, provide evidence of the decline of traditional crafts in Iran. This was caused by the increased competition from European imports, at a time when Persian industry had recovered from almost a century of devastation caused by invasions and wars of succession.

Although European trade played as yet no important role in Iran during the first three decades of the 19th century the signs of things to come could already be seen. Trade with Iran was regarded both by Russia and Great Britain to be of marginal importance. This is clearly demonstrated by the commercial treaty of 1828 between Iran and Russia, which in practice was turned into an advantage for Persian rather than for Russian merchants. It was only when Russia began to take an interest in Iran as an outlet for its industrial products that this situation was changed. The same lack of interest may be noted in the British case, where Iran was regarded as an object of political rather than of commercial interest.[2]

Although, European trade might "as yet be in its infancy a taste for European goods is but arising; it requires to be fed gradually and judiciously, until it becomes matured into a steady and regular demand. To do this it is necessary to become acquainted with the wants and habits of the people, and to remove, where it may be practicable, the obstacles which trade has to contend with."[3]

The avalanche of European imports did not take very long to come into being; in fact it had already started when Fraser wrote these words. For during the 1820s Persian manufacturers had become so alarmed about the quantity of textiles, which were imported from Europe "that they had petitioned the king to put a stop to the importation."[4]

However, the real onslaught began during the 1830s and especially in the 1840s when increased consumption of European manufactured goods had a dampening effect on the output of Persian crafts. This development was the result of a rise in industrial production and in the export of in particular cotton textiles in Great Britain. Also, Great Britain increasingly took a commercial interest in Iran and started to prepare the ground to remove obstacles for its trade. Not being protected like Russian traders by a commercial treaty, Great Britain tried to obtain the same privileges for its own traders. Although the *raqam* (decree) granted by ʿAbbas Mirza, the heir apparent, for the protection of British trade in northern Iran in 1833 for all practical purposes put them at the same footing as Russian traders, the British government nevertheless, urged by its chargé d'affaires in Tehran, wanted more. In fact, it wanted "most favored nation treatment."[5]

Mohammad Shah (r. 1838–48), however, opposed such an agreement arguing that "as the balance of the money trade was against Persia, any measure that encouraged the extension of trade with manufacturing nations would be injurious, the only exception admitted was the import of arms and military stores, the main point used by the Persian ministers in support of these principles were: the scarcity of coin in Persia; the want of mines of pre-

---

2. Lambton 1970, 224, 229; Entner 1956.
3. Fraser 1826, 378.
4. Fraser 1826, 368.
5. Lambton 1970, 228.

cious metals, the impossibility of making returns in produce, and the discouragement of domestic, from the influx of foreign, manufactures."[6]

The Persian government not only wanted to protect its domestic market against foreign imports because of economic reasons, but also because it feared political problems with Russia. In particular, it was afraid for new demands from Russia, if the latter perceived the rights granted to Great Britain as being more favorable than the ones Russia enjoyed.[7] Therefore, to support his national industry "the Shah takes every means to check the consumption of European manufactures, and to encourage those of Persia; to effect the latter purpose he has recently advanced money, and offered rewards to the makers of chintz, and he has insisted that the courtiers shall gradually substitute Persian woollens and Kerman shawls for the broadcloth now used in their dress. These attempts to compel the use of inferior, and, in fact, more costly articles of home production, in lieu of the superior and cheaper manufactures of foreign countries, find no support beyond the circle of the Court, and will fail in attaining their object."[8]

That Mohammad Shah failed was not for want of trying, but because of the economic system of Iran, especially its lack of possibilities for effective protection of its national industry. Moreover, such incentives as were given for innovation and better competition were of marginal importance and of an incidental nature. As we will see below these measures did not constitute an integrated component of a comprehensive reform policy, which was geared to the development of the Persian economy.

When Mohammad Shah's trifling economic measures failed to obtain the intended results it was not surprising that when in 1837 Persian merchants protested against the establishment of European trading houses in Tabriz both the prime minister and the Shah did not react favorably to these requests.

> The former is said to have remarked that he had once wished to see a stop put to European Trade and people were told not to purchase European goods, but that they did so secretly notwithstanding. The Shah is reported to have said that he had in vain endeavoured to encourage Manufactures in this Country and that he now must be content with the increased Duties which the European Trade brought to the State, however much the Country suffered by that Trade.[9]

From that moment, i.e., 1837 onwards, European trade increasingly penetrated into the Persian market. Although Mohammad Shah had given up the fight against European economic penetration the Persian manufacturers and traders carried on a rear-guard action. In 1844 the British consul in Tabriz reports that the merchants had asked the government to prohibit imports of European manufactures "on the ground principally of

---

6. Issawi 1971, 78.
7. Lambton 1970, 231.
8. Issawi 1971, 78-79.
9. Issawi 1971, 112.

the ruin Persian manufacturers are reduced to by the constant and immense importation of foreign goods."[10] This attempt, as well as a similar one in Kashan, failed to obtain government support.

Around 1849, the pinch of European imports was hurting Persian crafts quite badly. According to Consul Abbott, there were in Kashan only 800 silk looms where formerly there had been 8,000 silk looms. In Isfahan, unrestricted trade in foreign goods had seriously hurt local manufactories. In Yazd, crafts also were in decline.[11] However, the best document on the decline of crafts in Iran is Mirza Hoseyn Khan Tahvildar's *Joghrafiya-ye Isfahan* in which he, amongst other things, discusses some 160 guilds in Isfahan during the late 1870s.[12] There was hardly a craft that had not been damaged and had not suffered ruin, because of a change in taste, because of import of cheaper European goods, and because of the competition with these same goods in foreign markets. To get an impression of the seriousness of the ruin of many crafts a detailed list of these crafts described by Tahvildar is given in what follows:[13]

The *qadak* dyers (*sabbagh-e qadak*) have been halved; the confectioners (*qannad*) have decreased in number bringing ruin to the artisans; of the makers of chintz (*chitsaz*) not even half of the original number remain, the potters (*fakhkhar*) have been more than halved; of the oil-millers (`*assar-e rowghan*) only one-third has remained; the jewelers (*hakkak*) have become insignificant; the silver wire and gold wire drawers (*simkash* and *zarkash*) are only a few now; the gold brocade weavers (*zaribaf*) have been completely ruined and the craft has now fallen into disuse; the gold lace makers (*golabtunduz*) now number only a few and their products are not much in demand; the silver brocade makers (*naqdehduz*) have declined considerably; the same holds for the crocheters (*qollabduz*) and the makers of London cloth (*londrehduz*). The hat makers' (*kolahduz*) work is not much in demand anymore and their guild has been ruined; the fur hat makers (*kolichehduz*) have become few in number and their work is not much in demand anymore; the same holds for the *khaz* (silken stuff) makers (*khazduz*), fur cloak makers (*pustinduz*), leather shoe makers (*charmiduz*), boot makers (*chakmehduz*) and women's shoemakers (*gorjiduz*). The craft of the embroiderers (*naqshduz*) has completely fallen into disuse and the same holds for the one-tenth makers (*dah-yakduz*), the sequin sewers (*pulakduz*) and the flower sewers (*golchehduz*). Especially the crafts of the weavers (*nassaj*) had suffered; their craft constituted at least 10% of the total labor force in Isfahan and by 1877 not even one-fifth of the weavers had remained. The related guilds such as dyers, washer men, and cotton dressers had also been ruined. Women in particular were hit by the ruin of these crafts, and most of them were out of a job and had no means of livelihood anymore. The decline of the silk weavers (*sha`rbaf*) was even worse than that of the weavers. Of the 1250 looms around 1830 only 460 remained during the early 1840s, while at the end of that decade their number had even been further reduced to 249; in 1877 only 12 remained. The weavers of *meshki* (*meshkibaf*) were also completely ruined and the same holds for the weavers of *jahk* and

---

10. Issawi 1971, 103-104.
11. Issawi 1971, 267-268.
12. Tahvildar 1341.
13. The following selection has been taken from Tahvildar 1341.

ehrami. Handwritten book production had fallen into disuse, because of the introduction of lithography. The cotton beaters (*naddaf*) depended on the weavers and had declined proportionally. The making of *givehs* (cotton shoes) also had declined to one-tenth of its original output. The gold smiths (*zargar*) had declined much and the same held true for the gold engravers (*naqqash-e zargar*). The paper makers were not doing very well either, while the knife makers (*kardgar*) had also diminished in importance. Of the darners (*rafugar*) only two remained of the many that had been engaged in this craft. The sword cutlers (*shamshirsaz*) were only a few in numbers, the same held for the gunsmiths (*tofangsaz*). Of the gun-hammer smiths (*chakhmaqsaz*) only a few remained, of the water-pipe hose makers (*neypichaz-e qalyan*) not even half had remained. The making of chain mail (*zerehsaz*) had fallen into disuse; the same held for the helmet and cuirass makers (*kolah-e khod va chahar a'inehsaz*) as well as for the bowyers (*kamansaz*). Of the scissors makers (*qeychisaz*) some part was left; the mirror makers (*a'inehsaz*) had been reduced from many to five shops. The shoe heel makers (*pashnehsaz*) were less numerous than they used to be. The *khatam* (kind of mosaic) makers (*khatamsaz*) had become less important than they used to be. Compared with former times the carpenters (*najjar*) had declined too half their former number. The stone-cutters (*hajjar*) had been reduced to one-third of their original number, while of the architects (*me'mar*) only four to five remained. Of the masons (*banna*) only half had remained compared with the situation of 20 years ago, according to Tahvildar.

THE RECOVERY OF MANY TRADITIONAL CRAFTS

Although the picture drawn by Tahvildar of the crafts in Isfahan is a dismal one it would be wrong to draw general conclusions from it. Although there is no denying that a similar process was also taking place in other towns in Iran it is quite likely that these suffered less than Isfahan. In Yazd, for example, they continued to use native yarns for weaving, while elsewhere-foreign yarns were used.[14] Tahvildar also states that many of the unemployed craftsmen migrated to Tehran, Tabriz and towns in Khorasan, which apparently still offered employment opportunities.[15]

Moreover, in some cases craftsmen were able to increase the importance of their craft and their output, as well employment. Such was the case with the tinsmiths (*halabisaz*) which craft did not exist prior to the 1850s and had come into being in Isfahan, from where it spread to the rest of Iran.[16] Another new craft that came into existence was that of the makers of Russian shoes (*orusiduz*), which formed quite a large guild in 1877 in Isfahan.[17] The brass workers (*davatgar*) who formed a small group formerly had increased considerably by 1877 due to the introduction of the samovar.[18] Even more successful were the weavers of `abas (`ababaf) who formerly likewise formed a small group only, but by 1877 had become a

---

14. *Berichte* 1910, 412.
15. Tahvildar 1341, 97, 98, 103, 108, 112.
16. Tahvildar 1341, 109.
17. Tahvildar 1341, 98.
18. Tahvildar 1341, 106.

very big and important guild, which sold its produce all over Iran.[19] Their importance was in fact even greater in the countryside around Isfahan, for "it gives employment to the women of the district, some 30,000 looms, it is said, exist in the various villages, in the town itself there are none."[20] The last part of this statement was not true anymore by 1910, for by then there were 120 master weavers of `abas in the city of Isfahan.[21]

Similar remarks can be made about other crafts in the different towns of Iran showing that some crafts were holding their own or were even able to expand their output. The most important manufacturing branch, however, was that of carpet-weaving, which experienced an unexpected and enormous rise in output during the last quarter of the 19th century.[22]

Although carpets already figured among Persian exports to India and Turkey in the beginning of the 19th century carpet weaving nevertheless did not represent an important craft in Iran.[23] It was only after 1873 that carpets started and continued to have an ever-increasing role in Persian exports. An increased interest in oriental carpets was only to be noticed in Europe after the World Trade Fair of 1851, and this especially held for old and antique carpets. The demand for Persian carpets, however, increased substantially after the World Trade Fair of 1873 in Vienna. The display of a collection of many costly antique Persian carpets created a demand for this commodity. This demand fortunately coincided with growing affluence in Europe and the United States and with the need of European merchants trading in Iran for export products.[24]

Already in 1840 British commercial interests found that "the importance of finding in the productions of Persia some available return for British manufactures is daily becoming more evident, not only because of the deficiency of bullion, in which the returns have up to this time chiefly been made, but also because of the extreme jealousy with which the Government regards British Commerce in consequence of the great quantity of the precious metals which it yearly carries but of the Kingdom."[25] This situation had not changed some thirty years later and in fact had acquired more weight. For, because of the lack of a formal banking system, as well as the credit system, which prevailed in Iran, it was more profitable for European merchants to convert their proceeds into Persian commodities for which there was a demand abroad. Another reason was the continuing depreciation of the Persian currency, which made the purchase of Persian products relatively cheap, and the export of specie even less interesting.[26]

Thus, it may be said that the European economic penetration of the Persian market did not only have negative consequences for the Persian economy. For foreign capital played a decisive role in developing the carpet weaving industry, in particular the British-Swiss Company of Ziegler & Co and the Dutch entrepreneur Hotz & Zoon. After having

---

19. Tahvildar 1341, 102.
20. DCR 1662, 10; Janab 1303, 79.
21. Issawi 1971, 259.
22. Fraser 1826, 363.
23. Wirth 1976, 28.
24. Issawi 1971, 91.
25. On the banking system see Floor, 1979, 263-281; Jones 1986.
26. Issawi 1971, 339 ff.

skimmed the market for old carpets these firms soon realized that to sustain their efforts in this trade the production of new, high quality carpets would have to be organized by them. This was necessary because the demand for carpets had increased between 1872-1874 by more than 100%, while the as yet unorganized home industry, which carpet weaving basically was, was too unreliable a base to guarantee continuity of output and quality.[27] The prevailing putting out system prior to the organization of a manufacturing system was described as follows by a contemporary observer:

> The bulk of the carpet industry is carried on in the weavers' homes, the women and children doing the weaving. The so-called manufacturer supplies to the weaver the design and the quantities of wool in different colours required for one carpet. He also advances sums to account of the price arranged, the balance being paid on delivery of the finished article. The practice has the usual disadvantages of home employment, slovenly and dilatory work, with little progress towards skill and finish, as the looms, scattered over a wide area, cannot be constantly inspected.[28]

Ziegler & Co, therefore, sent a representative to Soltanabad in the Farahan district to establish a carpet factory (i.e., mainly dyeing rooms, offices and stores) and to organize and develop the carpet production along standardized lines, as far as quality, designs and size were concerned. Ziegler & Co soon was followed by their competitor. At that time (around 1870) there were only some 40 looms in Soltanabad, while already 10 years later there were some 1,200 looms in the town itself and some 5,000 looms in about 150 carpet weaving villages around Soltanabad, employing a total of more than 10,000 persons.[29]

But Europeans were not the only ones that organized and developed the carpet production and trade. In fact we may observe the coming into being of a specialized class of carpet merchants in Iran, amongst whom the Tabrizis were the most prominent. This was especially the case in Kerman, where the Tabrizi merchants had almost complete control of the carpet trade. Persian capital and entrepreneurship competed with the European firms in the same towns, but they also, and mainly, organized and developed the carpet production in the rural areas, both in the villages and among the tribes.

> The Tabrizi merchants were not content merely to place orders with the village weavers and leave it at that. They soon established small factories with a few looms in the towns, where the weaving production could be more easily and more properly controlled. The movement began in Tabriz itself; but then extended it before long to Meshed, Kerman and Kashan. In each locality the moving spirit was the Tabrizi merchant. Besides the work in the towns they began to organize and manufacture in a number of village areas as well—in the Heriz district, east of Tabriz itself, and among the hundreds of villages east of Soltanabad. Some of the names of those noted families of traders—some of whose descendants are trading still [are]: Sadiqiani,

---

27. Issawi 1971, 301-302.
28. MacLean 1904, 95.
29. DCR 1376, 57.

Ipekji, Mamaghani, Mahmedoff, Urdubatli, Dilmaghani, Tehranji, Salmasi, Antikaji and Ehrabi.[30]

According to Abdullaev there existed even a group of Persian merchants, which had specialized in the trade of peasant and tribal rugs.[31] Both where output and employment were concerned the weaving of carpets was a continuing success story. By the beginning of the 20th century some 65,000 persons were employed in carpet making where a mere few 1,000 had been working in this craft around 1860.[32] The rise in employment and organization of this industry was also reflected in the rise of output.

TABLE 1.1: Main Exports of Iran (in percent)[33]

	1850s	1880s	1911-13
Silk and products	38	18	5
Cotton and woolen cloth	23	1	1
Cereals	10	16	12
Fruit	4	6	13
Tobacco	4	5	11
Raw Cotton	1	7	19
Opium	-	26	7
Carpets	-	4	12

In the early 1870s the total exports of carpets was estimated to be about £75,000, while in 1889 Curzon estimated the total export of carpets at £100,000. In 1903 exports had increased to about £500,000 and by 1914 they accounted for about 12% of Iran's total export, or some £1 million.[34]

THE RISE OF MODERN INDUSTRY

The attempts at modernization cannot be seen in isolation from the growing contacts between Europe and Iran in general, and the increasing penetration of European commercial and political power into Iran in particular. At the same time modernization was impossible without simultaneous similar modernizing attempts in the field of government administration. It goes without saying that the modernizing activities in both industry and government influenced one another.

After a period of relative isolation Iran was rudely awakened by the humiliating defeats, which it suffered against Russia in two wars (1812-14 and 1826-28). There were,

---

30. Edwards 1952, 56 and note 2
31. Abdullaev 1963, 59.
32. See below Table 1.4.
33. Issawi 1971, 136.
34. Issawi 1971, 302.

however, only a few people who wanted to learn from this experience. This first reform movement was in fact restricted to 'Abbas Mirza and his entourage. 'Abbas Mirza, the heir-apparent, had been in command of the Persian troops, who had been defeated, and he more than anyone else wished to modernize his army after the European model. French and later British military missions came to Iran to assist in training, reorganizing and rearming the new Persian army.[35] However, to sustain this modernizing effort beyond its initial stage of a pilot project "a total change must take place before the new system of defence can do more than paralyze the old," as Sir John Malcolm astutely remarked at that time.[36] For modernizing the army did not only mean assuring its financial upkeep, but a change in administrative and organizational practices, which would have far-reaching consequences for Persian society. It also made it prerequisite upon the Persian bureaucracy to guarantee that the new technology could be absorbed, adapted, modified, maintained, and innovated upon by Persians themselves. This meant that not only foreign technology and experts had to be brought to Iran; it also meant that Persians had to be trained in the sciences and systems, which gave the Europeans a head-start over Persians.

Notwithstanding the lack of support for his modernizing ideas from his father, Fath 'Ali Shah (r. 1799-1834), 'Abbas Mirza already in 1811 sent two Persians to Great Britain so that "they shall study something of use to me, themselves and their country."[37] In 1815, 'Abbas Mirza again sent a group of Persians to Great Britain. The group of five students had to study artillery, engineering, chemistry, languages and gun-smithery. From the choice of subjects it is clear that 'Abbas Mirza's interest was mainly, if not exclusively, bound up with his modernization effort of his army. This is also clear from his other efforts in the field of mining and traditional metal crafts.[38]

The attempts at innovations remained, however, restricted to Azerbaijan and 'Abbas Mirza's entourage. This was partly due to a great ignorance with regard to Europe and European science, which existed in Iran. Nevertheless, several young courtiers were well aware of the advantages of European technology and administrative practices. This is clearly shown by the account of the Persian mission to Moscow in 1829, among which we observe Mirza Taqi Khan, the great mid-century reformer. The secretary of the mission recorded: "it would be a great pity if the steam engine which is the basis of a industries should not become prevalent in Iran."[39]

Notwithstanding these sentiments it must be realized that individuals like 'Abbas Mirza did not represent a reform movement which wanted to change the face of Iran. It was only under his son, Mohammad Shah (r. 1834-48), that again some students were sent to Europe to study military science, mining, and medicine. Mohammad Shah was in fact continuing his father's policy, but because of the number of trainees involved as well as the lack of comprehensive and effective policies and interventions European technology only scratched the surface of Persian society and remained an alien body. The policy of sending

---

35. Farmanfarmayan 1968, 119f.
36. Malcolm 1820, vol. 2, 360.
37. Farmanfarmayan 1968, 120f.
38. Donboli 1351, 143. See Floor 2003a, chapter 5.
39. Farmanfarmayan 1968, 124.

students to Europe was continued, so that until the establishment of the *Dar al-Fonun* in 1852, Iran's own institute of higher and modern learning, only 29 students had been sent to Europe since 1811.[40]

Although the number of students sent to Europe was small, they had some effect on the Persian socio-economic situation, because a few actually practiced what they had learned in Europe. Apart from the establishment of printing-presses we observe that the only artisan among the students, Mohammad 'Ali, was charged with the task to manufacture canons.

The self-sufficiency drive also extended to other sectors of the economy such as paper manufacture. When in 1837 the first Persian newspaper was published by Mirza Saleh, another of 'Abbas Mirza's students, a paper factory was established at the same time in Tabriz, "so that the country need not depend upon foreign paper."[41] Paper production also ranked high in Hajji Aghasi's plans. This prime minister of Mohammad Shah started a production program of paper, gun-powder, and guns for a second Herat campaign. Although this campaign only took place in 1854, under Mohammad Shah's successor, these guns and gun-powder were indeed used for that purpose.[42]

The transfer of other European technology to Iran came almost to a standstill under Mohammad Shah due to financial problems. But under his successor's energetic reforming prime minister, Mirza Taqi Khan, a vigorous reform policy was implemented. Mirza Taqi Khan's task was easier, because his drive for modernization and reform was shared by others, amongst whom Naser al-Din Shah (r. 1848-96), as well. The fact that after Mirza Taqi Khan's death in 1852 the modernization policy was continued showed that there at least was some political platform for it. Mirza Taqi Khan, the great initiator and planner of this policy, had helped to secure the throne for Naser al-Din Shah and in return the latter appointed him prime minister. We have already observed that Mirza Taqi Khan had visited Russia in 1829. He similarly had first hand experience of the Turkish reforms. It was therefore not surprising that Mirza Taqi Khan initiated a reform policy, which encompassed a great many fields, such as industry, administration, education and justice.[43]

Mirza Taqi Khan's industrial policy was aimed at import substitution. He wanted to modernize the economic base of Iran and thus enable it to complete successfully with European imports. The economic pinch was already quite serious at that time and Polak states, "in order to check the continuous outflow of money, the present Shah has made repeated efforts to set up European type of factories."[44] This referred to the establishment of two sugar mills in Mazandaran in 1850, and in Tehran to a calico and a broadcloth factory, and a spinning factory. Furthermore, a silk weaving factory was founded in Kashan. Moreover, artisans were stimulated to imitate and duplicate foreign products such as samovars, carriages, and American round stoves. To promote the consumption of the products

---

40. Farmanfarmayan 1968, 124-125; Ringer 2001, 47-51.
41. Farmanfarmayan 1968, 146.
42. Ardakani 1368, 1, 199-200. For more details on paper manufacturing see Floor 2003a, chapter six.
43. Adamiyat 1348.
44. Polak 1865, 2, 182; Issawi 1971, 275.

of these modern factories Mirza Taqi Khan even organized an exhibition of Persian industrial goods in Tehran.[45]

To train the necessary staff and to familiarize Persian artisans with European technology Mirza Taqi Khan continued to send students to Europe. In 1850 he, therefore, sent a group of artisans and craftsmen to Russia to work in factories there and learn new techniques of their craft such as crystal making, sugar refining, casting of iron, papermaking, carpentry, smith-craft and wheel making. To broaden the scientific basis of Iran's economy Mirza Taqi Khan also established the *Dar al-Fonun*, the first Persian institute of higher learning, where European modern science was taught.[46] The artisans and craftsmen returned from Russia in 1853 and set up factories such as a cut crystal factory in Tehran, a paper mill in Isfahan, a cast iron workshop, and carpentry workshop in Sari.[47]

Mirza Taqi Khan took similar measures with regard to the development of Iran's natural resources. He issued a decree allowing unrestricted operation of mines in Iran. Under the terms of this decree, first all Persian subjects were given the right to work the mines, and second, for five years they were exempt from all taxation.[48] Some mines were operated at Mirza Taqi Khan's orders, such as in Qaracheh Dagh (Azerbaijan) and the Masuleh mines of Gilan. But, although plans were in the make for a rise in mining activities, as well as for the teaching of mineralogy at the *Dar al-Fonun*, his fall from power and subsequent death prevented these plans from being implemented. After his death his mining policy was reversed and heavy taxes were collected from those who wanted to operate mines.[49]

In other areas, however, his modernization efforts were continued and had the support of Naser al-Din Shah. Not only were new factories established, but the policy to send students to Europe was continued too, despite the existence of the *Dar al-Fonun*. In 1858, again some 18 Persian students were sent to Europe, this time to France, to study the making of broad cloth, china, paper, and other useful industrial activities.[50]

The Persian government's continued interest and the sustained efforts to modernize its industry show that this policy responded to a real and felt need. This felt need was a strong urge to counter European economic penetration. This objective the Persian government hoped to achieve by developing a modern national industry, which would produce articles that were currently imported from abroad. Polak, for example, observed, "at the time of the British-Persian disputes [1854-56], to free the country from the British market, the government tried particularly hard to set up European type of factories."[51] Neither expense nor trouble were obstacles for the implementation of this industrial import substitution objective. The establishment of the cotton-spinning mill in Tehran is exemplary: "Steam engines and other machines had to be brought over from the Caspian Sea over the shortest and most difficult roads by human labor. Whole villages were conscripted; a

---

45. Issawi 1971, 292-295; see also Hedayat 1363, 72.
46. Issawi 1971, 293.
47. Issawi 1971, 293. For more details see Floor 2003, chapters three, five, and six.
48. Issawi 1971, 296.
49. Issawi 1971, 296.
50. Issawi 1971, 293.
51. Polak 1865, vol. 2, 182.

complete district was destroyed and depopulated, during which 50 people perished."⁵² The total cost of this operation was not less than 150,000 ducats, or 1,650,000 *qran*s. But these were not the c.i.f. cost, for further considerable additional expenses had to be incurred. In 1861, Eastwick gave the following write-up on this factory:

> It was, probably, the accounts of Manchester industry, which led to the establishment of a cotton factory near Tehran. Persons acquainted the establishment of a cotton factory near Tehran with the business were sent for from St. Petersburgh, and under the direction of M. Pankoff, a Livonian, a large factory was erected on high ground, about three and a half miles from the walls of the capital. The edifice is of brick, and the wood work of Oriental plane, which furnishes excellent timber, but the cost is said to have been out of all proportion to the work. The building is three stories high, each storey consisting of a large room. The machinery in the two upper rooms has never been put together. As soon as that on the ground floor was ready, viz., on the 24th of May, 1859, the factory opened, and has worked at intervals two days a week. There are 30,000 spindles, but only 1,600 are used. They were made at Moscow, and are moved by a steam-engine of 25 horse power. The machinery can be impelled by water if necessary. There are 150 work-people, whose pay of 25 ducats [275 *qran*s] a year each is always about that period in arrears. The total cost of the factory to the present day is reckoned a little short of 300,000 *tuman*s [3 million *qran*s], equal to about 136,000 £.⁵³

Since Iran had no qualified and trained technicians at that time to manage and run these factories qualified European managers and operators had to be hired in Europe. We have seen that a Russian managed the cotton-spinning mill; for the paper mill in Tehran likewise some Russians were employed, while two Frenchmen operated the glass factory. These expenses added to the already very high initial investment cost of these factories.⁵⁴

TABLE 1.2: New factories built in Iran (type, location, year, investor)⁵⁵

Type of factory	Location	Year	Investor
		1850s	
Rifle factory	Tehran	1850	Government
Sugar mill (two)	Gilan	1852	Government
Spinning mill	Tehran	1859	Government
Calico-weaving mill	Tehran	1850	Government

---

52. Polak 1865, vol. 2, 53-54.
53. Eastwick 1863, 70-71.
54. Polak 1865, vol. 2, 184.
55. Abdullaev 1974, 114-120; Issawi 1971, 258-310 (and literature quoted and translated); Haqiqat Rafi`, 1352, 439; Hedayat 1363, 129-131; E`temad al-Saltaneh, 1298-1300, vol. 3, 107, 222, 232, 246, 271, 281; Ibid., 1306, 82, 93-126; Ibid. 1368, vol. 2, 1245, 1348, 1390, 1392.

Type of factory	Location	Year	Investor
Silk-weaving mill	Kashan	1850	Government
Glass factory	Tehran	1857	Government
Paper mill	Tehran	1858	Government
Paper mill	Isfahan	1854	Aqa Rahim Esfahani
Cut crystal factory	Tehran	1854	Aqa Rahim Esfahani
Cast iron workshop	Sari	1854	Hajji Mohammad Tajer Esfahani
Silk weaving mill	Milan	185?	Unknown
		1860s	
Glass factory	Tehran	1869	Government
Candle making factory	Tehran	1860	Government
Cartridges factory	Tehran	1861	Government
		1870s	
Gas works (electricity)	Tehran	1879	Government
		1880s	
Glass factory	Tehran	1888	Amin al-Zarb
Porcelain factory	Tehran	188?	Amin al-Zarb
Silk reeling plant	Rasht	188?	Amin al-Zarb
Porcelain factory	Tabriz	188?	Hajji `Abbas `Ali - Hajji Reza
Gas works	Tehran	188?	M. Boital (French)
Silk reeling plant	Birikadeh	188?	Russian
		1890s	
Glass factory	Tehran	1891	Belgian
Power plant	Tehran	1891	Belgian
Sugar mill	Tehran	1895	Belgian
Match factory	Tehran	1891	Russian
Spinning mill	Tehran	1895	Sani` al-Dowleh
Cotton ginning mill	Sabzevar	1896	Hajji Mirza Esfahani
Cotton ginning mill	Nishapur	1896	Russian
Cotton ginning mill	Amol	1896	Unknown
Tobacco processing mill	Mashhad	189?	Mashhadi Ebrahim
Kerosene refinery	Enzeli	189?	Persian/Russian
Kerosene refinery (5)	Mashhad-e sar	189?	Persian/Russian
		1900s	
Spinning mill	Tabriz	1908	Hajji Rahim Aqa-ye Qazvini
Power plant	Tehran	1905	Amin al-Zarb
Power plant	Mashhad	1903	Government
Power plant	Tabriz	190?	Russian/Persian

Type of factory	Location	Year	Investor
Power plant	Rasht	190?	Russian/Persian
Power plant	Tehran	1907	Amin al-Zarb
Spinning mill	Semnan	1902	Hajji ʿAlinaqi Kashani
Spinning mill	Qazvin	1909	Hajji Abu'l Qasem Esfahani
Brick factory	Tehran	190?	Amin al-Zarb
Brick factory	Urmiyeh	190?	German
Toilet soap factory	Tehran	1910	Rabiʿzadeh
Brewery	Tehran	190?	Unknown
Brewery	Urmiyeh	190?	Unknown
Ice-making plant	Tehran	190?	Russian
Lime kilns	Qazvin	190?	Russian
Cotton ginning mills (12)	Northern Iran	190?	Russian/Persian

Although the military element in the industrial and modernizing measures initiated by Mirza Taqi Khan still played an important role, these at least were implemented within the context of a wider reaching and more comprehensive scheme of reform activities. But we may also observe a change in the direction of the modernization activities. Western penetration had come to Iran as a political and military threat. Quite understandably the Persian government tried to find and develop a political and military response to that threat. However, in the mid-19th century the need to correct the negative balance of payments was competing with the military needs. Both influences were reflected in the choice and selection of industries encouraged by Mirza Taqi Khan. However, after the humiliating defeat in the 'War for a Lady,' which ended with the Peace Treaty of Paris (1857), Iran acquiesced in the political and military hegemony of Russia and Great Britain in Iran. It is therefore not surprising to see that in the third modernization period (after 1870) the military influence was all but absent from the modern industrial activities that were undertaken.

One may well question the starting date of the third modernization period, viz. 1870, since hardly any factory was built during the 1870s. In fact, more were built in the 1880s, while the establishment of modern factories only gained momentum during the 1890s and thereafter (see Table 1.2). The reason that nevertheless 1870 was chosen is closely tied up with the role of Mirza Hoseyn Khan Sepahsalar, who was another of the reforming Qajar ministers of renown.[56] He, moreover, was the prime minister who negotiated the Reuter concession. Although the Reuter concession itself did not lead to any industrial activity it was nevertheless a landmark, that set the pace of things that were to come and heralded the age of concession-hunting leading to direct European investments in Iran. Moreover, the reasons, which had led to the grant of the Reuter concession are of importance and made themselves later felt even stronger than before.

The Sepahsalar had personal experience with the Turkish reforms and he was greatly impressed by them. He had high hopes and great expectations of European technology,

---

56. Bakhash 1978.

the European political system and its civic organizations. He, e.g., regarded a railway project connecting Basra with Iskanderun as if the Ottoman Empire had been given "a new lease of life."[57] Reformers like him felt that to withstand the European penetration, both political and economic, countries like Iran would have to reorganize themselves. In fact, he even accepted Western interference as a price that had to be paid to attain progress, "for it will eventually lead to salvation, success and progress."[58] He felt it as an affront that backward Iran was regarded with no respect by Europeans, whilst reforming Turkey was. It may have been his idea that Naser al-Din Shah had to visit Europe himself to see that Iran needed sweeping reforms.[59]

Although the Sepahsalar's objectives may not as yet have been caused by the balance of payments and revenue problems which were to play an important role later on in Persian politics, but his arguments were certainly not forgotten. According to the Sepahsalar and those thinking like him, Iran might as well give rights to Europeans to exploit "unemployed resources which up to now have conferred no benefit on the government and, should they remain in our hands, will after this confer no benefit either."[60] These ideas no doubt also appealed to troubled Persian governments in the post-Reuter days.

One may not conclude from the fact that hardly any factories were built during the 1870s that the Persian government did not take interest in the promotion of such enterprises. However, the opposition against the Reuter concession had made it very difficult for a while to import foreign technology, which, because of the absence of qualified personnel in Iran, had per force to lead to the hiring of European technicians.

Both the Sepahsalar and Naser al-Din Shah, however, wanted very much to continue implementing the envisaged reforms. The Shah wrote to the Sepahsalar, e.g., on September 26, 1871 that he was eager "to carry on out a broad programme of reform and produced a long and varied list of projects he wished to carry out. Among these he included: "the improvement and development of commerce, agriculture, mines, forests and the customs; construction of schools, hospitals, forts, bridges, factories, and irrigation works and a thousand other things."[61] At the same time he bewailed the fact that there was nobody whom he could turn to, who might implement such a reform policy. That Naser al-Din Shah was sincere in this respect is demonstrated by the fact that he recalled the Sepahsalar to Tehran, and later appointed him foreign minister, in spite of the strong opposition against the former reform minded prime minister.[62]

Although the Shah developed his reform policy in the field of administration and government he also paid attention to the encouragement of national industry. Naser al-Din Shah especially promoted the traditional crafts by ordering the army to wear uniforms produced by native industry, for which he ordered the necessary cloth from Kerman. Simi-

---

57. Bakhash 1978, 44.
58. Bakhash 1978, 46.
59. Bakhash 1978, 48.
60. Bakhash 1978, 114.
61. Bakhash 1978, 135.
62. Bakhash 1978, 136f.

larly he also indirectly contributed to the revival of the weaving of woolen cloth in Yazd, Mashhad and Shiraz.[63]

In view of the importance of the manufacturing of shawls in Kerman the government took measures to support this industry. Mirza Taqi Khan had promoted its production with great success. At that time the demand in Europe for Kerman shawls had increased to such an extent that Naser al-Din Shah had forbidden its export in 1857. Thereafter, its importance declined, so that in 1879 there were only 100 looms left. To turn the tide Naser al-Din Shah ordered in 1882 that henceforth all robes of honor, which he would grant, had to be made of Kerman shawls.[64]

His most innovative measure (may be also the least effective) was the creation of a Ministry of Industry in 1882, which, however, did not play an important role.[65] For after 1882 we do not hear anything from this Ministry anymore, and it, in fact, does not occur at all among the list of ministries that were published each year by the Persian government. Already prior to that date there had been a minister of mines, who also had other responsibilities, which changed in the course of the years. Although Naser al-Din Shah continued to take an interest in the economic welfare of his country as shown by the decrees which he issued with regard to the ban on imports of aniline dyes and aniline dyes yarns in 1882 and 1885 this interest was overshadowed by other problems which beset Iran, which were mainly political in nature.[66] Because of the growing pressure from Great Britain and Russia, the balance of payments problems, the decreasing revenues, and the lack of sufficient internal support for a reform policy Naser al-Din Shah's enthusiasm waned, and he instead started to look for short-term solutions to the many problems that faced him.[67]

Although the government held regular meetings with the most important merchants and entrepreneurs of Tehran to discuss economic problems, these discussions did not lead to a formulation of an economic or an industrial policy.[68] Regularly, both in and outside these meetings, the subject of the ban on European imports was raised, but as Amin al-Zarb pointed out: "what manufactories and industries do we have that we can say: we do not want European goods."[69]

Amin al-Zarb was one of the Persian entrepreneurs who tried to beat the Europeans at their own game by investing in all kinds of commercial and industrial enterprises. In fact, Amin al-Zarb was almost the only Persian capitalist who dared to run the risk of investing money in modern plants. Apart from the various factories, which he established (for example, glass, porcelain, silk reeling) he also constructed a railway connecting Amol

---

63. Floor 1999 b, 103-104.
64. Issawi 1971, 295; E`temad al-Saltaneh 1306, vol. 3, 208, 323; Polak 1865, vol. 2, 168; Stolze und Andreas 1885, 25.
65. E`temad al-Saltaneh 1306, vol. 3, 224, 378.
66. E`temad al-Saltaneh 1306, vol. 3, 383.
67. Bakhash 1978, 46.
68. See Floor 1976; Adamiyyat & Nateq 1356, 299f.
69. Floor 1976.

(Mazandaran) with Mahmudabad, the port at the Caspian Sea. Later on Amin al-Zarb also founded a brick making factory as well as power plants in Tehran.[70]

But Amin al-Zarb was not the only enterprising Persian capitalist. Until 1880 investment in industry had been an almost exclusive government affair, but after that year we see private investors stepping in the field vacated by the government. A number of big merchants erected a number of plants, which were not without success. There were also government officials who believed that money could be made by investing in modern industry. A fine example is the construction of a cotton spinning mill in Tehran by Mortazaqoli Khan Sani` al-Dowleh and the wholesale merchant Hajji Mohammad Taqi Shahrudi.[71]

At the end of the 1880s European investors also began to take an interest in direct investments in Persian industry. Belgian investors especially played an important role with their establishment of a sugar mill, a glass factory and a power plant. It must be pointed out, however, that the Belgians were rather intermediaries for capital from various sources amongst which Persian capital.[72] After the Belgians had spent their money and energy it were mainly Russian investors who constructed factories such as a match factory, many cotton-ginning factories, several kerosene refineries, power plants and various other industrial plants.[73]

The increased European activities in Iran in trade, industry and mining gave rise to resentment, nationalism and a demand for government intervention. Where the Shah had lost interest the various reformers of the late 19th century tried to awaken and encourage the Persian people. They warned them against the growing dependence on import of goods for their basic needs and their preference for foreign luxuries. Mirza Aqa Khan Kermani stated that he feared "that very soon, ignorance and stupidity will bring Iran to such a pass that even water will be imported from Europe and sold at the price of wine."[74] In the *Siyahatnameh-ye Ebrahim Beg* the narrator urges the government and the people of Iran to join hands and to promote national industry. The author of the *Ketab-e Ahmad* defends the notion that Iran might make great progress:

> If we wore cloth (*qadak*) of Isfahan and made clothes from the wool (*shal*) of Yazd and Isfahan; if instead of the felt of the foreigner, we made hats out of skins (*pust*) of Shiraz; instead of foreign chinaware, we used the silver-like copper plates of the kingdom; preferred our earthenware hubble-bubbles to the crystal of the foreigners; did not burn at a single party camphor candles of a foreign nation; did not become the object of envy or the poor.[75]

---

70. Issawi 1971, 409-410; for more information (with pictures of the various factories and the railway) see Ashraf 1359.
71. Hedayat 1363, 74 (with picture).
72. "I have organized a public subscription [in Tehran] for the sugar mill in the month of February. In a few weeks 800,000 francs were subscribed, and among the subscribers, most of the Shah's ministers and Prince Na'ib al-Saltana, His Majesty's son and minister of war were to be found." D' Erp 1893, 24.
73. See Table 1.3.
74. Adamiyyat 1346, 228.
75. Bakhash 1978, 351 quoting `Abd al-Rahim Talibof's *Ketab-e Ahmad*.

Notwithstanding the fact that these sentiments responded to the feelings of many of the artisan, commercial, and educated classes in Iran there were not many attempts to promote native industry. In 1897 a group of reform minded activists in Isfahan founded the Oriental Society (*Anjoman-e Sharqi*), which aimed at promoting the consumption of native goods and the creation of Persian trading companies to withstand the European penetration of the Persian market.[76] About the same time a similar organization was founded known as the Islamic Society (*Anjoman-e Eslami*) by Hajji Mohammad Hoseyn Tajer-e Kazeruni.[77]

Many other trading companies were founded, but only one of which explicitly aimed at the production, trade, and sale of native goods, and which in fact was forbidden by its charter to trade in foreign goods. The Islamic Company (*Sharekat-e Eslami*), as the new company was called, was founded in 1898 by the backers of the two aforementioned societies and directed by Hajji Mohammad Hoseyn Tajer-e Kazeruni. The company constructed weaving facilities in Ardestan and produced cloth, which was known as Islamic cloth (*parcheh-ye eslami*).[78] According to Majd al-Islam, many of the leading ulama used for their clothes only the Islamic cloth, and this even held for their turban.[79] Although the company was backed by the ulama, who declared European textiles to be unclean, bankruptcy was its fate. Apart from embezzlements, the reason for failure appears to have been that most people preferred to continue to use the cheaper and better quality foreign textiles. There were other proposals to establish companies producing and selling only Persian goods, but they all came to nought.[80]

THE IMPACT OF MODERN INDUSTRY

From the above it is clear that both the 'buy Persian goods only' movement as well as the drive to construct modern European type factories was of limited importance, if not a failure. Curzon's statement, "factories, as the term is used in Europe, do not exist in Persia"[81] is echoed by many other authors. Bharier, e.g., bluntly states that "large-cale manufacturing industry - defined to comprise factories with ten or more workers - did not exist in Iran at the turn of the century."[82] If we use Bharier's definition of large-scale manufacturing, however, we observe that such a phenomenon was not absent in Iran as is shown in the Table hereunder.

---

76. Majd al-Islam 1350, vol. 1, 313.
77. Safa'i 1344, 342.
78. On the Islamic Company see Ashraf 1359, 100 and chapter three and literature quoted there.
79. Majd al-Islam 1350, vol. 1, 313.
80. Chapter three; to propagate the formation of trading and industrial companies along European lines the famous orator Sayyed Jamal al-Din Isfahani wrote a book called *Lebas al-Taqva* (Shiraz, 1900). For a short discussion of the contents of this book see Saba, Mohsen. "A note on Lebas ol-Taqva," *Tahqiqat-e Eqtesadi* 8, no. 21 (1971), p. 103ff.
81. Curzon 1892, vol. 2, 523.
82. Bharier 1971, 170.

TABLE 1.3: European type factories in Iran and their number of workers.[83]

Type of factory		Labor force
	Prior to 1900	
Silk reeling Amin al-Zarb		150
Silk reeling Birikadeh		20
Match factory		50
Paper mill		60
Sugar mill/Kahrizak		300
Glass & Porcelain/Tehran		20
Brick-making/Tehran		20
Oil refineries/Gilan (five plants)		272
	After 1900	
Cotton spinning factory/Tabriz		100
Brick factory/Urmiyeh		30
Olive-oil plant/Rudbar		20
Cotton ginning (26 factories)		416 (16 per factory)
Power plant/Amin al-Zarb		20
Power plant/Tabriz		15
Power plant/Mashhad		15
Power plant/Enzeli		15 (Liazonov)
Power plant/Enzeli		15 (Khoshtaria)
Timber plant/Resht		15
Timber plant/Talesh		15
Tobacco plant/Mashhad		20
Brick factory/Tehran		20
Soap making plant/Nezafat		20
Brewery/Urmiyeh		15
Brewery/Tehran		10
Ice making plant/Khoshtaria		10
Lime kiln/Qazvin		10
Ammunition plant/Isfahan		15 (German)
Assembly plant/Tabriz		20 (German)

Apart from the industries mentioned in Tables 1.2 and 1.3 (for pictures of two of them see figs 1.1 and 1.2) we also observe that at the same time some traditional crafts were being modernized and organized along manufacturing lines. The rise in demand for carpets, for example, led to the appearance of carpet workshops of the manufactory type. One of them was even organized on a bigger scale than the largest European type factory. In

---

83. Abdullaev 1963, 198ff.

Tabriz, in 1898/99, a Russian subject, Ganjiev (Mamedov), constructed a carpet manufacturing plant in which up to 1,500 workers were employed.

> This enterprise was a large manufactory, consisting of several brick buildings, in which were workshops for carpet making and a dye-house. Mamedov also had his own bakery, in which ten thousand loaves were baked each week for his workers. In the large workshop, about one hundred carpets were in process at any one time. Annual turnover was 500,000 rubles [about £ 50,000]. We have not come across any other carpet making enterprises of that size, but establishments with up to one hundred workers and over were to be found in several carpet making centers. Such enterprises often belonged to representatives of foreign capital.[84]

The development of cottage industries towards manufacturing was to be observed in other branches of industry as well, such as in leather production, opium preparation, henna processing, and in mining. There is no doubt that the greater part of traditional crafts still was operated on handicraft basis or in the case of carpet making on the basis of the putting out system, however.[85] After the first initial efforts by the Persian government it looked as if after the mid-1860s no modern factories were to be build anymore in Iran. In fact all factories listed in Table 1.2, built prior to 1880, were closed by then and were either used for other purposes or were left and abandoned.[86] The British consul Thomson wrote in 1864:

> A paper manufactory has cost the Government 14,000 *tumans* [140,000 *qrans*]. The result was so unsatisfactory, that after a short time the Russian workmen employed in it were dismissed, and the place has since been allowed to fall into ruins. A further sum of 23,000 *tumans* has been expended on an establishment for making candles. This also proved a failure, and though the works are not closed, they cannot be expected to result in anything but further pecuniary loss to the Government. The glass-works have been equally unsuccessful. They were placed under the management of the French workmen, who do not appear to have fulfilled their engagements, and after a useless expenditure of about 14,000 *tumans*, these works have now been abandoned.[87]

When private investors took up the initiative in the 1880s it looked as if this was a last effort, for all the new factories failed very soon. It was only in the 1890s that some change occurred, although the big factories built by European investors proved to be failures as well. Nevertheless a few factories survived and the ones that were not closed succumbed to unfair Russian competition. It was only in the 1900s that it looked like that industrializa-

---

84. Abdullaev 1963, 115; see also Issawi 1971, 297 f.
85. Issawi 1971, 298-299.
86. Abdullaev 1963, 189f.; Seidov 1974, 114f.
87. *AP* 1864, 192-93.

tion on a larger scale than before would take place. However, the First World War and its aftermath put a stop to all that.

The limited role of industry is also borne out by the employment it provided for the urban population in Iran. In the beginning of the 20th century modern industry probably did not provide more than 850 jobs. Both in relative and absolute terms, this contribution to the unemployment problem was insignificant. Traditional crafts and mining played a much more important role than modern industry in this respect as is shown in Table 1.4. On the eve of the First World War the urban industrial labor force in Iran was estimated to amount to some 126,000 men, women and children. Industry accounted for less than 1%, while carpet making was by far the largest industrial branch offering some 60,000 jobs or about 50% of the total urban labor force.

TABLE 1.4: Composition of the urban labor force in Iran (around 1910)[88]

Factories	850
Anglo-Iranian Oil Company	7,800
Mining	200
Carpet making	65,000
Metal working crafts	20,000
Leather working crafts	900
Other handicrafts	10,000
Fisheries (Caspian)	4,200 (incl. 2,000 Russians)
Pearl fisheries (Persian Gulf)	4,000
Porters and Dockers	4,000 (incl. Russians)
Wood cutters	300
Leather production	3,000
Railway employees	200
Servants	5,000
Road workers (Resht-Enzeli)	300
Railway workers (construction)	3,000
Printers	300
Total	125,500

The little effect that modern industry had, both in economic and employment terms, is in contradiction with the considerable capital investment that was required to establish these factories. Although data are very scanty there is enough evidence to state that during the Second phase of industrialization (1848-70) more than three million *qrans* were

---

88. Abdullaev 1963, 212. The data given by Abdullaev have been corrected where the labor force in factories are concerned, because he also counted those laborers in factories which had been abandoned by 1900 (see Table 1.3). There were also some 5,070 Russians working in Iran, which are included in the numbers given in Table 1.4.

invested, leaving apart recurrent cost. Moreover, it must be stressed that the data given here refer to initial investment only.

TABLE 1.5: Capital investment in some modern factories in Iran (1850-70)[89]

Type of factory	Investment (in *qrans*)
Spinning factory	950,000
Candle factory	230,000
Paper mill	140,000
Glass factory	140,000

Although data are lacking it must be assumed that total investment costs in these factories were much higher. The last government efforts after 1870 were the construction of two power plants, one in Tehran (1879) and one in Mashhad (1904). The capital investment required for these two plants were considerable and amounted to respectively more than 800,000 *qrans* and 200,000 *qrans*.[90] Even more considerable was the scale of direct foreign investment during the 1890s as shown in Table 1.6. Although precise data are lacking the amounts that are mentioned indicate a very high initial capital investment level.

TABLE 1.6: Direct foreign investment in modern industry in Iran (1890s)[91]

Type of factory	Investment (in *qrans*)
Glass factory	5,300,000
Power plant	1,600,000
Sugar mill	5,000,000
Match factory	1,000,000

The spinning mill constructed by Persian investors in 1895 in Tehran, although using very "inexpensive machinery" nevertheless required an investment of 570,000 *qrans*.[92] However, as is shown in Table 1.2, foreign investors dominated the industrial scene after the 1890s, while native capital was scarce and reluctant to risk investments in industrial enterprises. Apart from the fact that Persian capitalists preferred to invest their money in cash-crop production or to finance commercial ventures, which had a quick turnover and could be easily liquidated, there were other reasons why they took less interest in the industrialization effort. These other reasons have mainly to do with the high failure rate of modern factories, which in turn was caused because of the following reasons.

---

89. Jamalzadeh 1335, 93; see also Issawi 1971, 308.
90. Jamalzadeh 1335, 94-95; see also Issawi 1971, 309-310.
91. Issawi 1971, 306f. (quoting Lorini); D'Erp 1893, 24; Government of the Netherlands 1893, 24.
92. Issawi 1971, 309.

FIGURE 1.1: Woodworking machines in the Alleman, Mossig & Schünemann factory in Tabriz (1910), from Walther Küss, *Handelsratgeber für Persien* (Berlin, 1911)

FIGURE 1.2: The Interior of a Modern Spinning factory in Tabriz (1912), from Eberhard-Joachim Graf von Westarp, *Unter Halbmond und Sonne* (Berlin, 1913)

REASONS FOR FAILURE OF MODERN INDUSTRY

Some scholars have taken the position that the Persian government took no interest in the plight of its industrialists and artisans, or that its role in manufacturing was restricted only to granting concessions to foreigners.[93] This, in truth, is a one-sided and altogether unfair assessment of the government's role, which in several instances had tried, and that at great financial and social cost, to provide Iran with an independent industrial base. That this policy failed was not for want of trying, but because the government was too weak, too ignorant with regard to economic affairs and the requirements of modern technology, and in fact unable to protect its nascent industry.

The government was unable to protect Persian goods against foreign imports, because of the commercial treaties that it had signed with a great many countries which stipulated that customs duties were fixed at the uniform level of five percent ad valorem on all goods. Although both Persian business leaders and high government officials had urged the government to change the level of import duties to protect its own industry the Persian government was unable and powerless to act upon such suggestions. For to do so the Persian government required the consent of all these foreign states which enjoyed the 'most favored nation' status. This especially held for Iran's two most important trading partners, Great Britain and Russia. For both countries trade with Iran was of no great importance from an economic point of view. This particularly held for Russia, for which the Persian trade was but an instrument of political policy. Contrariwise, Iran was dependent on Russia for its export trade. Russia took at least 50% of Iran's exports after 1890 and up to 70% after 1904. Moreover, the heavy subsidization of Russian export to Iran made goods such as tea, kerosene, and woolens cheaper in Iran than in Russia itself.[94]

When at the turn of the century Iran entered into negotiations with Russia to discuss a new customs tariff the Persian government did not do so with a view of raising import duties to such a level to protect its industry. Its intention was to increase its customs revenues and to balance its unfavorable trade balance. The new tariff concluded in 1901 was not high enough to protect Persian industry, and made it possible for Russia, for example, to dump its competitive goods on the Persian market.[95]

Apart from the disadvantageous political-economic context in which Persian industry had to operate one of the main reasons of the failure of modern industry in the 19th century was bad planning and project execution. This not only held for raw material delivery, but also for power availability and other foreseeable input obstacles. When Polak warned the government that it should plan industrial investments properly before taking any action he was rebuffed and accused of "wanting to impede the industrial development of the country."[96] In case of the paper mill, Polak observed that it had been built "where water power was insufficient."[97] The glass factory (1860), although being managed by two

---

93. Bharier 1971, 15; Gilbar 1978, 198.
94. Entner 1956, 70.
95. Entner 1956, 53f.
96. Polak 1865, vol. 2, 182.
97. Polak 1865, vol. 2, 184.

experts, could not obtain fire-resistant, refractory clay in Iran.[98] This same problem was one of the causes of the fiasco of the Belgian glass factory built in the 1890s.[99] The first spinning mill, although having cost a lot of money and lives during its transportation, had been built "in the desert, and because of no other reason than because it was situated near the hunting grounds of the Shah and this site was particularly adequate for *tamasha* or show."[100] The Russian match factory built in the 1890s also suffered from its wrong location, namely two hours outside of Tehran, where locally there was no labor available. Also, labor discipline of the workers was different than required in European factories. Moreover, Persian workers were not accustomed to night shifts, while the month of Ramazan was a period of reduced, if not lost income, because labor productivity was not high.[101] The British consul in Tehran, Thomson, commented in 1864:

> During the last five years several attempts have been made by the Persian Government to establish factories for cotton and silk manufactures, glassworks, &c., in the neighbourhood of Tehran, but owing to the defective system upon which they have been organized and worked by the agents of the Government no advantage has hitherto been derived from these establishments. Large sums of money have already been expended on these unprofitable experiments, and work is still carried on at some of them, though there is no prospect of their ever affording anything like an adequate return for the capital employed.
>
> The largest and most important of these factories is that for spinning cotton-thread. It is capable of employing 300 hands, but half that number have rarely been at work. The quality of the cotton used is inferior, and the work is, moreover, frequently interrupted without any apparent reason for weeks together. Under such a system it is not, therefore, surprising to find that the Persian Government [have] not realized from it even the interest of their money.[102]

The Belgian sugar mill was a showcase of bad planning and has been described with much gusto by Lorini:

> To make a long story short, everything had been studied, everything had been provided for, but one thing – a trifle which yet had a certain importance had been forgotten: to ensure that the area under cultivation would be sufficient to provide the required raw material. Ditto for the establishment which had been built, and which after all these studies remained without beets, except for the small amount in Varemin. Besides, the only buyers of

---

98. Polak 1865, vol. 2, 184.
99. Issawi 1971, 306.
100. Polak 1865, vol. 2, 53.
101. Government of the Netherlands 1893, 12, 27.
102. Thompson 1864, 193.

beet were the Belgians; and as they wanted to set conditions and impose
prices on sharecroppers, the latter preferred to revert to their grain, to
barley, and run the risks of the free market. The more so as the land owners
would have nothing do with new crops, still less use their money to effect
the desired shift. Moreover, in fact it turned out that the native do not know
how to grow beets, sometimes watering them too much, sometimes too little
and so on.[103]

A particular impediment for the development of Persian modern industry was the energy problem. This problem already bedeviled the first factories constructed in Iran, but later in the century they still had not found a satisfactory solution to this problem. The Belgians intended to use the coalmines at Hiveh to supply the required coal to support their power plant as well as the sugar mill. However, here another problem arose, namely that of transportation. Towards the end of the 1880s coal cost 8-10 *qrans* per *kharvar* (300 kg), but in the autumn of 1892 the price had risen to 20-28 *qrans* per *kharvar*. The reason for this sudden rise was the fodder situation, which was bad at that time. This resulted in higher transportation rates and consequently the price of coal increased proportionally.[104]

Roads were another problem and it were especially the Russians after 1890 who exerted themselves to built good roads connecting Iran with Russia. Notwithstanding Russian success in this field the cost of transportation remained exorbitantly high and constituted an obstacle for Iran's development.[105]

Labor also was a handicap which modern industry had to overcome in Iran. This held for both management and manual labor. The unskilled labor, about half of them were seasonal labor, were not accustomed to factory discipline, which caused all sorts of problems with management. For the latter, practically always Europeans, work in Iran was not easy, and often they were not flexible enough to adapt themselves to the local conditions. The result of this situation was a low level of productivity in most modern factories[106]

Nevertheless, it is reported that some factories were performing quite well, and in fact, were able to compete with European machine-made products. It is quite possible that such plants would have been able to perform well for a longer time, if they could have been protected against the cheaper (subsidized) foreign imports. The oil refineries in Enzeli and Mashhad-e Sar constituted such a case. These were able to market kerosene at lower prices than the Russian produced kerosene, which alarmed Russian producers. To destroy the Persian refineries the Russian government abolished the export tax on kerosene and in this way ended this successful competitor in Iran.[107] For the same reason, i.e., the Russian Loan and Discount Bank was the most important importer of sugar into Iran, the Russian government lowered the export price of sugar to Iran, so that the Belgian sugar mill could

---

103. Issawi 1971, 306.
104. Government of the Netherlands 1893, 10.
105. Issawi 1971, chapter four.
106. Government of the Netherlands 1893, 27.
107. Seidov 1974, 119.

not compete anymore, since the Russian price was equal to its cost price of sugar. The sugar mill, therefore, had to close down.[108]

We therefore can observe that foreign powers, mainly Russia, did not allow Persian industries to develop in those areas where Russian and Persian interests clashed. All factories built after 1900 and which survived were industries, which either were in branches in which there was no competition with Russian trade interests, or which served Russian industry. This latter point is especially brought out by the fact that the largest number of modern factories was to be found in the sector of agro-industries. Here the Russians had exerted themselves to improve the quality of the cotton crop and its processing. It is therefore not surprising that 26 cotton-ginning factories were built in the cotton growing areas in northern Iran, which exported most of its produce to Russia.

Conclusion

We have seen that there was a severe crisis in many of Iran's traditional crafts, which was not compensated for by the creation of employment and revenues in the nascent modern industry. At the same time it must be said that some crafts rebounded while important new ones like carpet weaving came into being, and, that therefore most traditional crafts still played a preponderant role around 1910, being the largest employers of the urban labor force. It were these traditional crafts which absorbed a great part of the migrant labor which left the rural areas to look for a living in the towns. Another important part of the rural migrants found employment abroad, especially in the adjacent Russian provinces. Therefore, de-industrialization may not have been as drastic as the impressionistic accounts of Persian and foreign commentators want us to believe. According to Bharier agriculture "constituted 80-90% of GNP at the beginning of the century"[109] which suggests that Iran had not become more agricultural in nature than at the beginning of the 19th century. There probably was a minor decrease of the industrial and the agricultural sector, which was off-set by the growth of the tertiary sector. This development manifested itself at least quite unequivocally after 1900.

---

108. Seidov 1974, 119.
109. Bharier 1971, 59.

CHAPTER TWO

Labor Unions, Law and Conditions in Iran (1900–1941)

Part 1. Labor Unions

INTRODUCTION

Iran in 1900 was a pre-industrial country and one of the poorest and least developed in the world. It had a small urban labor force, which for the greater part worked in traditional artisanal workshops, whilst a small but increasing part was formed by wage earning workers. The majority of the urban labor force was organized in traditional craft and trade guilds, which represented the interests of the employers rather than of workers. This labor force moreover did not share any socialist or trade union ideals.

Nevertheless some sort of labor movement can be observed as of 1906 until 1912 which was often the result of activities by Iranian social-democrats preaching their gospel in, for example, Tabriz; sometimes such labor activities were obscured by simultaneous political objectives such as anti-Russian actions in Rasht and Enzeli. Since the labor class in Iran had no true representative, for the guilds cannot be considered as such, the few labor movement activities expressed themselves through (or at least were felt to be) opposition. A weak government and some sympathy among reform-minded politicians were the main reasons why the purely labor demands were met. However, when reaction set in and Russian influence increased after 1910, these labor activities were no longer tolerated. The most coherent (or is it just the best documented?) action of labor was that by the printers' union in 1910 in Tehran, which at the same time was the last turn-out of the labor movement prior to the first World War.

It was only at the end of this war in 1918 that the labor movement was reactivated. From the beginning, the trade unions and other forms of labor activities were influenced by the Communist Party of Iran (CPI). From 1921 the Iranian unions were affiliated with the Moscow-based Profintern, the International Trade Union Movement This control of the labor movement by the CPI was an important reason why the labor movement remained alive for some time, while at the same time it was one of the main reasons for its demise and lack of success.

The CPI, being a Marxist party, regarded the state as the most powerful tool for the liberation of the working class. The workers therefore had to gain control of the state for, in order to overcome hostile legislative, political and social resistance, workers had to acquire political power. There was another reason why the worker organizations tended to become instruments of political interest groups: there was a rather strong movement among the leading political groups in Iran to modernize the country, which led to conflicts with conservative groups. Although the worker organizations were weak, they, because of their concentration in the important political center of Tehran, constituted one of such modernizing groups, while at the same time they constituted an important political instrument to promote the cause of the progressive forces. The leaders of the CPI and the labor movement therefore were more interested in political matters than in bread and butter issues. This development was enhanced by the fact that the leaders of the labor movement did not originate from the working class itself, or from the class of artisans who were or felt threatened by foreign imports or the establishment of modern industrial plants.

For both the CPI and the trade unions were started and led by men whose material and cultural background made them members of the middle class. The workers in general had neither the time and energy, nor the understanding and capability to organize labor activities, let alone a labor movement. These members of the intelligentsia, being Marxists moreover, considered labor problems as being an integral part of the socio-economic and political system in which imperialism and capitalism were the moving forces. The influence of Great Britain on the Iranian economy, the links between the governments of Iran and Great-Britain, and the fact that Iran's most important and modern industrial activity, the oil industry, was owned and managed by Great Britain, supported such an analysis. It goes without saying that the Soviet Union was regarded as friendly towards the labor movement and the main bulwark in the fight against imperialism and capitalism. The presence of foreign-owned and/or foreign-run enterprises on Iranian soil made labor activities a rather complex and difficult affair, since such labor action automatically acquired political overtones other than purely national ones. It meant on the one hand that the labor movement had to cope with two opponents, the national bourgeoisie and the foreign (British) power, while on the other hand it presented labor with an important instrument of political mobilization in the form of anti-British or xenophobic sentiments.

The primary aim of the labor movement in Iran therefore was the destruction of imperialism and capitalism. In the early 1920s the labor movement scored some notable successes with bread and butter demands, which partly explain its early growth and relative success. This development was made possible by the existence of a rather fluid and unstable political situation and the absence of a strong government between 1918 and 1923. The weak cabinets were in constant fear of attacks by the 'progressive' groups with which the labor unions were affiliated and therefore preferred to give way in some of these labor matters in order to hold their own in the political field.

This early success of the labor movement in Iran is the more striking since the unions were rather weak organizations to carry out effective bargaining. This was because of their low degree of organization due to a low level of class consciousness and fragmentation of the urban labor force itself. Moreover, owing to the extreme poverty of their members, the unions lacked proper funds, and even the financial subsidies from the Russian legation could not properly deal with that problem. Finally, purely economic action was therefore a rather ineffective weapon, the more so since the relationship between labor demand and labor supply was not favorable. Although we do not have data on the level of unemployment in the urban areas of Iran, the mass character of the seasonal pre-1914 migration to Russia, for example, is an indication that there was a considerable labor surplus.

With the advent of a strong centralized government in 1923, led by the autocratic Reza Khan, there was no room for rebels against society. He persecuted both the CPI and the labor movement and finally forbade their existence. The suppression of the labor movement was executed with great ease, which underlines its weakness. During the 1930s, several observers therefore could rightly state "there are no labor unions" in Iran. For, apart from a few isolated labor disputes, the labor movement was unable to organize itself either locally or nationally. The fact that after 1941, when labor unions could legally be formed again, it took some years to do so, only strengthens this observation.

THE BEGINNINGS OF THE LABOR MOVEMENT (1906–1911)

The year 1907 was an important year for Iran, for it acquired a Constitution as well as its first trade union and experienced its first labor strikes. The constitution established, inter alia, the right of free speech (art 20), free association and free assembly (art 21) and thus constituted the legal basis for union activities.[1] Under the influence of social-democratic ideas, which had been disseminated among certain sections of the urban labor force in Iran, the printers of the *Kucheki* printing shop in Tehran established the first trade union in Iran in 1907.[2] The creation of this trade union was the result of the dissemination of 'modern' ideas from Europe among the intelligentsia in Iran. In general these ideas dealt with other, democratic forms of government. Their influence on the reform-minded sections of Iranian society were instrumental in bringing about and deciding the course of the Iranian Constitutional Revolution of 1906–09.[3] With regard to the position of the lower classes, and labor in particular, the main source of information was formed by the social-democrats in the Caucasus.[4] The presence of tens of thousands of Iranian migrants, however, did not lead to a discernible and effective sensitization of that labor force to social-democratic ideals. It is therefore misleading when Abdullaev asserts that Iranian

---

1. For an English translation of the Constitution of 1906 see Browne, 1909, 362. For an analysis of the constitutional movement of 1906–1909 see, for example, Abrahamian 1982.
2. The data on the establishment of the first trade union in Iran are conflicting. Some sources give the year 1906, others give 1907, while both dates are quite possible ones. See e.g. Chaqueri 1978, 7, 10, 78, 92, 97; Bashkirov 1948, 24.
3. See for example, Abrahamian 1982; Haeri 1977, chapter one; Ravasani, n.d. chapter two.
4. Ibid.

migrants in Russia in general were of great importance for the formation of the Iranian working class.[5]

It was only in 1904 that the social-democrats in the Caucasus created an organization called *Hemmat* with the express purpose of organizing Moslem workers in Russia politically.[6] Although its prime purpose was to sensitize Iranian labor to political matters, the *Hemmat* organization did not neglect to pay attention to the important question of labor rights. Its program therefore also aimed at:

—the eight-hour working day, and

—the right to strike to settle labor disputes.

Shortly after the creation of the *Hemmat* organization a similar one was founded in 1905, namely that of the *Ejtema`iyun-e `Amiyun-e Iran* (Socialists) which also stood for the right to strike. Although founded in the Caucasus, this organization soon also created branches in Tabriz, Mashhad, Tehran, Khoy, Isfahan, and Enzeli.[7] In Tabriz, the Armenians played an important role through their *Dashnakiyun* party. These groups had strong contacts with the social-democratic party in Baku, while contacts also existed with progressive thinkers such as Sur Esrafil, Malek al-Motakallemin and `Ali Akbar Dehkhoda, who later would play important roles in the constitutional movement.[8]

In view of the fact that the social-democrats constituted only a small insignificant group with some kind of organization in only a few Iranian cities and with hardly any contacts in the labor force, it is surprising that in 1907 a great many strikes occurred in Iran. These strikes were partly the result of the political situation at that time, partly the expression of growing labor unrest sensitized by social-democratic ideas. It is indeed noteworthy that these activities were restricted to those areas which had been both the scene of strong support for the constitutional movement as well as the areas exposed to social-democratic influence.

The first labor strike appears to have taken place on November 21, 1906 when the fishermen of Enzeli protested against Liazonov, the Russian fisheries concessionaire. The fishermen gathered in the telegraph office of Enzeli and made it known that henceforth they would keep all the fish that they caught for themselves. Liazonov paid them only one *shahi* for each fish, an amount they considered too small. The government sent troops against the strikers and in the ensuing scuffle one fisherman was killed. The fishermen were not beaten, however. They also refused mediation by two local influential leaders, Vazir-e Karma and Shari`atmadari, whom they sent packing with a shower of vilifications. The strike was very popular among the population of the North, and the inhabitants of Rasht wanted to boycott Russian goods to show their feelings.[9]

---

5. Abdullaev, 1963, 40; for a translation see Issawi 1971, 50.
6. Ravasani, n.d. 128 ff.
7. Ravasani, n.d. 128 ff.
8. Abrahamian 1982; Haeri 1977, chapter one; Ravasani, n.d. chapter two.
9. Malek 1357, 63 quoting Rabino, 1352, 183.

In January 1907 a strike of telegraphers occurred in Tabriz to enforce the payment of their arrears,[10] while in the spring of 1907 the printers in Tehran went on strike out of solidarity with one of their colleagues, who had been beaten by E'temad al-Saltaneh, the chief of the government printing office. The strike lasted until E'temad al-Saltaneh had been dismissed.[11]

In April 1907 the telegraphers went on strike in Tehran and other cities to demand higher wages and better treatment.[12] One month later, in April 1907, a strike occurred in Enzeli. The dockers and sailors of the Enzeli-Baku shipping line demanded a rise in wages. The dockers wanted more for unloading Russian ships, a demand which was refused. The dockers then refused to unload ships until their demand had been met. After that ships were unloaded in the estuary of Enzeli, which had not been customary up till then.[13] During the summer of 1907 the printers of Tehran again went on strike, this time to demand shorter working days. Their strike was successful, for their working day was reduced from fourteen to nine hours.[14]

The strike wave continued, however, for on August 2, 1907 the workers of the electricity plant of Emin al-Zarb in Tehran organized a strike. They demanded paid leisure days, just like government officials. Further, they wanted clothes paid for by the employer, since, because of their work, their clothes were torn and they had to get several suits each year. Finally, they wanted a certificate of good behavior on dismissal and the establishment of a health and safety fund. For "it is customary all over the world that in case of industrial accidents the workers get paid until they are healed, or in case of death that the wife and children receive assistance." The strike lasted three days during which time no electricity was supplied to the city. It is not known whether the strike had any success.[15]

Strikes were contagious owing to the political climate created by the recent acquisition of a constitution in Iran. For on August 11, 1907 the tramway workers in Tehran demanded better working conditions, although they held permanent jobs. They wanted

---

10. Hezb-e Tudeh 1349, 183. On January 1, 1907 the fishermen still refused to come to terms with Liazonov or to hand over the fish called *suf*, FO 248/906, 3. It has not been recorded when this dispute ended.
11. Hezb-e Tudeh 1349, 173.
12. Hezb-e Tudeh 1349, 173. The number of striking telegraphists (1600) as given by this source is much too high.
13. Malek 1357, 63; Rabino 1352, 13. The strike of the mainly Russian sailors probably ended at the end of April, for later it is not mentioned any more. While asking some reasonable concessions, they also asked impossible ones, according to Rabino, for "they ask that they should be engaged for 12 months in the year instead of for nine as at present and this notwithstanding that the port of Astrakhan is frozen in winter and that all shipping of the Caspian is stopped. They also require accommodation or quarters on board for the crew, an increase of their pay by 100% and a certain sum for their food. They also demand that Sundays and feasts should be regularly observed whether at sea or in port." In mid-April this strike had not yet ended a strike broke out amongst the Iranian "sailors who man the kerejis which are used as lighters to unload steamers which do not enter the harbour of Enzeli. They are claiming for an increase in the freight paid them. Their strike has so far been ineffective, as there has been scarcely any shipping of late owing to the strike at Baku." FO 248/906 Rasht local news, f.129–133.
14. Hezb-e Tudeh 1349, 174.
15. Malek 1357, 64 (quoting from *Habl al-Matin* 1, 84, 27 Jomadi al-Akhar 1325 Q).

paid holidays "as is usual elsewhere in the world."[16] Government officials also caught the infection, even at an unexpected Ministry such as Foreign Affairs. On October 1, 1907 the Ministry had already been on strike for a few days because the minister had not shown a proper reaped for his collaborators.[17]

It would appear that other trade unions were formed in those days besides that of the printers in Tehran. For, later in 1922 the recollection of these earlier groups served as an incentive to try to resuscitate them.[18] One such group was no doubt the *Anjoman-e Ettehadiyeh-ye Telegrafi* led by Besharat al-Saltaneh, which was founded in 1908 to provide its members with mutual support.[19] The existence of similar groups among the dockers and boatmen of Enzeli, the shoemakers in Tehran, the printers in Isfahan, the tramway officials and *droshksechi*s in Tehran and the carpet weavers in Kerman is also reported.[20]

The establishment of such groups undoubtedly helped to maintain solidarity among the workers concerned. It also made it easier to start new strikes demanding better working conditions, pay and rights. In 1908 Enzeli was again the scene of strikes by fishermen against Liazonov. Although, in December 1908, the Government sent the Cossacks against the strikers, in April 1909 they again organized a strike.[21] Earlier that year - April 1908 - the boatmen of Langerud had struck for higher wages.[22]

On October 28, 1908, Tabriz had a strike on its hands, for 150 workers of three tanneries demanded improved working conditions and more labor rights. They had been organized by Russian social-democrats, who also directed the strike. The workers made the following demands.

1. A pay rise of one and a half *shahi* per skin;
2. That the appointment and dismissal of workers and apprentices should; take place with the permission of the workers;
3. Improvement of health conditions;
4. Payment of doctor's bills by the employer;
5. Payment of 50% of the salary in case of illness;

---

16. Malek 1357, 6 (quoting from *Habl al-Matin* 1, 88, 2 Rajab 1325 Q).
17. Malek 1357, (quoting from *Habl al-Matin* 1, 129, 22 Sha'ban 1325 Q).
18. RMM, 1922, 52, 148.
19. RMM, 1908, 5, 167.
20. Hezb-e Tudeh 1349, 174, Shidfar 1339, vol.1, 165; Ivanov. n.d. In the FO files there is, however, no evidence to be found at all of the existence of a union of carpet weavers. There is evidence to the contrary rather, see for example FO 248/1030, Kirman Diary (July 1911), f.157. There was, however, a union of cultivators of henna aiming to got fixed prices for their products, while at the same time there was a union of buyers of henna, FO 248/906 Kirman Diary (September 1907), f.386. In Rasht the servants formed a kind of servants' union to protect them from oppression at the hands of their employers. From the context it is clear, however, that these people also had political objectives, because they also wanted to join the local *Majles* and started negotiations to come to a kind of compromise after having first been turned away, FO 248/906, "Rasht local news" f. 161.
21. Hezb-e Tudeh 1349, 185.
22. Hezb-e Tudeh 1349, 184.

6. Less overtime;
7. In case of overtime, payment of 200% of the normal salary;
8. No dismissal of strikers during the strike;
9. Payment of wages during the strike;
10. No exclusion of workers who participated in the strike.

The strikers had formed a committee to negotiate these demands with the employers. The result was that the strikers returned to work on October 30 when three of their demands (1, 8, 10) had been met. Although solidarity among the workers had been strong during the strike, the negotiating committee wanted to establish a strike fund for workers who were without means.

When one of the employers did not stick to the agreement (he dismissed a foreman, a member of the negotiating committee), the workers used the weapon of boycott against the employer. At the suggestion of their social-democrat mentors, the workers first found another job for the foreman and then persuaded prospective candidates for the vacancy, not to apply. Although the employer offered better terms for this vacancy there were no applicants. The result of this action, unfortunately, is not known. Although the social-democrats wanted to form a trade union in the future, for the time being they preferred to organize and interest the labor class politically.[23]

Notwithstanding the early enthusiasm shown by various groups of urban workers to fight for better wages, rights and working conditions, they lacked organization, funds, political backing and support from the working class in general to withstand the political changes in Iran, which were inimical to the rights and interests of the lower classes there. For, although the constitutional forces were able to defeat the counter-revolution mounted by Mohammad 'Ali Shah, they were not able to cope with their own inadequacy. The Democrats, who favored all kinds of reforms, including the adoption of labor laws, were faced with a strong majority of so-called Moderates, or rather conservatives, who, backed by Russia and Great Britain, proved to be too strong for them. Many potential bazaari supporters, moreover, joined the Moderates at the urging of the ulama. "The clergy, who had a vested interest for opposing reform, fooled the public, especially craftsmen and tradesmen, into believing that the Democrats were the sworn enemies of Islam."[24]

Not only were the guilds effectively barred from representation in the *Majles* (Parliament), but all 12 trade unions were forcibly dissolved as well.[25] Although these trade unions were said to have put up a fight we have hardly any information on this issue to confirm, assess or gainsay such a statement However, it seems unlikely that labor put up a fight. The sections of the labor class that were politically aware were both geographically and numerically restricted. The majority of the urban working class were not at all

---

23. Ravasani, n.d., 388–89.
24. Abrahamian 1982, 102f, Malekzadeh 1325, vol.4, 212. For the programs of the progressive parties during the second *Majles* period see Mansureh Ettehadiyeh 1361.
25. Shidfar 1339, vol.1, 165; Shaje'i 1344, 184–189/

exposed to trade union ideas and remained within the traditional fold of the guilds. In the labor force dominated by the guild organization, affiliated as it was with politically traditional forces, there was no interest in labor matters. The unorganized casual labor in the cities was not fertile soil for the blossoming of workers' ideals either.[26] So the very few professions which were new and modern, namely, the printers and telegraphers, constituted in fact the only real organized labor organization in Iran. A similar situation may have existed among the workers (dockers, boatmen, fishermen) in Enzeli for they had been exposed longer to social-democratic ideas than any other group of workers in Iran. A unique situation existed here, viz. that a considerable number of these workers were influenced by Russians who took these revolutionary ideas 'en bloc' with them.[27] There is no sign whatsoever that exposure of Iranian migrant workers to trade-unionism and social-democracy in Russia led to any lasting activity among workers.

The above is also borne out by the fact that the best organized section of the labor movement in Iran, the Printers' Union in Tehran, put up the only real fight. As in European countries, the printers belonged to the best paid and educated part of the working class, with a high level of organization and class consciousness. They also supported the Democrats. In 1910 there was a constant exchange of portfolios by the Sepahdar's cabinet which the opposition newspapers ridiculed, while they also spoke in disrespectful tones about the Sepahdar and his new ministers. On May 25, 1910 the offending newspapers were suppressed by order of the cabinet and their editors were ordered to appear in the courts of justice to be tried, but this they refused to do.[28] The printers, protesting against the cabinet's measures, organized a strike. When the police interfered, the strike leaders took sanctuary in the Parliament building to enforce the release of the arrested strikers and the acceptance of their demands.[29] These were the following:[30]

1. The working day is to be nine hours;
2. The minimum wage is the three *tumans* (about 75 p.) a month, wages to be increased on a scale varying between five and twelve percent,

---

26. Abrahamian 1982, 130, FO 371/20830, f.184 "A Memorandum on Economic Affairs in Azerbaijan" (31 December 1936), Bahar 1358, 139 states "socialist ideas can but fall on barren ground in a backward environment such as Iran where there are no industrial capitalists, no industrial enterprises, and thus no industrial workers."
27. Many Russians were working in the fisheries industry, the timber mills and in shipping. An example of the influence of Russian labor relations on the Iranian situation has been given in note 13 above.
28. FO 371/950, Monthly Summary, f.373.
29. Hezb-e Tudeh 1349, 185, Hushyar 1330, 51. According to the *Times* (July 19, 1910, 7) the general strike of all printers in Tehran took place on June 26. Its journalist reported "evidently rumours had got abroad that the printers had been paid to strike by persons in authority desirous of extinguishing the regular newspapers, for the authors of the new venture (i.e. the paper *Ettefaq- e Kargaran*) took care to base their action on economic grounds. They published a list of demands which throw an instructive light upon the relations between employers and workmen, and it is probably not too much to say that such a document is unique in this country".
30. *The Times* (July 19, 1910), 7 (English text, for the Persian text see Chaqueri, 1359, 117 f. with a facsimile of the first page of the first issue of *Ettefaq-e Kargaran*.

according to the amount. For instance, the highest wages mentioned, 20 to 25 *tumans* (£4 - £5) a month, to be increased by five per cent. Above all, the wages must be paid regularly;

3. If a workman is dismissed through no fault of his own after six months' service, he must receive fifteen days extra wage. If after one year, a month extra;

4. He has also the right to fifteen days' notice and, should the establishment change hands, he can demand wages for that period from the original owners;

5. The editors and managers must treat their employees with politeness;

6. In the case of continuous night work, a night staff must be employed at one and a half times the day wage. In the event of the day staff being employed on special occasions at night, they must receive a similar increase;

7. In addition to the usual feast days, one day a week must be free;

8. In case of illness, a workman must receive his full wage, but on recovery he must return to his work;

9. Every printing office must have its own doctor in attendance;

10. In case of temporary disablement, the workman is entitled to a full wage for as long as three months;

11. In case of complete disablement, the amount of compensation to be fixed by the employer and the representatives of the workmen;

12. In the case of death, the compensation to the family of the deceased to be settled as in the preceding instance;

13. Every printing office must have a manager;

14. The owners and the representatives of the committee of workmen have to draw up regulations for all printing offices.

In June 1910, under the leadership of the Central Labor Council (*Ettefaq-e Kargaran-e Markazi*), the printers carried on their fight. As a result of their strike there were no newspapers. In order to inform the general public about their grievances and demands, the printers published their own newspaper called 'Labor Union' (*Ettefaq-e Kargaran*), of which only five issues in all appeared.[31]

Although none of their demands was met, it did not break their fighting spirit. The more so, since Sardar 'Asad, the other strong man of the cabinet, allowed the papers to reappear again, upon which the Sepahdar withdrew from the cabinet. In 1911 printers all over Iran even created a national printers' trade union.[32] Nevertheless, for the time being they appeared to be a spent force. The atmosphere in Iran was hostile to the further devel-

---

31. See notes 29 and 30 above.
32. Bashkirov 1948, 24.

opment of trade unions in Iran, for, after 1911, northern Iran was virtually under Russian occupation and they stood no nonsense from Iranian workers as the dockers in Enzeli knew from experience. Moreover, after its 'surrender' to the Russian demands Parliament was not convened again until 1914. With the suspension of Parliament - the main controlling agency with regard to the implementation of Iran's constitutional rights - these rights, including the freedom of association, were suspended as well.[33]

In the South there was no labor organization outside the guilds. Nevertheless, some labor unrest occurred here also, when in April 1913 the deputy-governor of Kerman published a set of regulations on conditions to be maintained in the carpet factories in that town. However, it was not the weavers, but the employers who went on strike.[34] A similar lock-out took place in October 1913 in Kerman, again by the employers of the carpet factories. But this time the weavers, angry at this political act (the employers were protesting against some taxes), took sanctuary in the British Consulate, for they were most grievously hurt through enforced idleness by this strike.[35]

The unsettled political situation and the crisis occasioned by the violation of Iran's neutrality during the First World War, made Iran the scene of war, which excluded any organized labor action. Moreover, Parliament, which had begun its third session on December 6, 1914, was suspended again on December 14, 1915 and for the next five and a half years Iran had no parliament and no proper government. The country was on the point of dissolution, while factionalism, local uprisings and warlordism ravaged what had survived the vicissitudes of war. With the Russian Revolution of 1917, the role of Russia in Iran also changed. It still wanted to influence events there, and some Bolsheviks even argued that Iran was "the first nation to be conquered by the Soviets."[36] But the interference was thence-forth aimed at the 'progressive' forces and not at the elite. The new Soviet government wanted to organize the revolutionary power of the working and peasant class of Iran. Thus Russian support also provided an impetus to Iranian progressive forces, both inside and outside Iran. During the war, Iranians in Baku had established a group called *'Adalat* (Justice), which formally constituted itself into a party in 1917 under the same name. Its aim was to prevent the old conservative forces regaining control in Iran and one of the means would be the formation of trade unions. It was not the only progressive organization, of course, but it was the best organized party with the widest distribution of organizational structures, having branches in most big Iranian cities.[37] In June 1920, under the influence of a similar development in Russia, the *'Adalat* and *Hemmat* parties dissolved themselves and, together with other leftist organizations, formed the Communist Party of Iran. The intended activities of this and similar organizations coincided with

---

33. On this period see Abrahamian 1982, 102–111.
34. FO 248/1072, Kirman Diary, f. 62, 68.
35. FO 248/1072, f.222, 256.
36. Lenczowski 1968, 10.
37. Ravasani, n.d., 248 ff. the *'Adalat* party was not the only progressive party that undertook action in Iran, apart from another group mentioned. Ibid, 246 (note 1) there was also a *Ferqeh-ye Sosiyalist-e Iran* in Qazvin. For a copy of its program see FO 248/1259, *'maramnameh'*, May 1919.

labor unrest which had arisen spontaneously in Iran as a result of the miserable conditions under which the people existed.

THE GOLDEN AGE (1918–1925)

The situation in Tehran

Towards the end of World War 1, in the winter of 1917/18, thousands of people in Iran died of hunger and cold. This situation was further aggravated by hoarding and short-selling to customers by the bakers.[38] This provoked reaction on the part of the workers in the bakeries. They formed a trade union and forced the government to recognize them by organizing a strike and closing down all sales points for bread.[39] Although this led to a temporary improvement in the bread situation, (for hoarding was soon resumed), the first union had been born again. At about the same time, the printers formed a second trade union.[40] They organized a strike during the 'hunger demonstrations' in 1917/18 and, while waving red banners to express their support for the Russian revolution, attacked the shops of bakers and hoarders with the other demonstrators. The police broke up this demonstration, but not the new-found solidarity among the printers.[41]

In 1918 they organized another strike which lasted two weeks and forced the government to recognize them as an official trade union. By that time the printers' union had 2,000 members. The new union was able to force the employers and the government to accept their demands, the most important of which were:

1. An 8 hour working day for all printers
4. Overtime paid at the rate of 150 per cent of the normal wages
6. In case of illness, the employer to continue to pay the wages for a period of two months as well as the doctor's bills
15. In case of dismissal, the employer to give one month's notice and pay one month's wages
22. In case of an industrial accident leading to invalidity of a worker half a worker, the employer to pay the disabled month's salary for a period as long as the printing establishment has existed. Moreover, in addition to Fridays, workers to have a right to three days on festive days to a maximum of 25 days per year as well as the right to ten days of paid holidays for each year worked.

---

38. Chaqueri 1978, 7, 20.
39. Ossetrov 1922, 574.
40. Ossetrov 1922, 574.
41. Chaqueri 1978, 7, 20, 86.

Equally important was the fact that both the government and the employers had accepted the principle of collective bargaining and agreements in case of the Printers' Union.[42]

Another old acquaintance, the Telegraphers and Postal Workers' Union also came alive again and, with allegedly 2,000 members, was second only to the printers' union. This nationwide union was at first not recognized by the government, which did its best to have it dissolved, though without success.[43]

Although the printers and the post officials initiated the renaissance of the trade union movement, this proved to be an incentive for other trades to form unions too. Especially in 1918-1919 a few of these groups, such as the tramway and construction workers, were active in opposing the government led by Vothuq al-Dowleh as to the Anglo-Iranian Treaty. Apart from demanding expulsion of the British from Iran, who had still troops there, their demands centered on issues such as the hoarding of grain, the 8-hour working day and the right to form a trade union. The turn-out of the unions supported by other labor groups[44] was quite big in the autumn of 1919 during an anti-British rally, during which the demonstrators demanded the release of Soleyman Mirza, a Socialist leader,[45] who had been interned by the British in India during the war. Although several of these groups clearly only had short-term political objectives, as shown by their sudden demise, the trade union movement nevertheless was contagious and successful. The anti-British attitude amongst the population in general continued to be an important mobilizing factor for political and labor organizers.[46] As is shown by Table 2.1, the years 1920-1923 were the hey-day of trade unions in Iran. This held especially for Tehran, which was, with Gilan (Rasht, Enzeli) and Tabriz, the main center of trade union activity. From two unions in 1918 the movement grew to ten unions in 1920. By the end of 1921, of the 20,000 reported trade union members in Iran, Tehran accounted for some 8,000. At that time the trade unions claimed a level of organization of 20 per cent of the total urban industrial labor force in Iran, which they estimated to be about 100,000.[47] By November 1920 the trade union movement had gained such strength and popularity in Tehran that in November 1921 the union organizers decided to create a Central Union Council (*Ettehadi-ye Markazi-ye Koll-e Kargaran-e Tehran*), which at the same time joined the *Profintern*, the Moscow-based organization of international Red Syndicates.[48] At the summit of the trade union movement (1922-23) this central council represented sixteen unions. According to

---

42. Ossetrov 1922, 575 (partly translated by Ravasani n.d., 228).
43. Ossetrov 1922. 575 (22 union members in Tehran; however, nationally there were allegedly 2,000 members, Ravasani n.d, 227).
44. Chaqueri 1978, 86 these other groups were formed by construction workers, tramway functionaries and others.
45. On his career see Abrahamian 1982, 127–28; see also FO 416/79, f.94 for a short biographical note.
46. As Lenczowski 1968 remarks, "the Anglo-iranian Treaty of 1919 was denounced by practically everybody in Iran, and the prevailing climate in politics was decidedly anti-British", 100.
47. Lenczowski 1968, 7, 11, 13, 16, 76, 88, 97; the labor force, however, was much bigger at that time, see Bharier 1971, 34.
48. Mani 1325, 9; partly reprinted in *Taban* 1974, vol.1, 159f.

its secretary, Shokrollah Mani,[49] the membership of the central council in 1922 was as shown in Table 2.2. The task of the Central Council was to guide and instruct existing unions and to organize new unions. Each union was represented by three members on the Central Council, which met regularly every Thursday evening in the office of the *Haqiqat* newspaper and later in a rented house in the Khiyaban-e Naseriyeh.[50]

TABLE 2.1: Trade Unions and their Membership in Tehran [51]

	Name/Year	1921	1922	1923	1924	1925
1.	Printers	180	200	200	250	150
2.	Salesmen (mercers)	350	-	80	-	-
3.	Bakers	3000	2000	1800	-	-
4.	Trade clerks	250	200	-	-	-
5.	Postal workers	90	100	120	-	-
6.	Telegraphists	180	564	564	-	-
7.	Confectioners	300	400	400	-	-
8.	Shoemakers	1800	1800	1800	150	-
9.	Tailors	2000	1000	2000	15	-
10.	Lace-workers	150	150	150	-	-
11.	Teachers	-	480	400	-	-
12.	*Taftuni* bakers	-	-	720	-	-
13.	Municipal workers	-	-	500	-	-
14.	Cigarette makers	-	-	2500	-	-
15.	Textile workers	-	-	-	200	50
16.	Pharmaceutical workers	-	-	130	100	-

---

49. Mani 1325, 9 f.; he also mentions the names of the representatives of the various unions. According to Chaqueri 1978, 75, the important group of bakers was not affiliated with the Central Council, because it was not a proper union, being a religious kind of organization. Lambton 1954, 23 also states that the *Shateran-e nanva* (a section of the bakers' guild) may have retained a religious character. Could it be one of the last vestiges of a *fotovvat* association? On this issue see Floor, 1984a, 106, 114.

50. Mani 1325, 11; FO 416173, Intelligence Summary nr.29, July 21, 1923, f. "The Union of Workmen in Tehran has opened an office in the city. On the door is the inscription: Proletarians of all nations unite, with the Soviet crest of the hammer and sickle etc., above it. Meetings are held every evening about how to boycott English goods in the best way."

51. Table 2.1 based on Chaqueri 1978, 83; see however, 93. For 1926 see Ibid, 94; see also Ossetrov, 1922. 57; and FO 371/9027, "The Ishtamayun Party," f.176, which states, "1,350 artisans and workmen wore members of the Socialist party and organized into several unions - Union of Printers, strength 300, president Jehangir/Union of Editors, strength 40, president Nasir Saif/Union of Masons, strength 200; president Hussein Mehmar (sic)/Union of Bath Attendants, strength 100, president Ustad Hussein/Union of Bootmakers, strength 200, president Abdul Karim/Union of Tenants, strength 510, president Farokhi (editor of the extremist 'Tofan'). "The data show how unreliable these newspaper figures are, for in many cases they do not agree with one another."

	Name/Year	1921	1922	1923	1924	1925
17.	Construction workers	-	-	-	400	40
18.	Bath-house attendants	-	-	-	200	--

TABLE 2.2 Trade Unions Represented on the Central Council in 1922

1	Printers' union	9	Cigarette makers' union
2	Shoemakers' union	10	Bath-house workers' union
3	Bakers' union	11	Drapery workers' union
4	Pharmaceutical workers' union	12	Salesmen's union
		13	Textile workers' union
5	Teachers' union	14	Dockers' union (Enzeli)
6	Post office officials' union	15	*Taftuni* bakers' union
7	Municipality workers' union	16	Stocking makers' union
8	Construction workers' union		

Mohammad Khan Dehqan, the editor of *Haqiqat* and president of the Printers Union was a member of the Communist Party of Iran. He was a leading force in the trade union movement and he worked hard on its behalf. The Communist Party, which had declined considerably after the collapse of the Gilan Republic, tried to make a comeback[52] through men like Dehqan.[53] The Communist Party therefore had instructed its cadres to work in such a way that people did not make a direct link between the Party and the trade unions. Although the Communist Party did not formally control the unions, in reality it had direct control over them. Within each union the members of the Communist Party constituted a secret inner circle to influence the decisions and actions of the unions.[54] One might say the whole show was run by the Communist Party in collaboration with the Russian embassy in Tehran.

It is therefore not surprising to observe that the accredited Iranian delegate to the 1922 Fourth Congress of the Communist International confidently reported that the party achieved good results among the unions. "The party's main task was to strive for a common anti-imperialist front by establishing a democratic bloc to which all national

---

52. Zabih 1977, 50.
53. For particulars about Dehqan see Mani 1325/1946, 18 and Abrahamian 1982, 132.
54. Chaqueri vol. 1, Ovanessiyan 1974, 119–140, 114. In particular, a similar observation is made by Lahuti n.d, 21. Abrahamian's statement, 1982, (119 n.39) "although this book is a forgery - probably by the police" is not substantiated by a shred of evidence. Lahuti's book is borne out in most of his observations by other Communist authors such as Ovanessiyan mentioned in this note. It is therefore not surprising that Abrahamian ends his note with the (contradictory) statement "it provides interesting information on the revolt and the communist movement in exile".

and democratic groups might belong, but in which the leading role would be played by the CP."[55]

Apart from politicizing workers by urging them to form unions, for which purpose large amounts of money were later spent by the Russian embassy (through the CPI, unions, or otherwise) on propaganda aimed at influencing young government officials, progressive intellectuals and (skilled) artisans, the message was strongly anti-British, and very critical of the old feudal and aristocratic families. People were exhorted to be freedom-loving and to support the Constitution. It was moreover stressed that a modern progressive, if possible socialist, government was near. Care was taken that Russia should not be mentioned, unless to show how well people (especially workers) were treated there.[56]

The medium of the message were a few newspapers, amongst which was the so-called trade union newspaper, *Haqiqat* (Truth), which in reality was one of the organs of the CPI.[57] The same also held true for its successor *Kar* (Work), and other progressive newspapers such as *Eqdam* (Struggle), *Setareh-ye Sorkh* (Red Star), *Tufan* (Storm), *Siyasat* (Politics), *Shahin* (Pointer), *Shafaq-e Sorkh* (Red Twilight), and some others.[58] All these papers received financial support from the Russian embassy.[59]

The Russian embassy in 1922 also tried to organize a communist trade union.[60] One Shareman Khan, a tailor working in the Russian Legation, was asked to form this union. During the constituent meeting, Dehqan attended for the Printers' Union and 'Ali Mirza, a boot-shop owner, for the boot-makers. It was decided that Dehqan would be the

---

55. Zabih 1977, 50.

56. Lahuti n.d. 22; this observation is e.g. borne out by an analysis of the contents of these newspapers, Fatemi 1952, 280–92; see also Lenczowski 1968, 98.

57. Founded on December 30, 1921, it identified itself as a Socialist (*ejtema'i*) newspaper and as as supporter of the workmen (*ranjbaran*) and the trade unions, whose Central Council had been created in November 1921. The paper also printed at the top right-hand of each issue "Workers of the World Unite". For this newspaper see Chaqueri 1974–1978, vol. 7, 49 re-issues of the *Haqiqat* newspaper.

58. The CPI also published *Peykar* in Rasht, *Nasihat* in Qazvin, *Seda-ye Sharq* in Mashhad, *Faryad-e Kargaran* in Tabriz and *Enqelab-e sorkh* in Tehran.

59. The following papers supported Soleyman Mirza, leader of the Socialist Party, and therefore received subsidies from the Russian Legation in Tehran: *Peykar*, editor Mohammad Vothuq-e Homayun 125 *tuman*s per month, *Kar* editor Abo'l-Fazel Lesani,150 *tuman*s per month, *Kushesh* editor Shokrollah Sofri,100 *tuman*s per month, Baharistan Nowbakht,100 *tuman*s per month, *Shafaq-e Sorkh* editor 'Ali Dashti, 200 *tuman*s per month, see FO 371/9027, f. 176-77. It goes without saying that the British financed their own newspapers and men of straw, a methodology which still has not lost its value in today's ideological warfare. On British activities see Waterfield 1973, 71.

60. FO 416/70, Intelligence Summary nr. 4, January 18, 1922 "The military attaché Colonel Rogachef is of the opinion that the time has not come for this, but the other members of the Yarcheika (cell) committee considered it feasible and recommended a commencement".

president of the Union and Mohammad Khan,[61] its treasurer. The union's program was as follows:[62]

1. To bring together workmen of all nationalities together into one union for mutual support.
2. Each class of workmen e.g. chauffeurs, bakers, etc. to have their separate committees which will in turn be under the Central Committee.
3. Each group of workmen must be ready to support another group e.g. by strikes etc.
4. The newspaper *Haqiqat* to be the official organ of the Union of Workmen; the cost of running this paper to be paid from the treasury of the Central Committee.
5. Employees in Government departments can also become members.
6. Fifty per cent of the money collected in the treasury to be spent on unemployed members.
7. The Union to have a free school, library and hospital for the use of members and their families.
8. The Union to have close touch with similar unions in Russia.
9. The Union to arrange to have translated into Persian all papers and books received from Russia which relate to workmen's unions in order that they may be accessible to members.
10. Assistance in organizing unions for any particular trade may be obtained from Russia, whence expert organizers can be sent to assist.
11. Efforts must be made to start similar branches of the Union in other towns in Iran.
12. Only people who are genuinely employed in some trade can be enrolled as members of the Union.

On September 5, 1922 the Russian Legation decided to dissolve the Iranian Communist Union of Workers, for it had failed to draw a sufficient membership.[63] In its place, a professional union was created on September 10 which was open to all nationalities. It was the clear purpose of this union to fill its ranks with Russian citizens, who in this way would try and attract Iranian members. The president of the union was Romanovski, while

---

61. Mohammad Khan was "employed on the staff of the *Haqiqat* newspaper. Formerly a Major in the Gendarmerie and served with the Germans in South Persia. He is close friends with Sohrab Zadeh Mudabber ol-Molk who is a professional agitator ready to join any party for a consideration. Meetings of the Central Committee (of the union) take place once a week at the office of the Iran press. Each member pays a contribution of 3 tomans a month". FO 371/7809, Saunders to Minister, 28 February 1922 (secret).
62. FO 371/7809, Saunders to Minister, 28 February 1922 (secret).
63. FO 371/7828, Intelligence Summary nr. 36, September 9, 1922 "in accordance with the decision of Shumyatski and Apin".

its office was in the *Vneshtorg* premises.⁶⁴ The driver of the Russian Legation tried to organize a similar union in February 1922.⁶⁵

To what extent these Russian endeavors were successful is unknown. Since no other sources makes mention of them we may conclude that all these efforts came to nought. The Russians had some success with the organization of a union among the Armenians in Tehran to which end Nerces Nercessian had been specifically sent from Moscow.⁶⁶

In 1922, the CPI sent Reza Rusta and Pishehvari from Baku to Tehran to take over the running of the Central Council, which was very much resented by Dehqan and led to friction between them. But, since they had to work in secret, this dispute did not lead to open hostility.⁶⁷

To create a better political climate for the unions, the CPI tried to create a political platform for them by establishing links with the leader of the 'minority' faction in parliament, Soleyman Mirza, leader of the Socialist Party (*Ejtema'iyun-e 'Amiyun*).⁶⁸ This link was necessary, for the CPI had no representatives in the parliament and the unions still had to fight for official recognition. On January 22, 1922 the parliament deputy, Sayyed Ya'qub, declared that in Iran there was no working class, and thus there existed no labor problem.⁶⁹ Some other conservative deputies, led by Nosrat al-Dowleh, created a rural workers' union which tried to invalidate the labor movement.⁷⁰ Later the conservatives promoted the creation of an employers' syndicate, which was led by influential Tehrani bazaaris.⁷¹ The 'majority' in parliament clearly wanted to destroy the unions.⁷²

The CPI-financed newspapers attacked these conservative deputies and exhorted the workers to support the unions.⁷³ A publication by the Central Council, published in *Haq-*

---

64. FO 371/7828, Intelligence Summary nr. 36, September 9, 1922.

65. FO 416/70, Intelligence Summary nr. 7, February 18, 1922 f. "as part of the scheme for spreading the communist doctrine".

66. FO 416/72 Intelligence Summary nr. 33, August 19, 1922. f.145 "he is a trained Bolshevik propagandist"; see also Ibid., IS 15. April 14, 1923, which mentions the start of a club of workmen by an Armenian communist committee at the orders of the Russian legation.

67. Lahuti n.d, 21.

68. Ibid. see also Abrahamian 1982, 131–32 for an analysis of the political situation at that time.

69. "We do not yet have workers in Iran. Everyone is an employer. If God so desires, and our country becomes important, and trade and agriculture commence, and factories are founded, at that time a labor-employer law will be produced. However, at the moment we have neither workers nor factories or railroads for which to have workers", *Majles*, 1924, 424; see also note 26. See also "La Politique du gouvernement des soviets en Perse," in: *RMM* 1922, 150 and Floor, 1984b. For a reply by *Haqiqat* see below note 76.

70. Ossetrov 1922, 578; Mani 1325, 18 states that Reza Khan had established the unions of the five (low-class) quarters (*mahalleh*) to attack the newspaper *Haqiqat* and the workers' unions. These other 'unions' were composed of *owbash* (ruffians). On p. 18 Mani, however, states that Modarres had organized these ruffian-'unions', which is not unlikely in view of the good relationship that he had with Reza Khan and Nosrat al-Dowleh as well as with the city ruffians. On the use of the *owbash* as a political weapon see: Floor 1981, 83–95; for another example see Chaqueri 1978, 78.

71. Ossetrov 1922, 578.

72. According to Mani 1325, 18, Modarres induced the hooligans of Tehran to attack the *Haqiqat* office in the Lalehzar street.

73. RMM 1922, 150; *Haqiqat* nr. 59.

iqat, stated "it was necessary to show that there are workers who form a considerable class in Iran. Joining the union is an expression of loving your country and of support for the *Majles* and as a protest against those who sell our country."[74]

Of special importance was the fight of the postal officials against the government for the recognition of their Union and the role of the Belgian advisor Molitor. The Union accused Molitor of obstruction and efforts to have their Union dissolved and tried to have him dismissed. The Union fought and created an issue about Molitor by accusing him of fraud. This led to a fierce discussion in parliament. Qavam al-Saltaneh's cabinet then issued a decree forbidding government officials to be members of a trade union. This caused an outcry in progressive circles and, backed by the 'minority' group of Soleyman Mirza, they worked together to bring down Qavam al-Saltaneh's cabinet.[75]

Apart from establishing their political credibility and appealing to patriotism and xenophobia, the Union leadership also had more practical means to create unions. Shokrallah Mani, himself a textile worker, wrote that when Sayyed Mohammad Khan Dehqan approached him and his colleagues about the formation of a union they liked this idea "after he had explained what his (Printers) Union had done and achieved. The more so when he outlined that by unity they might get a raise of pay."[76]

The moment was well chosen, for the employers wanted to lower the wages by one `abbasi per ell (*zar*). When the workers had been given a small amount of money as an advance payment they liked the idea of a strike for a higher wage, since they could afford not to work for a few days. The strike took place in April 1922 and lasted one day. When the weavers won it was quite understandable that the Union became very popular and all 700 of the weavers joined.[77]

In those golden days the Central Council could indeed hold out the promise of a successful strike. In the second half of 1921 the record had been very successful with strikes by the Bakers' Union, the Printers' Union, the Postal Officials' Union and the Mercers' Union. In Enzeli, moreover, there had been a successful Dockers' Union strike.[78] On December 24, 1921 the teachers of Tehran went on strike because their wages had not been paid for six months. The strike also had another objective, namely to protest against the government decree that no government officials were allowed to join a union. After three weeks strike the government resigned, although it is not clear whether it was due

---

74. Reply by *Haqiqat* (nr. 2 January 1, 1922) to Sayyed Ya`qub Anvar Ardekani (see note 70).

75. See on this matter *Haqiqat* nrs. 51, 69 and 83; also Chaqueri 1978, 23, reproducing an article by Soltanzadeh which is probably the source for Ladjevardi's mistake of stating that Molitor was a Swede, see Ladjevardi 1981, 75. *Haqiqat* nr. 2 (January 1, 1922) states "foreign personnel forced the government to dissolve the union of postal workers and the Majlis, the same Majlis for whose establishment these same workers gave thousands of sacrifices does not raise a voice against the violation of one of the principles of the constitution". A union of dismissed finance officials was organised in Tehran about the 1st June 1923. They had been recently dismissed by Millspaugh on reduction of staff and numbered about one hundred, FO 416/73, IS nr. 22.

76. Mani 1325, 8, for the announcement of the creation of this union see *Haqiqat* nr. 78 (May 12, 1922).

77. Mani 1325, 8, *Haqiqat* nr. 69 (April 30, 1922).

78. Chaqueri 1978, 7–9.

to this strike or to other political reasons. On June 24, 1922 the new government formed by Qavam al-Saltaneh decided to ban seven newspapers affiliated with the opposition. He also had their editors arrested. As a result of these activities, the Central Union Council met and decided to call a general strike if the government did not release the arrested printers and lift the ban on the publication of the papers. On September 9, 1922 Qavam al-Saltaneh, faced with this threat, gave in to the Unions' demands. Another strike by the printers of the *Majles* printing office in 1923 was also a Union success. The government met all its demands - a wage increase, a vacation of ten days per year, and abolition of the rule that *Majles* printers (who were military personnel), could also be called upon to do duties other than printing.[79]

Not only success and financial support for strikes drew workers to the unions. The various individual unions led by the Central Union Council also organized a great many events to enhance workers' social life. The union member, 'Ali Zhaleh, for example, opened a reading room for workers (*qara'at-khaneh-ye kargaran*) in the Lalehzar avenue. This was not free from harassment and the lease was withdrawn from 'Ali Zhaleh, who, however, was soon able to re-open his reading room in the same street in May 1922.[80]

Apart from literature,[81] the Union also had several publications through which to disseminate their ideas among the populace. The most famous one was *Haqiqat* edited by Dehqan, which in fact was an instrument of the Communist Party.[82] According to Mani, *Haqiqat* had a readership of 4,000, while it was so popular that a copy of *Haqiqat* could be resold at much higher prices than the subscription rate. It appeared to have attracted the attention of conservative circles also, who eagerly read the contents of the paper.[83] But *Haqiqat* was not the only the paper dealing with union issues. After its demise there was the newspaper *Kar*, *Eqtesad-e Iran*, and of course *Komunist*, the official CPI paper.[84] In the provinces we see *Takammol*, the paper of the Workers' Party (*Hezb-e Kargaran*) in Tabriz.[85] In 1923, a new Armenian newspaper, subsidized by the Russian Legation, named *Banyor* (workman) was published in Iran.[86] The CPI, through the formation of Komsomols, also established links with the Unions and youthful members, trying to influence them through the handwritten journal *Bolshevik-e Javan*.[87]

The Union also had its own theatrical group, which performed all kinds of plays which they themselves translated into Persian. The leader of the group was Rezaqoli 'Abdollahzadeh (Seyfi), a printer by profession, and member of the Central Committee

---

79. Chaqueri 1978, 22, 94, FO 416/70. Intelligence Summary nr. 34, December 24, 1923; Hadow 1925, "Pay was until recently, often seriously in arrears"; Lenczowski 1968, 66.
80. *Haqiqat* nrs. 63 (April 22, 1922) and nr. 78 (May 15, 1922).
81. Dehqan for example translated works of Marx and Engels into Persian, Mani, 1325, 18.
82. See above note 21.
83. Mani 1325, 16.
84. Mani 1325, 16, see also note 22 above.
85. Ossetrov 1922, 576.
86. FO 416/73, Intelligence Summary nr.39. September 29, 1923, f.229.
87. Ovanessiyan 1974, 137; they also formed football (soccer) teams.

of the CPI.[88] Some unions also organized parties, for which some even had a club, such as the Armenian socio-democratic *Hanchak* party in Tabriz.[89] The Russian Legation also opened a Russo-Persian workers' school and workers' club in Tehran where all kinds of lectures were given.[90] A very famous club was that of *Farhang* in Rasht, led by Keshavarz, which received a monthly subsidy of 40 *tumans* from the Russian Legation.[91] The *Farhang* Club was founded in 1917, and formed the model for two other important similar cultural clubs, the *Farhakht* club in Enzeli, and the *Parvaresh* club which was founded in 1924 in Qazvin. Both these new clubs were founded with the help of members of the *Farhang* Club, which kept regular contacts with its younger counterparts. All these clubs staged plays, were active in the field of adult education, and in general worked to elevate the level of knowledge of its members.[92] The Socialists also had their own club in Tehran just like the Armenian *Hanchak* party in Tabriz, while the former also ran a co-operative shop in Tehran.[93]

The most important festivity for the labor unions was of course Labor Day. It would appear that the first Labor Day celebrated in Iran was in 1920, organized by the socio-democratic Armenian *Hanchak* party. It was reserved for party members only.[94] The first Labor Day demonstration in Tehran took place in 1922, about which the British reported that it was a failure and had been organized by the Russian Legation. "The only people who stopped working were the printers. Political meetings took place at the Shah's mosque and in one or two quarters of the town, but meetings were badly attended and no enthusiasm was shown."[95]

In the summer of 1923, during the parliamentary elections, Reza Khan took sudden and unexpected steps against the unions. He wanted to become the next prime minister and found the unions posed too much of an obstacle for his liking. Through his military commanders he had the unions suppressed all over the country. This action led to the near annihilation of the trade union movement of Iran.[96]

After Reza Khan had become Prime Minister, however, the union organizers took heart again and started to rebuild their organization. They also continued their political activities and concentrated on anti-British agitation. The excuse to do so had been offered

---

88. *Haqiqat* nr. 55 (April 5. 1922) and advertisement for the play 'Kaveh Ahangar' *Haqiqat* nr.63 (April 20, 1922), and Nadir Shah Afshar, and *Haqiqat* nr.69. (April 30, 1922 a comedy). On theater activities in general see Willem Floor, *The History of Theater in Iran* (Washington, DC: Mage, 2006)

89. Chaqueri 1359, 120.

90. FO 416/72 Intelligence Summary nr. 24, June 17, 1922, f. 72.

91. FO 371/13783, f.85 "20 per cent are said to be Russian subjects, leading spirit is Keshawarz, Munshi Bashi of the Russian Consulate"; see also FO 461/72 IS nr. 10, March 10 1923.

92. Kambakhsh 1972, 30.

93. See note 91; Ovanessiyan. 1974, 131.

94. See note 91 which has full text of the invitation for the May 1 celebration. The *Hanchak* party was an Armenian Communist party founded in 1887 in Geneva. In reaction, conservative nationalist groups established the *Dashnak* party in 1890.

95. FO 416/72 Intelligence Summary nr.18, May 5, 1922, f.15.

96. Chaqueri 1978, 83, 93; Ovanessiyan 1974, 135.

by the British who had expelled some Shi`a ulama from Iraq.⁹⁷ This led to popular demonstrations in Iran in July 1923, which was made intelligent use of by the tiny trade union movement to propagate its own message. During these demonstrations militant union members carried banners with texts such as: "Hail the Union of Workmen and the Religion of Islam"⁹⁸ in line with the policy of CPI to create an acceptable image for the unions and to appeal to the religious belief of the workers.

In November 1923 another such demonstration was held outside the northern gate of Tehran, which was attended by some 5,000 to 6,000 people. The trade union movement organized a strike that day and all shops were closed after 13.00 hours. The pupils of the Eslamiyeh school attended the meeting as well and sang the 'Workman's song.' A similar meeting was also hold in December 1923.⁹⁹

When Reza Khan returned to Tehran on November 11, 1923, he was welcomed by all kinds of social groups, who all displayed banners in the bazaar. The Union of Printers was represented by a banner with the text "The Union of Printers welcomes Sardar Sepah, the defender of the Workmen's Unions in Iran"!¹⁰⁰

How did this turnabout occur so soon after the suppression of the unions by Reza Khan? The CPI was hoping for the establishment of the republic of Iran by Reza Khan and his army. The party, therefore, supported by the Comintern, decided to support the republican objectives of Reza Khan, since his role was seen as an intermediate one in the progress to a socialist state.¹⁰¹ The unions therefore were instructed to support Reza Khan just as were the other instruments of the CPI. The opponents of Reza Khan were to be fiercely opposed and attacked, and as much support as possible had to be mobilized in his favour. The CPI and its supporters all joined the *Nahzat-e Melli* movement which constituted the focus of attention of all republicans in Iran. Funds were made available by the OGPU to Soleyman Mirza to buy *Majles* deputies.¹⁰² In this way the CPI and the unions contributed to Reza Khan's accession to the throne.

In 1924, the unions were only 1,300 members strong and, despite their political activities, were unable to attract the same attention as in former years. On May 1, 1924, the

---

97. See on this issue, for example, FO 371/9020.
98. FO 416/73, Intelligence Summary nr.28, July 14, 1923, f.84; for other similar examples see note 93.
99. FO 416/73, Intelligence Summary nr.44, November 3, 1923, f.4, Intelligence Summary nr.48. December 1, 1923. f.20 "The Workmen's Union had a banner stretched across the street inscribed 'Union will enable us to oppose English tyranny.'" As instructed by the Comintern, the CPI had "to do everything in their power to assist in boycotting British goods in Persia, Arabia, and Mesopotamia. It was also decided to set up a Committee of Action in Tehran with the indirect assistance of the Soviet Delegation", see FO 371/9026, f.110.
100. FO 461/73, Intelligence Summary nr.46 November 17, 1923, f.8.
101. Lahuti n.d. 23; Rezun 1981, 44 f.; *Haqiqat* nr.78, May 12, 1922 used the following arguments for supporting Reza Khan "because he is not from their class and has no peasants or estates or titles. For him it makes no difference if the upper classes profit or incur a loss. The upper classes cannot accept or tolerate a non-aristocrat gaining influence in a ministerial post." The CPI still hoped that this earlier assessment was the right one, and whole-heartedly supported this flirtation with the republican idea.
102. Lahuti n.d., 40; see for the Soviet-CPI analysis for this policy, Rezun 1981, 44f., 268-69; Zabih 1977, 51-54.

printers celebrated Labor Day with a one-day strike which was the last time they were able to do so publicly.[103] At that time Reza Khan still did not want to alienate forces who were supportive of his cause. In that same year the municipal workers went on strike, because they had not been paid for a long time. Although their demonstration led to clashes with the police, their demands nevertheless were met.[104]

All this changed in 1925. Reza Khan had to abandon his flirtation with the Republic after pressure from the ulama in Qom.[105] This turnabout led to clashes between the republicans and Reza Khan's supporters. During the parliamentary elections, which had to pave the way for his accession to the throne, Reza Khan ordered a total suppression of the unions and the CPI.[106] In both objectives his army was totally successful.

The Situation in Gilan

In other towns in Iran unionism was alive as well, principally in Gilan, Tabriz and Mashhad which, according to Ossetrov, was due "to their greater knowledge of workers' movements in Russia."[107] In Gilan unionism was strong among the dockers, fishermen, and porters. The Fishermen's Union was also affiliated to the Central Union Council and its leader Akhondzadeh, even replaced Dehqan, when he was away in Russia.[108]

In 1922 especially, these unions were reported to be very strong, although the data on their membership is conflicting. According to Ovanessiyan, the Porters' and Boatmen's Union, each had a membership of 700 to 800 and, together with the fishermen, of more than 1,000, although the latter had a fluctuating membership.[109] However, other sources state that 3,000 fishermen were unionized, of whom 30 per cent were Russians, while the strength of the Porters' and Boatmen's Unions was estimated to be only 150 to 200 each. Moreover, within this union a great variety of people had been brought together which gave rise to internal conflicts, for even big proprietors were members.[110]

The Russians by various means tried to propagandize for the Unions, both as an instrument for Marxist propaganda as well as a successful means to defend labor rights. At the end of 1922 the Russians set up the 'Caucasian Cooperative' (*Kavkaskaya Corporatsie*) in Enzeli. It was a kind of cooperative society for the benefit of the workers and a Russian called Sagaev led it. The society imported all kinds of goods, the profits of which went to the workers who were members of the society.[111] In Rasht, the unions were also quite

---

103. Chaqueri 1978, 94.
104. Chaqueri 1978, 94.
105. Hae'eri 1977, 142f.
106. Chaqueri 1978, 83, 93; Ovanessiyan 1974, 130.
107. Ossetrov 1922, 576; see also Abrahamian 1982, 130.
108. Mani 1325, 15.
109. Ovanessiyan 1914, 135.
110. RMM 1922; Ossetrov 1922, 576.
111. FO 416/72, Intelligence Summary nr. 46, November 18, 1922.

strong with some 3,000 workers organized from various trades such as printers, hat makers, and leatherworkers.[112]

The government did not appreciate the activities of the unions and in 1923 the military commander arrested their leaders, which was a blow to both the unions and the CPI.[113] Nevertheless, undoubtedly with help from the Russian consul, new activities were started again. In 1302 Ordibehesht/May 1923, an *Ettehadiyeh-ye Kargaran-e Bikar-e Gilan* (the union of unemployed workers of Gilan) was formed in Enzeli, which drew the attention of the *Majles* to their lot and asked that measures be taken to create employment for them and their colleagues elsewhere in Iran. In their published statement they exhorted other unemployed workers to follow their example, for only through the creation of unions and unity could they better their lot.[114] This union apparently belonged to an Ettehadiyeh Committee, whose existence the British reported in March 1924, which had a branch in Rasht. Most of its members were boatmen, porters and the unemployed. The head of the Enzeli committee was Safar, a boatman, and in Rasht it was headed by 'Abbasqoli, a tinsmith.[115] The unions were apparently strong enough to resume their various activities, for in the same year of 1924 they celebrated Labor Day in Enzeli.[116]

The Russians did everything they could to fix people's attention on socialist ideas, and the consul in Enzeli formed a workingmen's society for workers of all nationalities. He himself attended all their meetings, which took place on Thursdays.[117] Whether this club was similar to the cultural society *Farhang* in Rasht seems unlikely. Keshavarz, son of Vakil al-Tojjar, an influential member of Rasht society, led this club. The *Farhang* society also received a monthly subsidy of 20 to 30 *tumans* from the Russians.[118]

The Russians also created a union in Rasht which was led by Mohammed Aliov, an employee of *Persaznaft*. All those who worked for Russian enterprises and all Soviet citizens had to join this local union. However, the local military authorities used this compulsion as a pretext to prohibit the union and forced its dissolution. The military then organized a purely Iranian 'Union of Workers' of Gilan "and assured its immediate success by enrolling the large number of workers employed by the military on the construction of barracks and roads."[119]

Nevertheless independent unions continued to exist in Rasht and Enzeli, which continued to receive support from Russia. The latter sometimes used ingenious methods to disguise these financial subsidies. In 1925, for example, the Union of Rasht sent through

---

112. Chaqueri 1978, 10.
113. Ovenassiyan 1974, 135.
114. For the complete text see Chaqueri 1359, 126. The organization, or at least the attempt, of the unemployed workers is another indication that labor organizers did their utmost to rally any possible support for their (political) cause.
115. FO 416/74, Intelligence Summary nr. 9, March 1, 1924, f. 125. "Object of the committee is socialist propaganda," the British commented.
116. FO 416/74, Intelligence Summary nr. 19, May 10, 1924, f. 8.
117. FO 416/74, Intelligence Summary nr. 50, December 13, 1924, f. 24.
118. See note 57 above; FO 371/13783; for the published text see Chaqueri 1979a, 283.
119. FO 416/76, Intelligence Summary nr. 7, February 14, 1925, f. 67.

the Soviet consul in Rasht, a red banner to the workers of Russia, for which kindly act the Union received a gift of 1,500 *tuman*s in exchange.[120]

The Situation in Tabriz

In Tabriz in particular the labor movement appears to have been fairly strong. Here a Workers Party (*Hezb-e Kargaran*) was formed, which could only be joined by those who did not exploit other workers.[121] The Workers Party apparently had difficulties in applying this criterion to everybody's satisfaction, since it is reported that there were internal troubles. By the end of 1921 the Workers Party had a membership of 3,000.[122] At the same time a shopkeepers association was created, for the position of these shopkeepers did not differ much from that of the wage earners. These petty traders did not make much money and were completely dependent on a few rich people who owned their shops, and often also supplied them with their raw materials as well as organized the artisans on the basis of their craft, whose representatives elected a General Council which settled all important matters in collaboration with the Council of the union.

The result of the merger between petty traders, artisans and wage laborers was a membership of 12,000. Backed by this force, the General Council was able to enforce a decrease in shop rent of 20 per cent. The government tried to win over the Workers' Party to its own political position, but failed to create sufficient interest in such an affiliation. When the offer of collaboration was turned down, the government tried to use coercion. This led to a clash between the Mayor of Tabriz and the Workers' Party, which demanded the Mayor's dismissal. At first Mokhber al-Saltaneh, the governor-general of Azerbaijan, refused to accede to this demand, But, after a general strike by the bazaar, he gave in.[123]

In Tabriz, the Workers Party is not heard of again after its initial success. It may have been suppressed after the Khiyabani revolt.[124] Nevertheless union activities can also be observed in 1922, when a Teachers Union of Azerbaijan was created, the first of its kind in that province.[125] We further learn about a strike of railway workers in June 1922, while in 1925, a Workers Party (*Hezb-e Ranjbar*) was active in the national republican movement (*nahzat-e melli*).[126] In that same year the Russian trade organization in Azerbaijan was also trying to force workers of all crafts to join unions which they had formed, by underselling non-members in almost every craft.[127]

---

120. FO 416/78, Intelligence Summary, December 12, 1925, f.12.
121. Chaqueri 1978, 7-8.
122. Chaqueri 1978, 7-8. According to Ossetrov 1922, 576 its membership amounted to 800 only; according to *Haqiqat* nr. 15 January 1922, it was not a proper union and it had been organized by Mokhber al-Saltaneh to pre-empt activities by the progressive forces.
123. Chaqueri 1978, 78.
124. In a British report on political parties in Tabriz during the period prior to the revolt, no mention is made of the "Workers Party", see FO 248/1278.
125. *Haqiqat*, nr.49, March 29, 1922.
126. FO 371/7823, Bristow to Lorraine, Tabriz, June 20. 1922 f.
127. FO 416/77, Intelligence Summary, October 22, 1925, f. 174; Ibid., Intelligence Summary nr.5, June 13, 1925, f.6.

The Situation in Mashhad

In Mashhad we learn about a *Hezb-e Ranjbaran* (Workmen's Party) which was formed by 'the revolutionary committee', a group having links with the CPI. In view of the special local conditions, Mashhad being a holy city, the socialist message of its program was framed in Islamic phraseology.[128] Whether the party had any impact is unknown, since no further information is available about it.

In 1922 and 1923, the *Ettehad-e Khorasan* (Union of Khorasan) led by Mirza Ahmad Dehqan, editor of *Fekr-e Azad* (Free Thought), was very active in Mashhad, mainly in the political field. Dehqan and his ally, Sayyed Mehdi Esfahani, who founded the Tailors Union in 1923, were strongly anti-British and had good relations with the Russian Consulate.[129] Dehqan took care, however, to cultivate the ulama. During the expulsion of some ulama from Iraq by the British in 1922 he printed a long Congratulatory Address on behalf of the Union of Workers in his paper, which was presented to Sheikh Mohammad Sadr, one of the expelled ulama on his arrival in Mashhad.[130] In 1923 the Union of Khorasan organized a strike to protest against the fact that Dehqan was not only excluded by the governor of Mashhad from standing for election for the *Majles*, but was also excluded from the board of supervisors of the elections. Even the complaints of the Russian consul-general proved to be ineffective.[131]

All these activities came to nought, however, or so it would appear, for in January 1925 it is reported that "a new organization has recently been formed called the *Kumiteh-e Kargaran*," from which one may conclude that the earlier organizations either had ceased to exist or were ineffective. The moving spirit of the Workers Committee was a certain Aliev, the assistant of the Soviet consul-general. The membership included three editors of local papers and two police officers.[132]

The Situation Elsewhere

In 1925 the existence of an Armenian communist 'Workers Union' is reported in Qazvin, as well as one for Iranians called *Howzeh-ye Taraqqi-ye Azadi*, which was previously known as *Azad khvahan*, which was led by Mirza Abdul Samad" (Kambaksh?).[133] In other

---

128. FO 371/7821, Mashad Diary nr.10, March 11, 1922, f.58 "there was a discussion as to the cause of the present failure of the revolutionary movement in Khorasan. It was suggested that the name and aims of the party were too 'advanced' for the present—and it was decided to change the name to 'Ranjbaran Party' (Workmen's Party) and to moderate their programme. The Russian Consul-General is said to have approved of the change". For a translation of the Manifesto of the *Ranjbaran* Party see Appendix D.
129. FO 371/9034, Mashad Diary, f.173. At that time there was also a traders' union in Mashad, Ibid., f.195.
130. FO 371/9035, Mashad Diary, f.46, 117. The Address concluded with "Long live Islam and its preachers. Death and destruction to the enemies of Islam. Long live the workman class of Islam."
131. FO 371/9026, Prideaux to Lorraine, Mashhad, September 12, 1923 and FO 371/9035, e. 181; see also f. 110 and FO 371/9035, f.120.
132. FO 416/76, Intelligence Summary nr.2 January 10, 1925, f. 33. This is another indication that middle-class elements lead the labor movement.
133. FO 416/76. Intelligence Summary nr.5, January 31, 1925, f. 55.

towns of Iran we do not know whether unions existed. Ossetrov reported that they existed in Qom, but no further information is available on them.[134] Undoubtedly some interest existed among the working class in the new ideas, as indicated by the presence of "representatives of the laborers, tinkers, blacksmiths, and working classes who eulogized the Soviet government" during the opening of the Russian consulate-general in Isfahan in June 1922.[135]

The Situation in the APOC Area

The oil-industry in Khuzestan, which started its operations in 1908,[136] had to use for management and skilled labor, employees from Britain and India. The Indians, together with Armenians, filled the middle ranks. Iranians, mainly people from the surrounding tribal areas, met the demand for unskilled labor.[137] The workers were hired from foremen (*sarkar*), who each led a work-gang and who, received a small amount of money, from the men working for them.[138] Not only was it very difficult to keep these workers, but in the beginning it was very difficult to get them at all.[139]

It was only in 1914 that the first labor trouble is reported. Two workers were killed as a result of an industrial accident. Their colleagues asked the APOC to support the families of the deceased, and to take precautionary measures. The APOC, so it is claimed, refused to deal with the demands of the workers, who then began throwing stones at the living quarters of the British staff. All work in Abadan was stopped, and the APOC turned to the ruler of Khuzestan, Sheikh Khaz'al, for assistance. After Sheikh Khaz'al had dealt with the demonstrators, the APOC decided to form its own police force. This force was commanded by British officers and was instructed to prevent any untoward activities on the APOC grounds.[140]

New trouble arose in 1920. The Amritsar riots of 1919 had led to some political agitation among the 3,000 strong Indian labor force in Abadan. The agitators found fertile ground for their ideas owing to the bad living conditions, low wages, and bad labor relations. On December 9, 1920 the Indians went on strike, and they were joined the next day by the Iranian labor force. Their demands were:

---

134. Ossetrov 1922, 576.
135. FO 371/7836, Confidential Summary Persian Gulf, July 1922, f. See also the speech by Consul General Tombakov in Shiraz on May 1, 1923 in which he alluded to the power of labor, FO 371/9026, f.81–87.
136. Bharier 1971, 150 ff; Ferrier 1982.
137. Ferrier 1982; Ellwell-Sutton 1955.
138. Wilson 1942, 53; the system of hiring work gangs headed by a foreman (*sarkar*) existed prior to the APOC operations in Khuzestan, see e. g. Morgan,1905, 40 referring to the situation at the end of the 19th century. The contract labor employed by the APOC in the 1930s were still hired on the same basis, Elwell-Sutton 1955.
139. Wilson 1942 140, "Food is so cheap that the Oil Company must paradoxically, pay higher wages to get the people to work at all. Men's needs are few and they are 'lazy' – in other words their standard of living includes a large element of leisure, and who shall blame them?" (1910-Shush area).
140. Chaqueri 1978, 26-77 (quoting *Setareh-ye Sorkh*).

1. An increase in wages;
2. A reduction of their working hours per day;
3. Additional pay for overtime; and
4. Improvement of sanitary conditions and an end to vilification and molestation of workers by staff members.

The APOC was obliged to give in to appease the workers, and granted a rise in wages of 80 per cent. The newly-arrived APOC manager tried thereafter to improve the wage classification system, as well as the working and living conditions. Although some improvements were made, there was no structural change in living and working conditions.[141]

Labor troubles broke out in 1922 in the APOC area. It was again the Indian labor force which was active, probably due to some political agitation as well as their living conditions, which remained bad. According to newspaper articles in the Indian press, the labor conditions of Indians working for the APOC were very bad.[142] In particular the detailed charges made by one of the APOC employees, Mudliar, led not only to an investigation by the British political resident in the Persian Gulf, but also to a strike.

The charges made were as follows:

1. Insufficient accommodation for second-class passengers on
2. River steamers plying between Mohammerah and the river head, and inadequate arrangements for securing the comfort of passengers at halting places en route;
3. Insufficient accommodation on arrival at the oil-fields, including the absence of cook houses and latrines and the turning of a deaf ear to all complaints on this score;
4. Inordinately long working hours;
5. Exhibitions of class hatred, by which is meant differential treatment of Europeans and Indians based on the racial prejudice of the former;
6. Callous treatment of patients;
7. Inadequate supplies of furniture and provisions even on payment;
8. Insufficient pay, which did not admit of remittances to dependants in India.

---

141. Chaqueri 1978, 41 (quoting *Peykar*); Ferrier 1982, 432.
142. FO 371/7819, these are published in Chaqueri 1978, 196-98. On pages 199–200 is a breakdown of the composition of the labor force employed by the APOC (AIOC) at that time.

The investigation carried out by the British Consul found no grounds for the accusations made by Mudliar. In fact he noted that due to the liberal treatment of Indian clerks by the APOC, it was very difficult to recruit such clerks and maintain them in government service in Khuzestan and the Persian Gulf.[143] The possible detrimental effect on recruitment possibilities by such articles mentioned by the consul, however, did not materialize. In 1925 as many Indians were working for the APOC as in 1922.[144] From this one may conclude that, it anything, the treatment meted out by the APOC was certainly better than elsewhere.

Moreover, the consul found no proof of Mudliar's allegations either. It was true that accommodation on the river steamers was limited, but those who could not get cabins (which also held for better class Europeans and Iranians) could always avail themselves of the abundance of shelter which otherwise was available for deck passengers. The APOC, moreover, held that in most cases cabins had been available and that in view of the expected increase in numbers of passengers extra cabins were being constructed. The APOC would also see to it that any congestion would as much as possible be avoided in future and that applicants would be informed by their recruiting agents that in exceptional circumstances it might be necessary to travel as deck passengers. The arrangements for passengers on shore were quite adequate, rest houses and food were available and an APOC representative present.

The living quarters for the clerks and coolie lines in the field were on the whole good, it was found. However, due to bad planning and rains, congestion had occurred, so that some clerks, amongst them Mudliar, had experienced considerable discomfiture for a few weeks after their arrival. The APOC maintained that the living quarters had been ready before their arrival, but that heavy rains had destroyed outhouses and several walls of the living quarters, which could only be repaired when weather conditions allowed this. The consul confirmed that this situation had been exceptional and that he would therefore urge the APOC always to have more accommodation ready than required.

The consul did not find any evidence either for the claim that exceptionally long hours, about the length of which there was no certainty at all, had to be worked. Overtime was also found to be minimal, and in that case European staff had been present as well. Nor did the consul find any evidence for racial prejudice against Indians nor was he given any concrete examples.

Mudliar's statement about the APOC hospital he qualified as a "malicious falsehood," for the hospital was the most modern of its kind in the East where no distinction was made between the patients on the basis of their nationality.[145] The consul could not substantiate Mudliar's charge with regard to supplies of furniture and provisions either. The quarters of the clerks were well supplied with furniture and utensils free-of-charge by the APOC. Provisions could be obtained from the numerous local Indian and Iranian shopkeepers as well as from the APOC stores. The Consul appended a list of goods which Mudliar had bought at these stores during January 1922.[146]

---

143. FO 371/7819, E.G.B. Peel to Trevor, Ahvaz, ff.220.
144. See statistics in Ferrier 1982, Table 10.1.
145. On the hospital and hygienic situation in the Abadan area see Williamson 1927, 128 ff.
146. FO 371/7819, f. 221.

The consul held that Mudliar's article had been written to put pressure on the APOC in order to get a higher salary. A few weeks before Mudliar wrote the article, he and a few other Madrasi clerks had demanded that they be given an initial salary of Rs. 200 per month. These were all recent recruits and had been engaged against a salary of Rs. 150 per month "rising by yearly increments of Rs.10 to Rs. 17" per month. They based their claim on the fact that other Indian clerks had been engaged at Rs. 200 per month. The APOC told them, however, that they had signed on for Rs. 150 and that a contract was a contract. Moreover, it was up to the employer to pay higher salaries above the contracted rate on the basis of merit and the quality of the work delivered. In addition to their salary, the clerks also received a field allowance of Rs. 20 per month, and the consul ascertained that, among the most vocal clerks claiming higher pay, the ability to remit money to India was about Rs. 70 per month.[147]

Notwithstanding this situation, a number of Indian, Iranian and Arab laborers went on strike at Abadan on March 14, 1922 claiming higher pay. The APOC refused to give in and summoned Sheikh Khaz'al from Kuwait, who soon dealt with the Iranian and Arab workers; the British themselves dealt with the Indian labor. The political resident gave lengthy interviews to their leaders, who refused to give in. Since the APOC had raised their salaries in 1921 by 80 per cent it was considered that their demands were unreasonable. When the men refused to return to their work they were repatriated to India because of breach of contract. The leaders refused to go, unless all strikers were sent on one ship. This was impossible as they numbered some 2,000 or about 50 per cent of the total Indian labor force. With the aid of a landing party of HMS *Cyclamen*, which had arrived on March 18, and four companies of Indian infantry from Basra, the strikers were embarked on 2 ships without problems and the labor troubles were over.[148]

After these troubles the British legation took an active interest in any Communist activity in the APOC area. In July 1922 the Legation reports that eight Iranian communists had arrived from Baku and were reported to have instructions to obtain work in the APOC oil-fields with a view to organizing communism among the workers.[149] This, however, seems unlikely, for Lahuti reports that the CPI preferred not to draw too much attention to itself by creating trouble in the APOC area in view of the importance of the operations there for the Iranian economy.[150]

Nevertheless, in 1924 the British legation reports about the presence of an Indian, Mohammad Khan, a mechanic in the service of the APOC, who was engaged in forming workers' unions in Masjed-e Soleyman. Probably as a result of his activities, the Indian labor force went on strike in 1924, which the APOC management was able to put down. As a result of this experience the APOC decided to reduce the number of Indian workers and replace them with others. This development was already to be observed in 1927,

---

147. FO 371/7819, f. 220.
148. FO 371/7836, Intelligence Summary Persian Gulf, March 23, 1922 the ships were the *SS Barjara* and the *SS Varela*.
149. FO 416/72 Intelligence Summary nr.20, July 22, 1922, f.132 which perhaps refers to the arrival of Pishehvari and Reza Rusta, see Lahuti n.d., 21.
150. Lahuti n.d., 45.

but from the data available it cannot be deduced, as Ferrier has it, that Iranians replaced Indian labor. Although it is true that the number of Iranian workers increased concomitantly with the reduction of Indian workers, at the same time a similar increase of other foreign laborers is to be seen. In view of the level of development of Iran one must assume that these foreign laborers took over the jobs vacated by the Indians.[151] The Legation commented that the infiltration of Bolshevik agents into the oil-fields was considerably facilitated by the presence of the Russian consul at Ahvaz. About the latter, the Legation reported in January 1925 that it had received reliable information that the consul was trying to establish influence among the employees of the APOC.[152] To that end, the Russian consul-general in Isfahan had probably been ordered to "cease or reduce subsidies to Persian Communist or Socialist organisations and to devote the money so made available to secret service work in Fars and Khuzistan."[153] These activities undoubtedly resulted in the creation of the first trade union of oil workers in the end of 1925.

Guild Unions

The unionizing of workers coincided with the growth of activities among the guilds in several Iranian cities. Although these guilds had no links with the Communist party of Iran or with the Profintern, they nevertheless felt some kinship with the unions, as shown by the contacts which existed between the two types of organizations. In Tehran, a Central Guild Council (*Anjoman-e Markazi-ye Asnaf*) had been established in 1906, while at the same time the Guild Committee (*Hey'at-e Asnaf*) in Yazd, the Public Union Organization (*Majma`-e Ettefaq-e `Omumi*) in Kerman, and the Guild Council (*Anjoman-e Asnifiyeh*) in Shiraz came into being.[154]

In Isfahan, for instance, about 40 guilds had united themselves into one guild-union, while in Tabriz and Kermanshah respectively 40 and 20 guilds had created united organizations. In Isfahan each guild had two representatives on the Central Union Council, who were chosen for a period of four years. This Central Council was charged with the co-ordination of the political interests and activities of the guilds concerned. Its program consisted of the following objectives:[155]

---

151. FO 416/75. Intelligence Summary nr.16, April 19, 1924, f.5; Ferrier, 1982, 433, and Table 10.1.
152. FO 416/76, Intelligence Summary, nr. 3, January 17, 1925, f.43.
153. FO 416/76, Intelligence Summary nr.8, February 8, 1925, f.77. This information was based on "an unconfirmed, but fairly reliable source".
154. Dowlatabadi n.d., vol. 2, 116. RMM, 1907, 554; Lambton 1954, 29. The Russian Consul-General Tardov commented that the trade union movement in Iran was permeated by the petty bourgeois ideology of the narrow guild group, and that this form of organization turned out to be entirely antiquated and faced a period of disintegration. He believed that stratification would become more and more visible among the artisans, Lenczowski 1968, 102. A report to the Comintern also stated that "trade unions in the real sense of the word hardly exist; the majority of the unions are more on guild lines". Chaqueri 1979b, 1113 report to the VI. Comintern Congress 1928).
155. Ossetrov 1922, 571; partly translated by Ravasani n.d., 227–28.

1. The protection of the Iranian constitution and the Fundamental Laws;
2. The prevention of the rigging of the elections for the *Majles* and the election of trustworthy persons belonging to the middle class;
3. The implementation of measures aimed at improving artisanal production methods and its maintenance at a high level as well as waging a battle against false imitations;
4. The protection of the interests of artisans.

Although the objectives were clearly restricted to those of the petty-bourgeoisie and had nothing in common with those of the CPI or the labor unions organized by the CPI, the guilds in their fight to defend their economic interests occasionally recognized the unions as their allies. This kinship had been formalized in the *Hezb-e kargaran* in Tabriz. But when, for instance, a dispute broke out between property owners and shopkeepers in Hamadan about the level of shop rents, the Guild Union (*Ettehadiyeh-ye `omumi-ye asnaf*) in Hamadan sent a telegram to the editor of *Haqiqat* to report on this conflict. After an initial agreement on April 4, 1922 the shop owners withdrew from the agreement, whereupon the shopkeepers left the bazaar and erected stalls near the telegraph office.[156] The flirtation of some of these guild-unions with the labor unions had no permanence, however. After 1925, Reza Shah used the guilds as countervailing instruments against union activities by inducing workers to join the government-controlled guilds.[157]

THE REIGN OF REZA SHAH (1925–1941)

Introduction

Soon after his accession to the throne, Reza Shah dealt a heavy blow to the trade unions in Iran by having most of the cadres of the unions and the Communist Party arrested.[158] This did not mean, however, that both the unions and the Communist Party were annihilated. These severely battered organizations went under ground to await better times. The Party did not allow its members much breathing space, however. Already in 1926 it ordered its cadres to be more active and to form a united national front against Reza Shah. This was very difficult since no labor unions, labor newspapers, or labor activities were allowed. Often only face-to-face contacts could be used to set up or resuscitate the unions. It was therefore decided that the real leaders would remain in the background. For public affairs such as meetings and demonstrations, lower-ranking officials such as Mehdi Kemaran would be used as a front.[159]

---

156. *Haqiqat*, nr.66. April 24. 1922 and nr. 83, May 25, 1922.
157. Chaqueri 1978, S5, 99, 104–5 (resolution IV. Profintern Congress).
158. Abrahamian 1982, 138–39 on his policy, Chaqueri 1979b, 1114.
159. Lahuti n.d. 44; Ovanessiyan 1974, 130.

Since no labor newspapers were allowed, the publications financed by the Communist Party continued their earlier policy of an anti-British line, only mentioning the USSR when there was something positive to tell.[160] In preparing the ground for the resurgence of the 'progressive' forces, the Communists were assisted by the Russian Legation, and its various other organizations, such as the OGPU. One of the newspapers in Tehran subsidized by the Russian Legation for instance, carried an article in November 1926 in which the journalist tried to prove that the tenets of the Koran closely resembled Marxist principles and that therefore every faithful Moslem should follow the Marxist path as "blazed by the Bolsheviks" the British commented.[161]

Notwithstanding the very smallness of the group of organized workers (Table 2.1) that had survived suppression by the police, the unions celebrated May Day in 1927. The printers as usual figured as an important group among the unionized laborers, while the construction and textile workers had also been able to weather the storm. In addition bakery workers, leather workers, tailors and some others had retained some kind of cohesion.[162]

The situation in Tehran

The Communist Party had a Labor Day bulletin printed secretly in 1927 and distributed it in Tehran. The May Day celebration itself took place on May 3, which was a Friday, in a garden outside Tehran. In small groups, in order not to attract the attention of the police, some 700 to 800 workers and party members met there, listened to speeches and sang worker songs. The inevitable red banner was not missing. Most of the workers were weavers, bakers, shoemakers, carpenters, chauffeurs and other craftsmen. After the official part of the celebrations was over, all participants had lunch together. Later, the hardcore of the participants, about 150 men, went again in small groups into Tehran to the Socialists Club (*Klub-e Ejtema`iyun*) in order to have a Labor Day party there. Soleyman Mirza and Mirza Shehab Kermani,[163] who were the leaders of the club, had to tolerate their presence, for they did not like having communists in their club. Although the police had no prior information about either the celebration of Labor Day in the garden outside Tehran or the party in the Socialists Club, they nevertheless learnt about them later on. Soon thereafter there was a crackdown on communists and union members, and more than 100 of the latter were arrested. The government also closed the Socialists Club, though it is no certain whether this happened because of the Labor Day party.[164]

On May 10, 1928, Adib al-Saltaneh, the chief of police, had all printing houses searched, even to the lockers and desks of the printers, in order to get hold of the Labor Day pamphlets. When such pamphlets were found, the guilty owners were arrested. Likewise those printers who had not worked on that day were arrested as well. This effort to

---

160. Lahuti n.d.,22.
161. FO 416/79. Intelligence Summary nr. 23, November 13, 1926, f.200.
162. Ovanessiyan 1974, 130.
163. Mani 1325, 21–23; Ovanessiyan 1974, 130.
164. Ovanessiyan 1974, 130.

arrest the leading elements of the Unions and the Communist Party proved to be a failure. Those arrested were released again after four to five months in prison.[165]

Although forced into hiding and having to start practically all over again, the party cadres renewed their activities and recruited many new union members. This time especially, the textile workers were very active, who recruited hundreds of their colleagues, or so it is claimed. In this new wave of unionism, drivers, bakery workers, carpenters, shoe makers, and the printers of course, further participated. The meetings of these unions were irregular and held in secret. Their activities, moreover, were almost exclusively aimed at improving working conditions in the various industrial establishments.[166]

This new drive for unionism was the result of a decision by the Communist Party to establish a special union committee in 1928. Its task was to organize new trade unions. Members of this committee were Hejazi, Ostad Mirza 'Ali Banna, 'Ata'ollah, 'Abdollahzadeh, and Ovanessiyan. Their main area of operations was Tehran, although links with the provinces existed, however weak these were.[167]

This decision undoubtedly was the result of the III Congress of the International Red Syndicates in Moscow that year, during which the Iranian delegate Reza Gholam 'Abdollahzadeh (Seyfi) had stated that the Iranian unions had no policy, no guidelines and no experience. He added that the unions needed an experienced leadership and support from outside. The logical place to look for that kind of support was the Communist Party of Iran but, in his own words, that party was in the same predicament. Summing up the union situation in Iran, Seyfi submitted that they neither knew how to defend labor's rights nor how to organize unions!

The Profintern discussed the union situation in Iran and condemned the "erroneous policies of the Persian trade union movement," because of "their excessive emphasis on politics and the transformation of the unions into purely political organizations." Radical steps had to be taken and past errors had to be rectified. The Profintern to that end considered it necessary to adopt the following resolutions:

1. To devote the maximum of attention to the amelioration of the economic conditions of the workers and to inaugurate the campaign for the eight-hour day in basic industries like match factories, textile mills, and leather works;

2. To construct a wide educational campaign concerning the importance of the trade unions as the class economic organizations of the proletariat as against the guild organizations led by the agents of Reza Shah, into which the Shah's government wanted to drive the Persian workers;

3. In spite of all difficulties, to proceed to the organization of the most numerous category of workers, and the one most cruelly exploited

---

165. Mani 1325, 21.
166. Ovanessiyan 1974, 130; Zabih 1977, 53.
167. Lahuti n.d. 44, Ovanessiyan 1974, 130.

by foreign capital, namely, the Persian workers employed in the oil refineries of the Anglo-Persian Company.[168]

At the same time, i.e. March 1928, Agabekov, the head of OGPU in Iran,[169] was busy trying to organize trade unions as well. The unions, which were aptly named 'new companies' (*sharekat-e jadid*), were first formed among the cooks and domestic servants. It was also reported that attempts would be made to form unions among farmers and farm laborers as well as among cab drivers.[170]

The British also reported a meeting held by Reza Khan Saqatforush, during which Gholam Hoseyn Khan Nezam al-Dowleh delivered an anti-British tirade. He told his audience that the socialists had by now also accepted communism as their official doctrine and that henceforth there was only one real Communist Party in Iran. The British reported that this group was also making headway with the organization of all kinds of trade unions.[171]

The Iranian government apparently also had information about these activities, for the police raided the Barq press in May 1928. The whole staff was arrested and the press itself closed. In connection with these arrests the police made another 250 arrests on charges of distributing communist leaflets in Tehran, probably referring to the distribution of Labor Day statements.[172]

The trade union committee was of the opinion that Labor Day in 1929 should be a national event underlining the rebirth of the unions. Pishehvari was ordered to see to it that in planned demonstrations progressive intellectuals, students, workers, and even apprentices should participate. In speeches and songs a cautious line should be taken, so that the government would not consider this a challenge to its authority. The theme of all public statements and expressions had to be support for certain aspects of government policy such as: 'Help national revival against imperialism', 'Close all banks etc. owned by Imperialism', 'a law should be passed to protect labor rights.'[173]

The setting of the Labor Day celebrations in 1929 in Tehran was the Mo'iniyeh garden. Early in the morning the workers had gathered there in small groups and were making merry. Political speeches were given by Ja'far Ordokhani, while various representatives of the unions delivered short speeches. After lunch a special poem written for the occasion was recited, while the workers sung tunes accompanied by an orchestra formed by themselves. The organizers were very satisfied with the turnout as it had been the biggest Labor Day celebration ever held in Tehran so far, and more than 2,000 people had attended.

---

168. Chaqueri 1978, 102–104.
169. On Agabekov see Rezun 1981, 94–113 and 171–82.
170. FO 416/82 Intelligence Summary nr.6. March 17, 1928, f.193.
171. FO 416/82, Intelligence Summary, nr.7, March 31. 1928, f.203
172. FO 416/82, Intelligence Summary, nr.11, May 16, 1928. F. 341; according to the CPI this was only a pretext to silence opposition forces in connection with the approaching elections for the *Majles*, Chaqueri 1978,104(citing *Inprekorr.* nr. 57, June 15, 1928, 1937); on this matter see also Zabih 1977, 61.
173. Lahuti n.d., 54-55; for the reasons for this political line and the differences between the CPI and the Soviet Union see Rezun 1981, 268 f.

When the merrymakers returned to town, the police noted there was more traffic than usual and after investigation realized that Labor Day celebrations had taken place in the Mo'iniyeh garden. The next day the police arrested about 50 union members and about the same number went into hiding or fled.[174] Although the police tried to get information on their colleagues out of those they had arrested, they failed. They were all released finally under the general amnesty which had been declared on the occasion of the visit of Amanollah, King of Afghanistan. There was one exception, Mohammad Hejazi, who had been arrested on his return from Russia where he had attended a meeting of the third Comintern. He died in prison shortly thereafter.[175]

Although the police had released the union leaders, they kept henceforth a close watch on any kind of meeting or gathering. The security police, Mani claims, checked all groups of more than three people in coffee houses. The strict control made further activities impossible and May 1, 1929 was the last Labor Day celebrated in Tehran for the time being.[176]

The Situation in Gilan

Trade Union activities elsewhere in Iran were also given new life by CP members as well as by Russian diplomatic representatives. In 1927 new unions were formed in Gilan, such as that among the tinsmiths (*halabi-saz*), oil-bunker workers, and hat-makers in Rasht. In Enzeli the following unions had been formed: the Porters (*hammal*) Union, the Fishery Workers Union, and the Boatmen's (*gorji-banan*) Union. In both towns the CPI also formed youth organizations (*komsomols*) which were also active in organizing unions.[177] An important development was the final agreement reached in October 1927 between Iran and Russia about Caspian fishing rights. In a note accompanying the agreement, Iran had stated that it "was duty bound to regard all political propaganda, all agitation, and even the organization of trade unions among the working population of the Caspian as detrimental to Iran's interests, and that such activity was considered illegal. ... those persons of Soviet nationality found guilty of provocation would be fully penalized to the full extent of Persian law." For the Russians this Note was a sore point, since they had long been trying to gain influence and sympathy among the workers of the Caspian via the trade unions. Karakhan, the Deputy Foreign Commissar, replied in an official note that "with regard to the organization of trade unions for Persian workmen and their admission to such unions, I have the honour to state that the Soviet Government takes note of your communication, since this question is within the competence of the Persian Government and a matter of internal Persian legislation." The Russians could give no other reply, of course. The more so, since the organization of trade unions was always done via men of straw and the Rus-

---

174. Mani 1324, 22 f.; Lahuti n.d., 55 mentions that the leaders of the union of sweepers, the tobacco workers' union, the weavers' union, and the mercers' union were also arrested as well as Pishehvari. Ovanessiyan 1974, 136.
175. Mani 1324, 24 f, For a statement by the Comintern on this case see Chaqueri 1978, 24-25 (*Setareh-ye Sorkh*).
176. Mani 1324, 24.
177. Ovanessiyan 1974, 138

sians could always deny their own involvement. They had no intention whatsoever of stopping organizing Iranian labor and continued to do so.[178]

A setback was suffered in August 1928 when the porters in Enzeli petitioned the governor to be allowed to form a union which would be free of Russian influence. They stated that the Russian consul had been taking a portion of their wages for Russian political work. The governor then had an agent of the consul arrested on August 27. He was released later on, but was deported. The Porters Union also informed the military commander about the political activity of the consul and accused their union president Keredjivai Sorkhi, Shirinov, the chief Soviet agent in Rasht, and Rusto, another Soviet agent, of bearing the major responsibility for bringing their union into disrepute. It would appear that the cause of this complaint was occasioned by the fact that the Russian-organized Porters' Union under Mohammad Ja'far excluded Iranian porters, who were not members, from getting work at Russian establishments, a policy the Russians also followed in Tabriz. In Enzeli the Porters Union was the only one allowed to load and unload the ships of the Russian Company *Moragent*, and they would not permit porters employed by the customs department to work on these ships. Owing to the open hostility which had broken out between the two groups of porters, the Russians decided to change their policy and opened branches at all Iranian ports as well as giving a share of the work on Russian boats to non-organized porters, i.e., the customs porters.[179]

In January 1929 the Union of Railway Workers organized a strike in Mazandaran,[180] which may have been one of the reasons why, after the Labor Day celebrations of 1929, the new Governor-General cracked down on the CPI and unions in Gilan in a grand cleaning-up operation. It may also have been possible that this happened on the orders of Tehran, since a similar action was undertaken there. The Governor-General also dismissed the socialist telegraph master and broke up the Porters Union.[181]

Unionizing activities were also carried on among the fishery employees, whose pay was administered by the Russians. According to the Governor-General, fifteen per cent of their pay was deducted and put into a provident fund. At Hasan Kiadeh the Russians had also started a school, but the Iranian government insisted on taking it over. The Russians continued their propaganda via the radio and social clubs. The Iranian police therefore received orders to prevent the attendance of Iranian subjects at these clubs.[182] However, other, secretly formed, unions escaped the government's attention at that time. The same also holds for the

---

178. Rezun 1981, 122.
179. FO 416/83. Intelligence Summary, nr.18, September 1, 1928, f.115; Ibid. nr.19, September 15, 1928; Ibid., nr.22, November 3, 1928, f.196; FO 371/13783 (1929), Finch, vice-consul at Rasht to Clive, February 5, 1929, f.83 "the instrument for disseminating communist influence has been the porters' union."
180. Hezb-e Tudeh 1349, 188.
181. FO 416/84, Intelligence Summary, nr.9, May 4 1929, f.256.
182. FO 416/85, Report on the General Situation in the Caspian Provinces. July 1939, f.60–61. The school referred to may be the same as the one mentioned half a year earlier, when the British consul mentioned the opening of a school by the Russians in the fisheries at Enzeli for the free education of the children of Iranian employees, who were asked to subscribe five per cent of their wages for the maintenance of the school, FO 416/80. Intelligence Summary, nr.1, January 8, 1927, f. 34.

National Union of Railway Workers, which had started in Mazandaran in 1928 and operated in secrecy.[183] Nevertheless, the Gilan unions were severely hit in 1931, and because of the many arrests, completely destroyed.[184] This did not mean that the spirit of labor was totally broken, as shown in 1932 when the 800 port workers in Nowshahr, who were said to have an illegal union, went on strike because they had not received their wages for four months. After a strike which lasted eight days, the workers got their wage raise.[185]

The Situation in Mashhad

Towards the end of 1928 the CPI concentrated its efforts on Mashhad, although that town could hardly boast of an industry or of an industrial working class. Most success was achieved among the carpet weavers, the largest group of workers in the town, who were working long hours under miserable conditions for low wages. Hundreds of them joined and the union was even able to function partly in the open. To attract the workers, who were apparently organized by factory, a mutual assistance fund was founded, out of which workers could get loans or just financial aid. The party also organized adult education classes for union members and some 30 to 40 in fact attended these classes. To attract young people to the union and the CPI, a *komsomol* was created which cooperated closely with the union. Its main assets were a football team and a journal, *Bolshevik-e Javan* (young Bolshevik) which was handwritten and then copied.

Labor Day in 1929 was not a big affair, but this situation had already changed by 1930 when quite a number of workers joined the secret meeting in the mountains outside Mashhad.[186] Another event which focused workers' attention on the importance of having a union was the murder of an apprentice carpet weaver by his employer on June 22, 1930. The murderer paid blood money to his relatives in accordance with Moslem law, a pitiful amount of 25 *tuman*s. The union used this occasion to distribute a statement on this incident among the workers, in which they were reminded of their miserable lot and that only in unity lay their strength, only in unity could they take revenge for this murder, and only then could they demand the prohibition of child labor up to fifteen years, proper wages, and an 8-hour working day.[187] Soon thereafter the police arrested many members of the CPI and the union as well as the executive committee of the union about which we hear no more.[188]

The Situation in Tabriz

In Tabriz, union activities were also renewed. In 1930 the workers of the match factory went on strike to demand immediate payment of their wages, which were in arrears. The

---

183. Ovanessiyan 1974. 138
184. Hezb-e Tudeh 1349, 189
185. Bashkirov 1948, 28, Ovanessiyan 1974, 139.
186. Ovanessiyan 1974, 115–120, 137.
187. Chaqueri 1978, 15 (text from *Setareh-ye Sorkh*).
188. Ovanessiyan 1974, 115.

police arrested fifteen of their leaders and in this way broke the strike.[189] In 1931 some unions were formed among the soap makers, weavers and some other crafts. The unions participated in the Labor Day celebrations which took place in the mountains outside Tabriz. Gradually the CPI was also able to organize some unions in other towns of Azerbaijan, while a recently-formed provincial committee distributed a statement on its objectives.[190]

The Situation in the APOC Area

In 1925 the cadres of the Communist Party had been instrumental in forming a Trade Union among workers of the APOC.[191] However, this union remained totally inactive. As a result the Communist Party had to start all over again in 1927 when many new cells were created among the oil-workers. It appears to have been well-organized with a relatively large membership. One of its first acts was to organize a First Congress of Oil Workers, which met secretly in November 1927 and was attended by some 200 delegates. The Congress decided to expand its organization, to create workers' clubs and cooperatives, to take action against fines, beatings, vilifications and against the policy of discrimination among nationalities practiced by the APOC.[192]

Despite these decisions, not much was done. The labor leaders acted very cautiously with regard to the APOC in view of its importance to the economy of Iran. Labor feared that disruptive union action might lead to a severe crack-down by the government.[193] Moreover, the APOC had its own police force with a security branch. Any militant action by unionized laborers led to beatings, intimidation or even dismissal with banishment from the APOC area.[194] At the end of January 1929, on the initiative of the provincial committee of the Communist Party, a Second Oil Workers Union Congress was held. According to *Setareh-ye Sorkh*, 2,000 workers attended this meeting, which seems unlikely in view of the fact that the APOC would have found out about the meeting and would have broken it up. The congress discussed both organizational and political matters. Its program of action was:

1. To fight for a change in the oil concession;
2. To claim the right to hold Labor Day on May 1, and organize strikes.[195]

---

189. Ivanov 1356/1977, 81
190. Ovanessiyan 1974, 138.
191. Anon. 1973, 120; Chaqueri 1978, 82 reproduces a Profintern report, which states that this union of APOC workers had presented a report on their working conditions to the *Majles* in 1926. Another Profintern report, Ibid., 97-98 states that this was repeated in 1927. However, a Comintern report of 1928 states that there was no union of the oil workers, see Chaqueri, 1979, 1116.
192. Chaqueri 1978, 97–98; Anon. 1973, 120.
193. Lahuti n.d. 45
194. Chaqueri 1978, 26–27, 41.
195. Hezb-e Tudeh 1349, 188; Anon. 1973, 120.

TABLE 2.3: APOC Staff and Labor in Iran 1910-32[196]

Year	Iranians	Indians	Others	Europeans	Total
1910	2724	316	292	80	3412
1911	3602	758	254	112	4726
1912	4898	1106	194	87	6284
1913	5798	1834	350	88	8070
1914	5488	2148	750	128	8554
1915	4406	1958	374	160	6898
1916	4670	2732	208	240	7850
1919	3973	2641	47	117	6784
1920	8447	3616	35	244	12342
1921	9009	4709	51	271	14040
1922	18441	4285	2940	490	26156
1923	20762	4715	849	644	26970
1924	18384	4731	648	738	24501
1925	15820	4890	7201	994	28905
1926	15843	3588	6042	1020	26493
1927	17887	3772	7009	1055	29223
1928	16382	3050	5365	1000	25797
1929	15245	2518	5273	980	24016
1930	20095	2411	7549	1191	31246
1931	14797	1675	3178	989	20639
1932	10343	1420	2346	744	14853

The 1929 Strike at Abadan

Much has been made of the May 1929 strike in the APOC Abadan refinery, although so far neither thorough discussion of these events nor information about them is available.[197] The story, as it is told by the leftists, is that the workers of the refinery organized the strike to protest against the lamentable working conditions and low pay as well as to give vent to their sentiments on the freedom to form labor clubs.[198] Reading the British documents on the 1929 events, nothing of this kind is confirmed, although passing reference is made to the issue of the workers' clubs. The main pre-occupation of the British, both APOC and embassy personnel, had to do with alleged Russian agitation and with alleged government

---

196. Ferrier 1982, Table 19.1 and Table 7.2. On p. 154, Table 4.1. Ferrier produces different figures for the year 1910/11.
197. Rezun 1981, 158–59, 287–88 is totally uncritical and off-the-mark as to the 1929 events. The 1929 strike did not even merit enough significance to be mentioned in the Annual Report by the British embassy in Tehran.
198. Chaqueri 1978, 52–53.

support for these events. Whatever the truth of the matter, it is clear that the 1929 strike was a storm in a tea-cup, with no lasting influence on labor relations.

In 1928 the workers of Abadan, Ahvaz and Mohammareh organized semi-public clubs under such names as *Naderi* and *Shapur*. In March 1929 the workers organized a club which was restricted to laborers. The objective of these clubs was to promote sports activities and provide some social center for the men; they enjoyed enormous popularity. The security office of the APOC considered these clubs as a means to organize labor, so it ended the existence of the workmen's clubs and organized one itself known as the *Khayyam* Club. Membership was also open to administrative staff, and the club president and his assistant, Arfa' al-Saltaneh and an Englishman, respectively were 'chosen' by the security office. When the workmen tried to take over control of the club, the security office had these men blackballed. The dissatisfied workmen then founded a club themselves. Its opening day was said to have been attended by 700 men. The security office was also present and ordered the leaders of the club to close it since no permission had been given. The club leaders showed the security office a written permission by the provincial Department of Education, but this was considered to be insufficient since permission from Tehran was required, not from the local representative of the Ministry.[199]

Both Persian and English sources agree that the immediate cause of the 1929 strike had been occasioned by the club question. Frustrated in their attempt to form workmen's clubs, "those responsible for organizing labor in Abadan," according to the APOC, or, to the workers themselves, according to Soltanzadeh, decided to try other ways and means to achieve their objectives.[200]

From the British documents it is clear that attempts were being made to form labor Unions, a development which the APOC abhorred. It was only in January 1929 that the APOC and the Iranian authorities learnt about the creation of a cell system among the refinery workers. By May 1929 the British estimated that there existed 30 cells in Abadan, each of which had about 20 members and was hierarchically controlled by foremen and gangers "who rank in this organization as officers and sergeants." There were also indications that two cells existed in Masjed-e Soleyman, two in Ahvaz, and seven in Mohammareh. The APOC had been unable to find out who controlled the cells, but it believed this master organization included seven Russians, four Tabrizi Turks, and four Isfahanis.[201]

Elkington, the APOC manager, was informed that the strikers would occupy the site of the refinery and would demand from there what they wanted, viz:

1. Representation in the Labor Office and at Medical Examinations with special reference to the engagement and discharge of employees;

---

199. Chaqueri 1978, 52–53.
200. Chaqueri 1978, 52–53.
201. FO 371/13783, unsigned and secret letter to M. Abadan, May 2 1929. f.130-34. This letter is reproduced in Chaqueri 1978, 215–17. The British also reported that "no labourers have been hitherto admitted into the organisation which is confined at present almost entirely to clerks, foremen, and artisans, all of Persian nationality. They wanted to increase their numbers and its funds by subscription until they feel strong enough to challenge the APOC and the government".

2. The increase of wages of laborers to the equivalent of Rs.45/per mensem, which wage was formerly paid in 1923;

3. Leave with pay;

4. A six hour day;

5. Company quarters or rent in lieu;

6. No further demolitions to take place in Abadan or elsewhere;

7. Persian artisans to be placed on agreement in the same manner as indentured Indians;

8. All grievances to be investigated by the Persian Police authorities;

9. Persian clerks to be placed on the same footing as Indians;

10. Questions of dispute between Europeans and Persians or between the Company and Persians to be settled by the Persian Law Courts;

11. Pensions to be awarded as the result of long service or if discharged as surplus to requirements, instead of gratuities such pensions to be continued to the descendants of the employee after death.

The APOC induced the Iranian authorities to arrest 93 active union members on April 29, 1929 to abort the expected strike.[202]

Although the APOC manager did not consider organized labor, which consisted mostly of artisans, sufficiently organized to carry out their intended strike, he nevertheless alerted the Iranian authorities and the British Vice-Consul. What made the APOC panic was the fact that four Russians named Firuz Mohammadov, Khalil Esmailov, 'Abdorrahim Roshbilkov and 'Ali Qorban Niazochli were constantly visiting Abadan and were in touch with the cell leaders. These were reported to be anxiously awaiting the arrival of the Russian steamer *Michael Frunze*, which, it was feared, would land arms in the country with the help of a pro-Russian customs inspector named Mirza Mehdi Khan Mirzaban. During the night of May 2 1929 Elkington even telephoned the Vice-Consul asking when the *HMS Cyclamen* would arrive at Basra.[203]

---

202. Chaqueri 1978, 216; Anon. 1973, 120. In the FO files no information is available on these arrests. Unfortunately the British Petroleum archives are as yet closed to researchers. It is BP's intention to make these available to bonafide scholars (it sounds rather restrictive) after Ferrier has finished his writing of BP's history. Ferrier, in his second volume of his History of BP, will deal with these labor matters and hopefully will shed light on these questions, Ferrier, 1982, XXI. 432. The alleged pre-emptive arrests may have been caused by the experience of the strike which reportedly occurred in 1928 in Naseri, as a result of which 66 workers had been dismissed, Chaqueri, 1978, 26, 28. According to another report & similar strike occurred in 1927 in the oil fields, Chaqueri 1979b, 1114. For the list of demands see Chaqueri 1978, 216 reproducing FO 371/13783, f.133

203. The apprehension increased when it became known that two other Russian ships *SS Loos*, and *SS Kommunist* would also shortly arrive at Abadan. The Iranian authorities, at the behest of the British government and in order to quell the unrest and tension in the area, ordered the Russian ships to leave Iranian waters.

The arrival of the Governor of Abadan from Mohammareh, who, charged with full authority by the Governor-General, arrested some 25 persons immediately, did not succeed in setting his mind at ease, however. During the arrest, documents were found which, according to Elkington, proved beyond doubt that Moscow, through the four above-mentioned Russians, was behind it all, that is to say, an action aimed "not merely at causing strikes and sabotage in the refinery, but also at creating unrest in the Province."[204]

Elkington also informed the Governor of Abadan about imminent trouble. He handed him copies of all reports which he had, including all the names of the cell leaders and agitators. The Governor left immediately for Ahvaz to discuss this issue with the Governor-General. After some hesitation, the latter ordered the Governor and the Chief of Police Sarhang Rokn al-Din Khan, to return to Abadan. The Governor returned to Abadan on the morning of May 3 and immediately went to see Elkington. After some deliberation, it was decided to arrest as many of the ringleaders as possible. The arrests proceeded slowly, because the names of the ringleaders in the Company books did not tally with those used in the labor organization, "a significant fact," Elkington commented. It was only through the arrest of a cell leader, Sayyed Khalil, at 5.30 a.m. that a full list of the names of the leaders was found. By that time it had become known in Abadan that arrests were being made, though only nine men had been arrested so far. By 22.00 hours some 30 to 40 persons had been arrested and pamphlets, instructions, a list of names, and the matrix of a cyclostyle from which a circular had been taken, were found as well.

These documents, according to Elkington, were considered by the Governor to justify his action, although he adds in the same breath that "there had been no leisure in which to examine documents or carry out further investigations." On May 4 some further arrests were made, bringing the total to 45. During that day, the governor examined the documents and informed Tehran about the situation. Elkington was desperately curious to know what was in the documents, but he refrained from asking as he "had no desire either to harass them or to appear to arrogate to the Company a position which it had no right to assume." In the evening, however, the Governor, accompanied by the Chief of Police, paid a visit to Elkington. Both officials assured Elkington "that no further trouble need be expected at the moment," that the workers were quite ignorant of the true state of affairs, and that the workers had been influenced to join by the leaders because these told them that the "Government itself would welcome a step of this nature in order that it might take the opportunity to impose its will upon the Company and upon the British generally."[205]

Although the Governor had not yet completed examination of the documents, he nevertheless had proof enough that a Central Committee of the Communist Party in Iran controlled the labor organization, and that a branch committee had been established in Khuzestan. Instructions by this Branch Committee to four of the chief leaders, three of whom had been arrested, indicated that the movement was not only interested in the APOC, but interested to reach all workers in South Iran. The Governor believed that the Branch Committee had contacts in Ahvaz, Main Fields, and Haft Kel, to which places reinforcements were sent. Staggered by the deviousness of the operations, Elkington

---

204. FO 371/13783, f. 130–34; Ibid, "Bolshevist Activities at Abadan, May 4, 1929, f. 171–72.
205. FO 371/13783, f.179–181 (May 8, 1929)

again inquired after the whereabouts and sailing dates of the nearest sloop, which was at Basra.[206]

On the night of Sunday May 5, Elkington received information that a demonstration would be held on the morning of May 6. The Iranian morning shift had not come to work by 3.00 p.m., but the Iranian night shift was willing to continue working. At about 5.30 p.m. about 40 men, mostly ex-employees, under the influence of arrack and opium and armed with sticks and knives tried to prevent the laborers from entering the refinery. A group of townspeople, many of them women, all carrying *Moharram* flags, arrived somewhat later and mixed with the labor gang. In this way they prevented the men from entering, and through the general excitement tried to incite to join them in their protest. That this activity was premeditated and organized was clear from the fact that some men were detailed to picket the other main entrances of the refinery as well, where they also created a disturbance.

The group attacked the time office, but it was diverted from breaking into the refinery through the arrival of the Governor and the Chief of Police and a few men, who took refuge in the fire station barracks when the mob noticed them. People were really excited by this time and were throwing bricks. Troops had been alerted by telephone and arrived in APOC trucks in half an hour. The mob then dispersed, and a few who had broken into the refinery were arrested. The troops took up guard duties both inside and outside the refinery.

Although Iranian laborers wanted to return to work, the Company preferred to wait until all the agitators had been seized, in order to prevent the ringleaders from entering the refinery. At 3.00 p.m. on Tuesday May 7 the night shift of May 5 was finally relieved, having worked for 32 hours, for which they were suitably rewarded.[207] Elkington reported that the mob had made no demands; although he was informed they would make the demands mentioned above. He believed these so-called demands were only a smoke-screen for Communist activities. What these were he does not report, though he states that the majority of the labor force just did not know what all the trouble was about.

Since the governor had only 200 men available during the night, and since he did not know what to expect, he asked the Vice-Consul to move the *HMS Cyclamen* closer to Abadan, but to stay out of sight, for this action was not reported to the Iranian authorities.

May 7 passed without incident but, at the request of the APOC, the troops from Ahvaz were retained at Abadan. Those arrested the previous day had mostly been transported to

---

206. FO 371/13784, Fletcher to Barrett, Mohammareh, June 1, 1929 07; On May 26 and 28 disturbances at the Uhlan Company near Ahvaz occurred. Two workers refused their pay on the grounds that it was insufficient. The manager, after having contacted the Governor-General, refused to grant any increase. On May 28 "a band of some 20 Persians prevented the other workmen from going to work. The police intervened and some 20 to 30 men were arrested. Since the Uhlan Company is employed by the government in a government scheme this demonstration ipso facto is aimed against the government." Fletcher stated that the tactics employed on May 6 and 28 were similar, which indicated that they originated from the same source, FO 416/821 Fletcher to Barrett, Mohammareh, June 1, 1929, f.171

207. FO 416/821, f. 181–85. According to CPI literature 10,000 to 20,000 people participated in the strike and the confrontation with the army and the police. As a result of this the production of oil even (temporarily) decreased. However, this is not borne out at all by the British documents. Kambakhsh 1972, 36; Chaqueri 1978, 54; Abrahamian 1982, 162.

Ahvaz, from where they would be deported to places outside Khuzestan. During May 2 and 6 a total of about 200 men had been arrested which included practically all of the cell leaders. The APOC Intelligence Bureau reported that the Branch Committee of the Communist Party had now decided to call off their plan, and that a new plan was being prepared to be implemented in a few months.[208]

Trouble for the APOC was not over yet, for Elkington reported that disturbances were also to be created in Masjed-e Soleyman. The Governor-General, at his request, reinforced the garrison there with 50 horsemen. Action there, if successful, would affect Abadan, where the situation was still volatile. The relatives of the 200 deported men, who represented quite a large number of people, became the object of sympathy on the part of the population of Abadan. According to Elkington, outside agents stated that the deportees were martyrs for the community. A subscription list was opened for their relatives, which was well supported. The resulting focus on these people, the expected arrival of another Russian ship on May 16 and the advent of *Moharram* (*'Ashurah* was on June 17) had all the ingredients for a renewed outbreak of demonstrations.[209]

On June 2 it was reported that demonstrations of women were being organized for June 7 and 15 to mobilize support for the families of the deportees. There were still about 20 of these families in Abadan, who remained a focus of bitterness which lingered. Fletcher did not believe that Communists would carefully plan any demonstrations during *Moharram*. He considered it more likely that, if riots occurred at all, they would have been incited by Bushehr elements who were under the orders of one Sayyed Asadollah Esfahani, who in turn, was under communist orders. However, this was later found to be wrong, for the Bushehri connection was represented by the Member of Parliament Mirza Hoseyn Movaqer from Bushehr.[210]

Movaqer was deputy for Khuzestan; he was a rich Bushehri, who in 1928 had been involved together with his son and three sons-in-law in the creation of workmen's clubs in Abadan.[211] The APOC sent Mr. Gass to Tehran to discuss the problems in Khuzestan with the Minister of Court, Teymurtash. The latter at first created the impression that he agreed that the Communists were the cause of the trouble. At the same time, however, he stressed the need for an examination of workers' conditions, though he opposed any increase in the wages of Iranian employees. He promised that a special police squad would investigate the complicity of customs officials, two of whom would be removed. He further asked why the APOC had suspicions about certain prominent persons and expressed his

---

208. FO 416/821, SNO to Admiralty, May 26. 1929, f.200; for a list of the cell leaders see Chaqueri 1978, 218, see also p.106 (Rundschau Basel) where the names of "Yusif Eftekhari, Rahim, Ali, Ata Abdulaev, Ardashir [Ovanessiyan?], and Pishevari" are given as the leaders of the Abadan strike. Teymurtash, the Minister of Court, telegraphed orders on May 5 to take drastic measures and to deport the ringleaders of the strike, FO 371/13783, telegram to Clive, May 5. 1929, f.107. This is one of the telegrams not reproduced by Chaqueri 1978, 109, it is also noteworthy that "so far the Indians have remained unaffected, the Arabs too appear to have remained untouched'! FO 371/13783, f. 37.
209. FO 371/13783, telegram May 10, 1929, f.127.
210. FO 371/13784, Fletcher to Barrett. Mohammerah, June 1, 1929, f. 36.
211. For more background information on Mirza Hoseyn Germani (so named due to his pro-German sympathies during WW 1) Movaqer see Shaje'i 1344/1965.

annoyance about reports in British papers about the presence of warships. He threatened to withdraw Iranian protection for APOC operations in Khuzestan if British warships became a threat to Iran.[212]

Gass had another interview the next day, May 30 with Teymurtash in which the Minister took a completely different line. He denied that there had been any Communist influence, or that Movaqer was involved with them. The latter had a grievance against the APOC and the Governor of Abadan because he had not got the concessions he had wanted to establish an electric-light installation in Abadan, and a tramway. Teymurtash further stated that the Governor of Abadan was an intriguer and would be dismissed. However, he assured Gass that the troops would be retained in Abadan, while the force of security police, which was to be formed, would keep in close contact with the APOC.[213]

Clive, the British Chargé d'affaires, ascribed this change of attitude to the fact that Movaqer apparently enjoyed protection in very high places. So nothing could be done against him without documentary evidence, since any such complaint by a foreigner would be disbelieved as a matter of principle.[214]

Meanwhile in Abadan the Governor quarreled with the Governor-General and intended to resign anyway, whatever Tehran wanted to do. Although Teymurtash had expressed his doubts about Communist involvement, the authorities in Abadan obtained Communist documents on the evening of June 7. As a result, four non-APOC employees were arrested. The documents contained instructions from the Central Committee of the Communist party for Khuzestan at Ahvaz appointing Comrade Reza "as leader at Mohammereh and Abadan" and instructing all party members to "obey orders at the appointed date." The Governor-General, although promising reinforcements to Elkington, refused to arrest Comrade Reza since it was the beginning of *Moharram*, a month when feelings ran high anyway. The volatile elements in Abadan numbered by that time only 200 men, mainly Bushehris, both employees of APOC and others, who were expected to incite the general population of Abadan during *Moharram* against the APOC, and the British in general.

A new factor was the dissemination of nationalist and religious propaganda against the British, which led people to believe that the Iranian government was behind all this. Mirza Jalal and Mirza Esma`il, sons-in-law of Movaqer, were meanwhile having meetings in their house at which they assured their audience that Movaqer would secure the release of the deportees. The Iranian authorities warned both men to keep a low profile. Nevertheless, the APOC intelligence bureau had information that on the first of *Moharram* (the night of June 8), Movaqer's sons-in-law intended to attack the refinery with 150 armed Iranians, mostly Bushehris. These would incite the population with such slogans as "Down with the foreigners and unbelievers," "Khuzestan for the Persians," and of "let the sons of

---

212. The allegation about British warships putting down the Abadan strike is utterly unfounded, since it is nonsensical. The ship stayed out of sight and at no time during the period under discussion was it seen by the local population. Its presence only became known, both to the Iranian government and the CPI, from reading the British press.
213. FO 371/13784, f. 37 (note 211).
214. FO 371/13784, f. 37 and Clive to Chamberlain, Tehran, June 1929, f.16–17.

Darius enjoy the fruits of their land." Fletcher immediately contacted the Iranian authorities in Abadan and Mohammareh asking them to send reinforcements as had been promised. From his own sources of information Fletcher was firmly convinced of the reliability of the APOC information.

The Governor-General refused to arrest the ring-leaders when given their names by the British, because he said it would be fatal in *Moharram*. He nevertheless guaranteed the security of the refinery. Elkington wanted more troops, but the Governor-General refused, saying that he was prepared to face the riots which Elkington foresaw. It was clear that the Iranian authorities were very skeptical about the British reports of impending trouble. They held, moreover, that people would be disturbed if troops were sent right then. The authorities also stated that Movaqer had nothing to do with the unrest among the Bushehris and that anyway they had sufficient troops, which Fletcher estimated to be only 250. He also urged Tehran to take steps with the Central Government to ensure that sufficient reinforcements would be sent, that all ringleaders would be arrested after *Moharram*, that steps would be taken against Movaqer and his relatives, and that practically the whole Customs Department would be changed.

In the end, the Iranian authorities were proven right and no disturbances occurred at all during *Moharram*. The situation returned to normal again, that is to say that Russian agitators were still reported to be active among the APOC labor force. Meetings were still being held by Movaqer's sons-in-law, during which the benevolent Russian role *vis-à-vis* that of the British was discussed. Although the secretary of the Chief of Police of Mohammareh participated in these meetings, the authorities did nothing.

The long-awaited demonstration by the women of the deported demonstrators finally took place around June 22, 1929. The women came from Abadan to Mohammareh where they went to the telegraph office and sent a telegram to Reza Shah, then they "proceeded to the Shah's statue, where they prayed and wept." Although further troubles were expected on the fortieth day after *Moharram*, nothing happened, and the situation was back to normal again. Almost normal, for the special police squad sent from Tehran to investigate the cause of all the troubles, intimated to Fletcher that the causes were the APOC and himself, who were trying to create an excuse to land British troops. He also reports that the policemen tried to induce Iranian *farrashes* to obtain incriminating correspondence to that effect. Such a trend was in conformity with the general attitude of the Iranian authorities in the South, Fletcher reported, who appeared to favor the Russians and who refused to take any action against their alleged agents and the ringleaders of the troubles.[215]

When examining the events of May, one comes to the conclusion that it was much to-do about nothing. Apart from a scuffle with a few drunken men on May 6, and some demonstrations on May 2 nothing in fact happened.[216] The APOC manager was overcau-

---

215. FO 416/85, Fletcher to Clive, June 10. 1929, f. 22; Ibid, Fletcher to Henderson, July 27, 1929, f.50–, FO 371/13784 telegrams June 8 and 9, 1929. f.9.
216. It is interesting to note that Chaqueri 1978, 218f, was rather selective in his choice of material and did not reproduce any material casting light upon the rather insignificant occurrences of May 1929. He did not indicate either that he only reproduced part of the material and had left out the telegrams dated May 5, 6 and 7, 1929, see FO 371/13783, f,103, 105, 107.

tious and ready to believe any story that was reported to him. Although Fletcher, who took a more down-to-earth view of events, bore him out as to the activities of the various elements hostile to the APOC and the British, he nevertheless characterized the policy of APOC throughout the trouble as a continued alternation between "cringe and scream," and the Governor-General of Khuzestan told Fletcher that he and those associated with him were frankly tired of Mr. Elkington's never ending cry of 'Wolf.'[217] A similar attitude also prevailed in the Royal Navy towards the APOC, which only had given filtered and selected information and wanted the Royal Navy to do its bidding.[218]

The Abadan strike is hailed by contemporary commentators, and also by authors today, as an important event in the struggle for labor rights. Lahuti is one of the few dissenting voices, he states that the Abadan strike showed how inexperienced and awkward the few CPI members were who had been involved. In his version he also tones down the involvement of the CPI which had only sent a few agitators to Khuzestan to tell people how badly off they were. The conclusion cannot be but that the Abadan strike was much to-do about nothing, which nevertheless had great propaganda value. However, the British ambassador in Tehran did not even refer to this event in his Annual Report.[219]

The Vatan Strike at Isfahan

In Isfahan the first organized strike took place in May 1931. A committee that was affiliated with the Communist Party prepared it. This committee had decided that on May Day the workers would strike to protest against the unjust conditions under which they had to work. In order to induce the workers to do so, the committee carried out a lot of propaganda and canvassing among the workers. Their effort was inadvertently aided by the management of the factory which, some time prior to May 1, issued a kind of labor contract in which amongst other things the following was mentioned: "if a worker does not give one month's notice before he quits work in the factory, the wages of one month will be charged to him and appropriated for the benefit of the factory fund." This, more than the communist propaganda, persuaded the workers to strike. The purpose of the management had been to weaken the determination of the workers to strike, and to prevent it taking place. On May 1, in reaction to the invitations which had been extended to them, already some time earlier, some 60 to 70 workers arrived in a garden near the city. A red banner on which was written "Proletarians of the World Unite" was fixed to a wall.

---

217. FO 371/13784, SNO to CIC Fast India Station, July 1, 1929, f.129.
218. FO 371/13784, June 30, 1929, f.126.
219. Lahuti n.d., 56. It may also be possible that the demonstration was indeed engineered by local notables such as Movaqer with the silent consent of Tehran. Both Barrett and the SND in the Gulf considered this a serious possibility. For "peaceful strikes with the object of increasing wages, reducing the number of foreigners employed and increasing Persian influence in the firm were to be expected and it is not impossible that such strikes will have the secret support of the Central Government" FO 371/13784, f.126; see also Ibid., Clive to Chamberlain. June 1, 1929 f.16. "I had the impression that Movaqer enjoyed protection in the highest quarters, and there is no doubt that this is so!"; For the Annual Report see FO 416/112 (1929).

After long speeches by the party leaders and discussions, it was decided to strike on May 7 (16 *Ordibehesht*).

The management of the factory had prior knowledge about the strike, for May 7 fell on the *Ghadir* festival and a Thursday, and the management therefore declared an extra holiday and said that the workers had to come instead on Friday, their normal leisure day. This of course incensed the workers further. On May 15 the management put pressure on the workers to sign the new contract. They singled out one worker and told him that either he must sign or be dismissed on the spot. The worker refused and the others stopped work out of solidarity. A group of workers from another factory hall who wanted to know what had taken place were confronted by a closed factory gate and were forced to go back to work.

The strike was almost total, and even 8-year old children participated. A few workers of the weaving department who wanted to continue to work, were induced to strike as well. On May 15 and the night of May 15-16 the factory did not operate, the director even wanted to take on hand-weavers to continue production, but it was to no avail. After the workers had left the factory, they went to a site nearby. Some officials from the factory joined them there, and tried to persuade them to return to work. The workers refused, and they marched in orderly fashion in rows of four to the Chahar Bagh Theological School, where they formulated their demands to the factory owners. These were as follows:

1. Freedom to organize a union;
2. Changing from piece-work to a monthly salary in order to prevent the early incapacitation of the workers;
3. An 8-hour working day with sufficient pay, which should not be less than 5 *qrans*;
4. Leisure time for half a day with pay in order to be able to enjoy a leisure day properly and to fortify themselves, so that they could perform the tasks in the factory the next week properly;
5. Abolition of the control system at the gate of the factory;
6. Abolition of the system of punishment with the stick, the bastinado and the branding-iron (the case of the dyer 'Abu'l-Qasem) and of vilifications, money fines and groundless dismissal of workers by the chiefs, supervisors and the instructors of the factory;
7. Establishment of a fund for wages for those who have fallen ill or had an accident as a result of work in the factory,
8. Payment of all costs of treatment of the workers by the factory;
9. A special subvention in the way of double pay in case of overtime (just as the money fines were levied at twice the level of the wages);
10. Total time off on Fridays and public holidays in accordance with the government calendar for all parts of the factory,

11. The maximum working day not to exceed 10 hours, i.e. only to include a maximum of 2 hours of overtime;

12. Complete attention to the maintenance of hygienic conditions by the factory in the interest of the workers in order to get rid of the dirty work and of sacrificing worker health in the interest of the employers. For example, the establishment of a dining-hall with furniture; the provision of clean drinking vessels in all parts of the factory, so that 400 men should not be forced to drink from the same vessel as was the case then; provision of warm tea in one big tank, so that every worker could drink warm tea with sugar; the construction of a ventilation tube in the cleaning department so that dust and refuse could be vented.

13. Arrangement for the payment of wages so as not to be exposed to the vexations and vilifications of the pay-master Sayyed Mohammad Taqi.

After written demands had been handed to the factory manager, the workers expected that their representatives would be invited by the director to discuss them.

During their rally in the Chahar Bagh, the police had arrived, and they arrested some of the labor leaders. The Police Chief threatened the other workers and told them to return to work. A delegation of the workers then went to see the State Attorney, who told them that their accusations were unfounded.

On the second day of the strike, the strike committee held a meeting in which the written demands were finalized and prepared for a plenary meeting. In spite of the fact that the police and factory management tried to prevent their meeting, the next day the strikers assembled on the public road. In their public and plenary meeting, the demands were adopted and eight men elected as their representatives: (one party member, three union members, three unaffiliated). The eight representatives went to visit the director in his private home, who received them in a friendly manner. After having listened to their demands he said that he gave his word of honor that all these demands would be agreed to, except the eight-hour day, which had to be at least nine hours. The party member among the strikers' representatives did not trust the director at all, and suggested that he give this promise in writing. Thereupon the director had the party member thrown out of his house. The others then also left the house. The director invited them back again saying that he had been serious about it. He took one of the representatives aside and tried to cajole and threaten him but, finally seeing that this did not work, told him to report his remarks to the workers. At the same time it was learned that the unaffiliated representatives had wavered. It was therefore decided to call a plenary meeting the next day or May 17. The workers believed the promises made by the director and returned to work.

On the afternoon of May 17 the workers stopped work after eight hours and went home. On the next day they saw armed policemen in the factory, who, when the workers had calmed down, arrested some of the leaders in the afternoon. In this way 25 to 39 workers were taken away by the police. Finally only six remained under arrest - all members of the action committee. Five of them were released after 50 days and one was banished for two months to Abadeh. He was apparently recognized as a CPI member when his picture arrived in Tehran. He was then taken to Tehran, but succeeded in escaping.

The main results of the strike were:
1. The working day was reduced from twelve to nine hours;
2. The examination at the gate of the factory was abolished;
3. A separate area was set aside exclusively for drinking tea and for eating breakfast;
4. A pay rise of 20 per cent was promised;
5. The vilifications and the money fines were to be reduced;
6. Vessels with iced water were to be put in all departments;
7. The lunch-time to be changed from half an hour to one hour; and
8. The main thing, however, was the withdrawal of the labor contract.

Although the CPI was very pleased with the outcome of the strike, at the same time it also analyzed some of the defects in the organization and handling of the strike: not only had the strike committee neglected to contact other factories in Isfahan, but women and children working in the *Vatan* factory had not been allowed to join the strike either. The strike leaders were also criticized for concentrating on purely bread-and-butter issues and the total neglect of showing the people in Isfahan the links between their own position and the bond that existed between the Iranian government and international capitalism. The CPI ascribed these defects to the inexperience of the strike leaders, which also explained why they had not organized the strike after the *Ghadir* festival, in which case to strike would have been more effective, or so the CPI believed.[220]

The Suppression of the Unions

After the *Vatan* strike of May 1931, there was hardly any further activity by unions. This had also become very difficult, for in June 1931 the *Majles* had adopted the anti-communist bill which, inter alia, forbade the formation of trade unions. As a result of this law, more than 2,000 CPI or suspected CPI members were arrested. This had serious results for the activities of the unions, which, as we have seen, were in fact creations of the CPI. Another reason for the disappearance of the unions was the fact that the Soviet Union preferred to remain on good terms with Iran and its ruler, Reza Shah. To that end it had already given orders to break off all contacts between the Russian Legation and the CPI in 1929. What contacts existed with Russia were mainly via the Comintern.[221] A last reason for the lack of attraction of unions may have to do with the greater employment

---

220. The story of the *Vatan* strike is based on letters in the Persian paper *Setareh-ye Sorkh* (published in Germany), which is reproduced (in translation) in Chaqueri 1978, 43–47, 63–66.
221. Abrahamian 1982, 139f.,162; Rezun 1981, 293 ff

opportunities which existed in Iran after 1931 owing to the wave of industrialization. The small group of skilled workers, the main target and support of the unions in Iran, were in great demand.²²² Under the political circumstances, they may have decided to let things be for the moment.

Not all workers were of this opinion. It is reported that the workers of the Northern section of the railway secretly formed a union in 1938.²²³ But, even it this is true, it cannot change the fact that unionism as a political and social force played no role whatsoever during the 1930s. The few strikes that occurred during this period more than likely were wildcat strikes, such as the one in Shiraz in the factory of the Dehqan brothers in 1936. The workers demanded better treatment to which the employers acceded.²²⁴ A strike by railway workers in the North in 1932 for higher wages and continued pay for the strike period was also successful.²²⁵ But these are the only ones reported during a period in which the industrial labor force increased by 250 per cent. In 1939 some militant APOC workers prepared a strike but before this could materialize their leaders were arrested and the danger of a strike averted.²²⁶ It is therefore not surprising that the British could state in 1936 that there were no trade unions in Iran.²²⁷

THE REASONS FOR THE FAILURE OF UNIONS IN IRAN

It would be wrong to conclude that the rise of the labor force in modern industry in the urban areas had led to the development of something like an industrial proletariat. The possible impact of industrial labor looks even more favorable for such a development when we look at the growth of large-scale factories with a big labor force (Table 2.4). As we can see, the relatively small number of factories with a labor force of more than 500 workers employed a disproportionate number of laborers. When we further realize that the majority of these large-scale factories were concentrated in only four urban areas, such a supposition about the growth of a militant industrial proletariat seems likely. However, as far as is known, the only strike that occurred in those four urban areas of highly concentrated industrial activity (Tehran, Tabriz, Mazandaran, Isfahan) took place in Isfahan in 1931, that is to say before all these large-scale factories were built.

---

222. Simmonds 1935, p.37. This was a great change as compared with the situation in the 1920s, when unemployment for unskilled labor was reported to be as high as 50 percent and for skilled labor as high as 20 percent, Chaqueri 1978, 75, 90.
223. Ivanov 1356, 82; Bashkirov, 1948, 28–29.
224. FO 371/20835, f.21 (Report on Economic Conditions in Fars 1936).
225. Bashkirov 1948, 29, Hezb-e Tudeh 1349, 189.
226. Hezb-e Tudeh 1349, 190.
227. FO 371/20830, f.184 (A Memorandum on Economic Affairs in Azerbaijan 1936).

TABLE 2.4: Growth of Large-Scale Factories and their labor Force 1930–40[228]

	1930		1940	
No. of employees	factories	workers	factories	workers
3-50	255	4600	283	3985
51- 500	17	6400	67	11030
501-1000	-	-	17	14862
1001-2000	-	-	11	15068

There are several reasons why no (militant) industrial labor class came into being during the 1930s additional to the inhibiting factor of the political context of Iranian society.[229] The most important reason is, I submit, the fact that a considerable share of the industrial labor force had not been divorced from its traditional agricultural and pastoral pursuits. Especially in the agro-industries such as the eight sugar-mills, the fish and fruit-canning industry, the wool-cleaning and carding, and the cotton-ginning industry, the large majority of the labor force were seasonal workers. During off-season, these would be easily absorbed by the agricultural sector. A similar situation also existed for such an important sector as the construction industry, which during winter-time had to lay off substantial part of its labor force.[230] It is even true for the oil industry, where the turnover of wage-earners was very high. Even as late as 1948, for example, 59 per cent of the wage-earners leaving the APOC's employment had less than one year's service, and 28 per cent less than two years' service. This high turnover was caused by the fact that tribesmen wanted to earn some extra money in the off-season of the pastoral sector. Another reason was that unskilled workers dodged the draft by returning to their villages, where control was less effective than in the urban areas.[231]

Another obstacle to the formation of a proper industrial class was the prevalence of female and child labor, which was especially to be found in the textile industry. In Kerman, 7,000 workers were employed in the carpet industry of which 75 per cent were children between six and twelve years and women. The remaining 25 per cent were almost exclusively composed of adolescents of fifteen to eighteen years. The older workers were the masters, mainly men, who numbered only a few hundred.[232] This pattern was only to be expected in an industry which was basically still a cottage industry. The same pattern also occurred in modern industry, here mainly in the textile industry. In Table 2.5 the labor force is shown in twelve cotton spinning mills. From this Table it is clear that employers showed an increasing interest in child labor. Women and boys received lower wages and were more amenable to the employers' wishes, although they only worked to obtain a little extra money for their families.

---

228. Abdullayev 1968, 89.
229. Abrahamian 1982, 132–65.
230. Floor 1984b; Bharier 1971, 71ff.
231. ILO 1950, 24-25; employers also dismissed older, militant workers for younger and cheaper ones, who also were less militant. Chaqueri 178, 14
232. ILO 1938, 89.

Another factor which inhibited the formation of a militant working-class outlook among the labor force was its high rate of illiteracy. Of those employed by the APOC in 1935, only eight per cent were literate. The corresponding percentage in the other industries, with a high level of female and child labor, was undoubtedly even lower.[233] Although illiteracy in itself is no obstacle to acquiring a class consciousness in terms of a sense of belonging to an industrial proletariat, as events since 1945 have shown, this, combined with the others, was nevertheless an inhibiting factor.

TABLE 2.5: Workers in the Cotton Industry, by Sex[234]

Mills	March 1935			March 1936			March 1937		
	male	female	child	male	female	child	male	female	child
1	-	-	-	-	-	-	443	58	212
2	-	-	-	-	-	-	127	-	79
3	270	60	120	350	150	180	355	142	190
4	200	50	150	500	100	200	600	200	300
5	-	-	-	-	-	-	695	342	262
6	70	-	50	120	-	80	280	20	150
7	-	-	-	-	-	-	378	42	140
8	-	-	-	-	-	-	300	-	500
9	-	-	-	160	-	180	170	15	315
10	-	-	-	70	-	50	130	-	120
11	440	52	-	544	15	-	625	122	-
12	180	20	100	180	20	100	210	20	110
Total	1160	182	400	1924	285	790	4313	961	2378

Nevertheless, the beginnings of an industrial proletariat appeared towards the end of the 1930s. Although the second generation of industrial workers only started work in the various factories towards the end of the 1940s, something had already changed in employer-worker relations. The wave of new state and private modern factories, which often offered higher salaries than the traditional small-scale workshops, attracted many workers. The result was that "for an additional rial or two per day the factory worker has lost the personal association with his employer. There is not, as yet, adequate provision for injury or for unemployment to replace the moral responsibility of the old-type employer."[235]

This situation was mitigated by the fact that just as there was no true industrial population in Iran neither were there old industrial families "with deep-rooted experience of

---

233. ILO 1950, 42; added to the relative isolation of the towns this resulted in a rather low class consciousness, Chaqueri 1978, 76
234. ILO 1938, 87.
235. See note 70 above.

industrial methods, organization and finance."[236] The above is also confirmed by the names of the most important shareholders/directors of the factories in Isfahan and Shiraz. In Isfahan the following factories existed in 1936:

Vatan: Hajji Muhammad Husain Kaziruni (eight heirs).

Risbaf: Hajji Abbas Akbari, Haidar Ali Immami, Hajji Sayyid Javad Kasai, Hajji Muhammad Kazim Mithqali, Ali Almasi

Zayandarud: Hajji Sayyid Abdul Rahim Mahmudiya, Hajji Zainul Abodin Amin, Muhammad Jafar Kaziruni

Ata al Mulk: Fazlullah Dehesh Ata al-Mulk

Nakhtab: Ishaq Sassoon, Eliahu Derlian, Qasim Rashti, Azizullah Maghen, Azizullah Shekib (mostly Jewish).

Chit: mainly the same as of Risbaf, Zayandarud and the Kaziruni family.

Shahreza: Hajji Sayyid Mustaffa Bunakdar, Hajji Hasan Ali Hamadani, Hajji Muhammad 'Ali Sahaban, Muhammad Javad Nilfurush.

Rughani & Cy.: Hajji Rughani Rahimzada (+ son, 70% of the shares)

Pashm: Muhammad Herati, Ali Agha Hamadanian, Hajji 'Abdul Hosain Akhavan Dehdashti, Hajji Hasan Vaffadar.

Kaghaz: Akbar Mas'ud Saram ud-Dawla, Hasan Sultani, Javad Kasai. Zainul Abidin Amin, Muhammad Shaikhzada, Sayyid Muhammad Atzal, Martin Essai.

Ittihad Shahrez: Many shareholders.

Kanva: Martin Essai, Miles Essai, Muhammad 'Ali Sahiban (mainly Armenian).[237]

In Shiraz the following situation existed:

Fars Electric Comp, & Sharikat-i sanayi`-yi dasti:

Abdul Husain Dehqan, Ali Muhammad Dehqan (Majlis deputy), Mehdi Namazi (Majlis deputy), Jalal Aryan, Hajji Muhammad Hasan Bihbahani.

Nassaji-ye Fars: Hajji Muhammad Hasan Bihbahani, Abdul

Husain Dehqan, 'Ali Muhammad Dehqan, Jalal Aryan, Mehdi Namazi, Muhammad Taqi Shankal.[238]

Most of the new industrial employers had only five or six years of experience as industrial managers by 1941. They originated for the greater part, moreover, not from the old

---

236. ILO 1950, 66; Conolly 1935; Korby 1977, 20–23; Anon. 1946, 311 "the men who have emerged as the directors and owners of these mills come from the merchants Class." FO 371/402222 f.79-80 (Labour and Industrial Conditions in Fars).
237. FO 371/20050, f.137–43 (Report on Economic Conditions).
238. FO 371/402222 f.79-80 (Labour and Industrial Conditions in Fars).

tradition of handicrafts and small-scale industry, but rather from trading and non-commercial families, or, as in the case of state factories, the managers were 'modernized' Iranians (military or civilian), with a totally different outlook on life and the future of Iran from that of labor force. Although the new class of managers treated their labor force in a paternalistic way, which was accepted and even expected by the workers, this attitude did not compensate for the moral responsibility felt by the traditional employers. The new managers were, with few exceptions, totally indifferent to the safety and health of their workers. "The employers feel somewhat outraged that such important persons as themselves should be treated in this disrespectful way by mere workers. Their sole thought is money and more money and they refuse to listen reasonably to the grievances of their workers and treat the latter in a hostile way when they try to submit complaints, which in many cases are genuine. The owners for the most part have no idea at all of how to deal with their men and no thought of maintaining good relations with them."[239] It was this attitude of total indifference and aloofness that, more than anything, caused resentment among the Iranian workers. Similarly, the different treatment accorded to British and Iranian workers by the APOC, in short, discrimination, more than low wages and bad working conditions, created a fertile soil for the acceptance of union ideals in the 1940s. The lack of experience and isolation of the working class, which was still steeped in tradition and its own moral values, led to the failure of the trade union movement in Iran during the 1920s.

---

239. FO 371/40222 Bullard to Eden, Tehran, March 5, 1944; see also note 67, f.75.

Part II. Labor Law

INTRODUCTION

The Iranian Government neglected the whole area of social legislation. Although, as we shall see, some legislation was adopted with regard to the prevention of accidents and of industrial diseases, it was insignificant compared with the lack of attention paid to such matters in practice and the lack of government enforcement of these laws. Surprisingly, even the workers neglected these issues, and did not go beyond demanding payment of compensation after an accident or illness rather than fighting for the adoption of preventive measures as well.[240]

We can distinguish three distinct periods between 1900 and 1941 with regard to labor legislation. The first period was that prior to 1921. During this time Iran boasted hardly of any modern industry and was beset by political and economic problems. The central government after 1911 held no power over the provinces. It is therefore not surprising to observe that, apart from an ineffectual and minor attempt at labor force regulation in 1904, little was done during that period. Only in Kerman was some effort made to regulate working conditions in the carpet industry. Owing principally to self-interested objectives of its proponent the whole effort came to nought however.

The second period (1921–1929) is characterized by Iran's efforts to become a modernizing state. After the 1921 coup, led by Reza Khan, various social reforms were proposed. Apart from being unrealistic from an economic point of view, these were also politically unattainable, and thus soon shelved. The discussion in the *Majles* of the need for a Factory Act underscored this lack of political support for such a step. Iran was not yet ready for it, socially, economically and institutionally. Nevertheless, Iran had joined the ILO in 1914, and it was by this organization that the issue of labor conditions in Iran was raised. The ILO's enquiry remained restricted to the carpet industry, which to the outside world was Iran's principal, if not sole, industry. As a result of this ILO activity, the first labor law in Iran was passed, although it only applied to one industrial sector (the carpet industry), and to one area (Kerman). After its publication in the ILO legislative texts, everybody's mind was set at ease, and no further interest was shown in its implementation.

The third period coincides with Iran's large-scale effort at industrialization in the 1930s. The majority of the legislation was aimed at the modern sector of the economy, with particular emphasis on state functionaries. The small-scale industry sector, such as the carpet industry, was not regulated at all, may be because of its increasing economic importance.

Although social legislation gave the labor force in the modern sector some measure of rights and protection, it did not give labor any bargaining power. The 1936 Factory Act even explicitly excluded this right. Labor laws therefore were more of a cosmetic than a material nature. Although labor laws conveyed some ideas of labor rights to the labor force, such rights were not yet to be exercised.

---

240. See Part One on the activities of the trade unions.

FIRST LEGISLATIVE ATTEMPTS (1900-1914)

Nevertheless, it was the field of occupational health and safety legislation that received relatively much attention from the Iranian Government. However, the first government measures concerning working conditions were associated with the Moslem character of the country. On 10 September 1902, at the orders of Mozaffar al-Din Shah, the Minister of Foreign Affairs informed the foreign legations that, after an interim period of two weeks, no Moslem women were allowed to work in factories owned by foreigners (i.e., non-Moslems). This decree, so the legations were informed, had been issued to prevent unrest among the population. The factory owners were advised to employ boys of ten to twelve years instead.[241] From the situation later in the century, it is clear that this decree was completely ignored by the authorities and the factory owners, a fate which befell most, if not all social legislation in Iran.

Another instance of Government interference with working conditions occurred in 1913 in Kerman. The Deputy Governor of Kerman had laid down conditions to be maintained in carpet factories, which he made public in April 1913. This caused discontent among the employers who took sanctuary at the British consulate to protest against the 'social regulations.' According to the British Consul, the Regulations:

> For the most part were in themselves desirable, an opinion in which the Agents of the European Carpet Firms concurred. Some of them were however scarcely practicable, and to a large extent they could only be made effective after the lapse of a reasonable period of time, while in fact they were declared operative at once. On the other hand the conditions of the trade are notoriously scandalous and highly injurious to the health and well being of the workers who are largely small children.[242]

The situation was complicated by the fact that the employers (owners of the carpet looms) worked on a contract basis for the European firms. If they had to work according to the new Regulations, they would be unable to fulfil their contracts, which would cause serious loss and inconvenience to the European firms. Moreover, the consul believed that the publication of the Regulations had not been occasioned by any humanitarian sentiments on the part of the Deputy Governor, but rather because of "a desire to turn a dishonest and oppressive penny." The employers, knowing this well, and being against any reform, made use of this knowledge to try to force the British consul and the European firms to support their case.

The consul (Lorimer) tried to outmaneuver them by stating that he would take no sides unless good arguments could be given to him to do so. He therefore invited both the strikers and the European firms to draw up a list of arguments against each single article of the Regulations. At first the employers did not comply with this suggestion, and the num-

---

241. Legatie Perzië, letter nr. 196, note verbale September 10, 1902.
242. FO 248/1072 folios 62 (April 7, 1913), 68-70 (April 14, 1913).

ber of strikers (*bastis*) swelled to several hundred. After two days the strikers finally, on the evening of 11 April, 1913, presented Lorimer with their case, the Europeans having submitted a "more effective statement" earlier. To prevent the case being taken to the Russian consul as well, Lorimer discussed the matter with the Deputy Governor, and explained it "from the point of view of H.M. Consulate and the interests it represents, with appropriate remarks on the principle of *festina lente*." He was able to persuade the Deputy Governor to issue an order stating that the enforcement of the Regulations was suspended pending deliberations to be held in connection with the representatives of the foreign firms and of the weaving community.

The strikers at first did not want to accept this alternative, and demanded total abrogation of the Regulations. Lorimer made it clear to them that nobody could deny that there was a clear case for reforms and that he would support no action which was aimed at suppressing such measures. He had seen to it that the government did not act wantonly and irresponsibly; it they rejected the new order, he would cause it to be withdrawn. After some discussion, the strikers were finally satisfied and returned home. Lorimer did not expect the Deputy Governor to raise the issue again in a hurry, but he also was against bringing up the matter of reforms at once. He proposed to make an inventory of the working conditions prevailing in Kerman and, with collaboration of the European firms, gradually to have "improvements introduced where necessary in regard to overcrowding, ventilation, and cruelty to children."[243]

PROPOSED REFORM BY ZIYA AL-DIN'S CABINET (1921)

The new government led by Ziya al-Din had indeed prepared various measures which were to be executed by the Welfare Organization of the Municipality of Tehran (*Edareh-ye Omur-e Kheyriyeh-ye Baladiyeh-ye Tehran*) which were made public in April 1921. Apart from measures in the fields of public health and consumer protection, action would be taken to combat unemployment. To that end a Labor Council (*Shurah-ye Mashaghel-e Kargaran*) was established, which was charged with finding jobs for unemployed workers, both skilled and unskilled. It had, moreover, to assist them when destitute, and to defend their rights, especially where their working hours and weekly rest period were concerned. For this purpose, the Council was also given powers to mediate between workers and employers, while it had to see to it that hygienic working conditions were adhered to. Finally, it was also responsible for the building of cheap housing, the provision of free schooling (both general and professional), and the establishment of crèches for working mothers. To enable the Labor Council to carry out all these tasks in a satisfactory manner, it would be put in charge of an 'Assistance Fund' for the needy and a 'Loan Fund' for municipal functionaries. Another instrument to combat unemployment, municipal workshops (*Karkhanehha-ye Baladiyeh*), would also be created, which would be open to both sexes.

---

243. FO 248/1072 folios 62 (April 7, 1913), 68-70 (April 14, 1913). Unfortunately, the FO files do not contain a copy or description of the Regulations.

These modern projects were not carried out. Not only was Ziya al-Din dismissed, but the projects were neither economically feasible nor technically practical. Iran was too poor a country to be able to afford such trimmings of a welfare state. Moreover, it also lacked the technical capabilities, in terms of manpower, management and technical know-how to implement such a policy. Nevertheless, something of the spirit of these projects was retained by succeeding governments as shown by their efforts to improve working conditions in the carpet industry in Kerman, and, later in the decade, by the beginnings of an industrialization policy.[244]

THE FIRST DEBATE IN THE MAJLES (1923)

Although Government's activities in the field of legislation and regulation were almost exclusively concerned with the carpet industries during the period 1910–1939, there was a notable exception to this rule. For on November 29, 1922 the *Majles* discussed the welfare of the workers in connection with the Bill granting the Khoy'i brothers concessionary rights for the manufacture of matches in Azerbaijan. Article 10 of the Bill obliged the employer to compensate workers for any damages suffered as a result of proven negligence or fault on the part of the employer. Several deputies opposed this provision on the grounds that the protection of the workers required a general law applicable to all factories and companies, for it would not be realistic to impose such rules on one company only. Modarres supported this view, saying that Iran had plenty of workers, but hardly any factories. Two deputies (Mohammad Hashem Mirza and Amir Naser) submitted that they had prepared such a general bill, but others argued that the *Majles* should not frighten off scarce entrepreneurs. Bahar, however, supported the adoption of such a general law but in its absence, argued for this single case to serve as an example and a precedent. He also observed that the discussion was of historical importance, since it was the very first time that the *Majles* had discussed employer-worker relations. On January 5, 1923 the Khoy'i bill was passed including Article 10, obliging the employer to compensate workers for damage suffered on the work floor.[245]

REGULATIONS FOR THE CARPET INDUSTRY

In the same year of 1923, the Government of Iran issued social regulations with regard to another branch of industry, the carpet industry in Kerman. This Government interference did not have as much to do with a felt need on the part of the Iranian Government as the effect of the law shows. It was, rather, foreign influence which prompted the Iranian Government to take action. Iran was one of the first members of the International Labor Organization (ILO) created in 1914. The ILO, after having received reports on the miserable working conditions of female and child laborers in the Kerman carpet weaving

---

244. RMM 1921, 125-27 quoting from the newspaper *Iran* of April 26-27, 1921.
245. Majles-e Shura-ye Melli 1924, 1380-84.

workshops, discussed this problem in the Fifth Session of its Governing Body in 1920. It was decided that the Director of the ILO would "address a friendly representation to the Persian Government on the subject on the condition of the carpet weavers in Persia."[246]

The ILO, supported by the British Government, contacted the Iranian Government in early 1921. On May 16, 1921 the Minister of Foreign Affairs, Mo'azzez al-Dowleh, informed the British Legation that necessary instruction had been sent to "the local authorities in Kerman province and authorities in other places where there are carpet factories."[247] These had reported that certain measures had been taken to improve the situation. The new Iranian government (for in February 1921 the coup d'etat led by Reza Khan had taken place), took this matter seriously and had appointed a commission in the Ministry of Public Works to study "the means by which the condition of child labor can be improved and drawing up regulations which will be put into operation when passed by the Government."[248]

On October 2, 1921 the Iranian Government informed the ILO that the improvement of labor conditions in general was a priority of the government program and that it was likely that positive results might be realized shortly.[249] On December 18, 1921 the Minister of Foreign Affairs informed the British Legation that, pending a final decision, the local authorities in Kerman had been instructed to implement the following measures:

1. Employment in the factories must be perfectly free;
2. The owners of the factories must undertake not to employ the laborers more than eight hours;
3. Children under ten years of age were not to be employed;
4. At midday the laborers must be allowed to go out of the factories and have a rest;
5. Factories must not be damp but properly ventilated and their sanitary condition must be perfect;
6. Proper seats must be provided for women and children so that they may be in comfort when working and no harm done to their nerves.

In addition, the local authorities had to see to it that employers did not cheat the laborers with regard to their wages and other necessaries.[250] Meanwhile discussion had started in Kerman and other towns about labor conditions, for the British Legation had asked its various consuls to report on labor conditions in the carpet weaving industry. These enquiries precipitated an initiative by Bishop Linton, of the British Church Missionary Soci-

---

246. Chaqueri 1978, 202 quoting FO 371/9030 f. 197.
247. Chaqueri 1978, 208 quoting FO 371/6450 f. 17.
248. Chaqueri 1978, 208 quoting FO 371/6450 f. 17.
249. Kechavarz 1934, 51.
250. FO 371/7829 f. 160 Assadollah, Moshar es Sultane to Norman, Tehran, December 18, 1921.

ety in Kerman, who called together nine managers of carpet weaving factories in Kerman at his office to discuss the improvement of working conditions on December 5, 1921. He induced the managers to sign an undertaking which they would carry out in their own factories, viz.

1. That the factories themselves be properly ventilated and be kept clean and in good sanitary condition, and be well-lighted;
2. That there be no overcrowding;
3. With regard to the sitting position of the workers:
   (i) that the carpet beam be eleven inches from the ground, i.e., that there be at least eleven inches between the bottom of the beam and the ground;
   (ii) that the seat be a flat board, at least eleven inches broad;
   (iii) that, if children were employed, the seat must possess a back-rest.
   (iv) that the seat must not be raised to such an extent that the feet of the children cannot reach the floor;
4. That the minimum age of workers in the factory be eight years for boys and ten years for girls;
5. That no children under fourteen work more than eight hours a day.

Bishop Linton also tried to raise the question of wages for those who could not live on their present wages. The employers, however, were not prepared to raise them. For "if a child getting ten shahis a day is raised to fifteen shahis, the fifteen-shahi worker will want a Kran, and so on, and the cost of carpets will be raised by 50 per cent." Bishop Linton pointed out the fallacy of this argument, for a 50 per cent rise in wages did not mean a 50 per cent increase in the cost of the finished product. However, he was anxious to make a start and had already faced great difficulties over the question of the minimum age. Bishop Linton intended to have a meeting with the *ostads* (foremen) next to put this undertaking to them. Finally, he wanted all employers to agree to these minimum conditions, for which he counted on British support.[251]

The Government meanwhile had also initiated negotiations with the employers who made strong objections to the eight-hour working day, the sanitary measures, and Government interference in the fixing of wages. Finally the Governor-General (*Vali*) of Kerman was ordered to issue the following decree on December 17, 1923:[252]

1. The working day shall not be more than eight hours;
2. On Fridays and public holidays work shall be suspended and workers will continue to receive their normal wages;

---

251. FO 371/7829 f. 163–64; the undertaking was signed by representatives of nine Companies who are mentioned on Ibid., f.163
252. Chaqueri 1978, 206; for the official text see ILO, *Série Législative* 1923, Perse 1.

3. Boys under eight and girls under eighteen years of age shall not be employed;

4. Boys and girls shall work in separate workshops; mixed workshops are absolutely forbidden;

5. Foremen (those who dictate the pattern to the workers) shall not enter the girls' workshop, where forewomen shall be employed

6. Employers shall not engage anyone with an infectious disease,

7. Workshops should not be underground or damp, and must have windows on the south side;

8. The weaving loom must be at one meter above the floor of the workshop and the seat high enough for children to be comfortable;

9. The head of the Public Health Service of the municipal office shall inspect each factory each month. In case of non-compliance with the decree it will be reported and proper action will be taken;

10. For every contravention, a fine of not less than 100 and not more than 500 krans, or imprisonment for not less than one day and not more than 20 days shall be imposed;

11. The police shall be responsible for the supervision of the carrying out of these provisions.

According to Kechavarz, the Government also appears to have ordered a provisional pay rise of five per cent. The employers protested against this measure, for it did not take into account good and bad workers. However, this instruction was probably carried out.[253] Although, as reports by British consuls show, working conditions in other parts of Iran needed improvement as well, the Government did not order implementation of the Kerman decree in other provinces. It nevertheless realized the need for wider application of the decree and appointed a commission to draw up new regulations of a more general nature, which could thus also be applied outside Kerman province.[254]

Meanwhile, both the ILO and the British Government were satisfied with the result of their activities. The British Minister responsible for ILO affairs declared in the House of Lords that the workers' situation had improved, though admitting that his remarks held only for Kerman.[255] The British Government's assertion was based on reports from its consuls in Kerman, Hamadan and Tabriz written in August 1923. In Kerman, according to Dr. Schaffter, the physician of the missionary hospital, the situation had much improved compared with that of 1913. Lighting and ventilation were satisfactory, hours of work had been shortened and wages increased, while very young children were no longer

---

253. Kechavarz 1934, 60.
254. Kechavarz 1934, 60.
255. ILO, 1928b. 381–82.

employed.²⁵⁶ The British Consul concluded that "the tendency is toward general improvement" as far as Kerman was concerned.²⁵⁷ The situation in Hamadan was considered to be favorable where working conditions, wages, ages, and health were concerned. The manager of the two European factories boasted that many weavers had been with his company for twelve years already, and he invited the authorities to have the women examined medically to "dispose of any suggestion of prejudice to child-bearing."²⁵⁸

In the Soltanabad area there were no factories, only cottage industries, which made control and inspection an almost impossible proposition for the Government, the consul commented.²⁵⁹ But he, like his colleague in Kerman, was of the opinion that in most cases the working conditions in the cottage industries were good. It was only in Tabriz that the British consul reported very bad working conditions in the Iranian factories. He had a favorable opinion of the conditions prevailing in the European factory where shorter working hours and better hygienic conditions obtained.²⁶⁰

The ILO had a similar impression and concluded that the matter had been dealt with in a satisfactory manner.²⁶¹ Meanwhile when the Governor of Kerman tried, in early 1924, to enforce the regulations, he met with opposition from the employers. They protested to the British consul about "the injury to their interests which these rules seemed to threaten." After discussions between the Governor and the consul, some trifling modifications were agreed upon which the employers accepted. However, shortly thereafter the 1923 decree was cancelled by order from Tehran, "on account of protests, it was said, from the master weavers, and nothing was heard anymore of the matter."²⁶²

The ILO began having doubts about its earlier assessment of the working conditions in the carpet factories in Iran when in 1928 an article appeared in the newspaper *Shafaq-e Sorkh* entitled: "The Kerman carpet or the extermination of the young generation of that

---

256. FO 371/9030, f. 205. C.M. Schaffter's statement, Kerman, August 19th 1923. The report also notes that "Bishop Linton visited Kerman in May 1923 and expressed pleasure at the improvement already noted in the carpet industry."

257. FO 371/9030 f.204 Haworth, L. to Sir Percy Loraine, Kerman 21st August 1923. He considered Schaffter's report on the local looms somewhat cold. "All the workrooms I have seen are excellent." He also remarked "Indeed with the standard set by European firms I doubt if the work could be done in bad conditions and I consider that cause for complaint no longer exists."

258. FO 371/9030, f. 218–19 F. Hale to Loraine, Hamadan, 24th October 1923 "The bazaar factory contains 110 looms in one large hall. The office factory contains 64 looms in two large halls. Both factories are well lighted and ventilated, with waterproof roofs. In winter they are warmed with stoves. Each factory employs a special water carrier who brings in drinking water in a clean skin throughout the day. Water closets are of the usual type. The cesspools are emptied thrice annually. Each factory is swept daily."

259. FO 371/9030, f.220 F. Hutton to Loraine, Sultanabad, October 30th 1923; an obstacle here was "the established custom of the country by which no one, Government official or otherwise, may enter a carpet factory without previously informing the agent of the owner of the carpets on the looms, who may accompany him. (This recognized custom is due to the fact that many carpet designs are private prop" and have to be kept secret). FO 248/1072 f.96 Kirman Diary (April 1913).

260. FO 371/9030 f. 215-17 consul to Loraine, October 25 1923.

261. ILO, 1928a, 109.

262. FO 416/11 Z 1. 104.

province."²⁶³ The author of the article stated that wages were not enough to live on. The workers he described as a collection of famished, pale, emaciated and deformed beings. In fact the article showed that not one single item of the 1923 Act had been implemented. The journalist nevertheless had some hope for improvement in the situation, because a Government Commission was preparing a new set of regulations for the carpet factories. This commission was not apparently the same as that created in 1924, since it was specifically stated that it had been created at the initiative of Teymurtash, the powerful Minister of the Court. In view of the good relationship between 'Ali Dashti,²⁶⁴ the editor of *Shafaq-e Sorkh*, and the government it seems quite likely that the article was a commissioned one. For in that same year, a Government decree was issued entitled "Regulations for carpet manufactories and workshops," which contained instructions with regard to the layout of the buildings, hygienic conditions in the factories, working conditions, working hours and wages. From these regulations it is clear that it was based upon the 1923 Kerman decree, as we shall see.²⁶⁵

According to the instructions on the layout of the buildings, the Regulations stipulated that weaving looms had to be at least one and a half meters above the ground; the building should not be humid, and should be constructed in such a way that the sun shone in. Ventilation should be provided, as well as a proper durable floor. Each worker should have a working space of at least three square meters. The height of the building should be at least four meters (art. 1 and 2).

The hygienic measures to be taken were the following: the building had to be in a good state and properly maintained. Workers were to have a seating arrangement that prevented physical deformation. In winter, space heating had to be provided by way of stoves and chimneys; open fires were not allowed. During working hours, adequate light had to be provided, while drinking water had to be clean and fresh. Each worker should have his own mug. Bugs and insects had to be dealt with properly, while care had to be taken that no flies, bugs, and dust could enter the working areas. The use of unprocessed and unwashed wool was forbidden in the manufactories. Clean and proper washrooms, which had to be maintained and disinfected regularly, had to be provided; one per 25 workers. After work the working areas had to be cleaned and aired for at least one hour. Once a week the working areas had to be disinfected. Prior to engagement, and once a month during employment, workers should have a medical examination. If workers had a contagious disease or consumption, they could not be employed until they were declared ready for work by the medical authorities (art. 13-14).

Workers below the age of ten (boys) and twelve (girls) could not be employed, while male and female workers had to work in separate areas. Women who had to give birth were entitled to five weeks vacation on half pay (arts. 15–17).

The regulations on working hours and wages were as revolutionary as those on working conditions. In the carpet industry, henceforth a working day of eight hours and a week of 48 hours, rest periods excluded, were declared. Overtime was possible if both employers

---

263. ILO, 1928a, 109-110 for the full text of the article.
264. FO 416/112 1. 180 calls Dashti a lackey of Teymurtash.
265. For the complete text of these Regulations see Kechavarz 1934, 112-119.

and employees agreed to it with a maximum of two hours per day and twelve hours per week for which the workers were to receive a proportional increase (50 per cent) in pay. The rest period during midday was fixed at one and a half hours. Salaries were to be paid in cash, and payment in kind was forbidden unless the employee agreed to it. In case of an industrial accident or illness, the worker was entitled to shorter working hours, sick-leave, as well as to his full wages. The employer, moreover, had to pay the worker's medical bill. In the case of dismissal or death, all wages due to the worker had to be made over to him or his heirs (arts. 18–22).

These Regulations held for all workshops with more than three workers, and were to be effective six months after the date of publication. The municipality was charged with supervising their implementation. The punishment for each contravention would be one week's imprisonment or a fine from three to 50 *qrans* (arts. 23–28).

Unfortunately, information is lacking on the level of practicality which the Iranian government itself attached to these Regulations, which were quite revolutionary. For even in Europe, the battle for the eight-hour working day and the 48-hour working week had yet to be won. It is therefore not surprising that these Regulations remained a dead letter. Working conditions continued to be bad, child labor was still the rule, wages were pitiful, children and women suffered from their working conditions and nothing changed. The Government of Iran apparently had second thoughts about the whole scheme, for it did not even report the 'leap forward' to the ILO. In 1932 an Iranian economist noted that the wages of the workers, mostly children who looked emaciated and even sometimes crippled, were insufficient. The resulting indebtedness to the employer led to bonded labor, but no outcry was raised. Although an ILO mission visited Iran in 1934, no visits were paid to the traditional establishments, but only to the new, modern model factories.[266] In that same year the American Legation reported on the implementation of the 1923 decree and stated that "no such reforms have been made and probably were never a matter of serious consideration, except to the officials charged with the duty of drafting an appropriate memorandum on the subject."[267]

THE FIRST SOCIAL AND LABOR LAWS (1931–1941)

On March 21, 1931 the first social security fund started to function in Iran when the cabinet approved the regulations for this fund for the benefit of road workers.[268] Those entitled to insurance were navvies, masons, carpenters, smiths, miners and other workers. The fund had to be financed from the contributions paid by the insured workers. The navvies, for example paid one *shahi* per day. From those laborers who had a contract: a tariff of two per cent was deducted from their wages. In exchange the fund provided the following services:

---

266. Weaver 1933. 516–522
267. Ladjevardi 1981, quoting Raymond Hare, 15 October 1934 (891.655/30) US National Archives.
268. ILO, 1932 135; Majmu'eh-ye qavanin-e mowze'eh va mosubat-e dowreh-ye panjom-e taqniyeh, *Majles* Printing Office, n.d.

1. Medical help to those fallen ill or wounded on the job. This included medicine, food, and medical services in the larger centers;
2. In case of illness or accident as a result of employment the workers would be paid 50 per cent of their daily wage for a maximum of two years;
3. Those permanently disabled would get a lump sum. In case of total disability, the sum would be equal to the contributions paid during the last two years with a maximum of 2,000 *tumans*. In case of partial disability, the indemnification would vary between 50 per cent and two and a half per cent of the contributions paid during the last two years depending on the kind of invalidity;
4. Payment of a lump sum to the heirs, and to those for whom the deceased was responsible. The sum to be equal to the payments made during the last two years.

The management of the fund was in the hands of the Ministry of Communications in Tehran and its local branches. It is not known how effectively this Fund operated, but some activities in this field were undertaken. Dispensaries, hospitals, and large accommodation barracks were built for the railway workers. In the north, where malaria was endemic, the *Kamsax* (the company in charge of constructing the railway) doctors practically eradicated malaria among the workers on the northern section of the line.[269]

Following the establishment of this social security fund, there was no activity for some time on the social legislation front. However, in 1933, this period of inaction was followed by a burst of social legislation. It started with the Municipality of Tehran issuing a decree regulating labor conditions in the bakeries in Tehran.[270] The decree also stipulated some hygienic and other public health measures. The impact of this set of regulations remained restricted, however, to the newly established modern bakery in Tehran. The traditional, private bakeries, where labor and hygienic conditions could certainly do with some regulation, were not included in the decree's sphere of reference.

This municipal decree was followed by a number of labor regulations issued by the central government. On August 30, the cabinet approved the establishment of a social security fund for workers in state industries and mines. Its regulations were the same as those laid down for the fund for road workers.[271] The creation of this fund was followed on December 25, 1933 by a set of regulations defining the labor conditions of all personnel involved in primary education.[272] A law, passed on March 10, 1934, regulated the working conditions of teachers at teachers' colleges.[273] A further law, regulating the position of state

---

269. Conolly 1935. 45.
270. ILO 1933a, 335.
271. ILO 1933b, 11.
272. ILO 1934, 185–86.
273. ILO 1934, 185–86.

employees, was passed on May 2, 1936. Apart from giving them the right of a paid annual vacation, the law regulated the conditions of leave of absence in case of illness.[274]

THE FACTORY ACT

The bulk of social legislation during the 1930s had been almost exclusively concerned with state employees. Moreover, the regulations all had a sectoral objective, i.e., they were only applicable to certain groups of state employees or (sub) branches of industry. However, on August 10, 1936 the *Majles* adopted the Factory Act, which was general in nature and required factories with ten or more workers to install a wide range of health services, including washing facilities, lavatories, working clothes, crèches and the like, as well as a comprehensive scheme of accident insurance. On paper the Act looked quite revolutionary, but in practice workers did not benefit from its results, since there were hardly any.[275]

This was due to the fact that the Government did not create an inspection agency, while the penalties for employers were very light (fines ranging from 20 to 70 riyals; imprisonment of three to seven days). In fact it could be argued that the Factory Act actually made the position of workers worse, for their obligations were enforceable and, ironically, the employers themselves were charged with part of the implementation of the Act. The salaries of the workers could be diminished, they could be fined and imprisoned, and all this at the whim of the employer. These sanctions were considerable ones, for the fines for example (five to 50 riyals) constituted a one-day to two-weeks' salary for a worker! Workers, moreover, could also be forced to compensate the employer for any loss due to their negligence. It is, however, difficult to assess the effect of this Act since data are lacking. From data from a later period can be inferred that, as a result of this Act, some improvements were made in working conditions as far as hygiene was concerned. In general, however, it made the workers even more dependent and subservient to the employers than they were before.

The biggest employer in the country, the APOC, did not implement the Act either. According to Elwell-Sutton, "an APOC circular criticized as impractical many of the provisions of this act, it indicated that the company would find it impossible to modify its practices in order to bring them into line with the new law. The Act no doubt became a dead letter in many parts of the country - but nowhere more than in the oil districts of Khuzistan."[276]

After passing the Factory Act, the government appeared to have spent most of its energy. After that date only a few social laws were passed dealing with marginal groups. In 1937, a law was passed regulating the employment of prisoners in industrial and agricultural establishments. They were to receive the same salary as non-prison inmates. However, political prisoners and those sentenced to hard labor were excluded from this law.[277]

---

274. ILO, 1936b, 222.
275. An English translation has been published by Elwell-Sutton 1941, 213–24.
276. Elwell-Sutton, 1955, 97.
277. ILO 1936a, 32 and ILO, 1937a, 342.

On September 1, 1937 a law was passed regulating labor conditions of pearl-divers.[278] This was followed by a decree (dated January 14, 1939) regulating some aspects of employment of pilots in Iranian ports.[279] In that same year the working conditions of medical personnel in government services were regulated,[280] while the last act in the field of social legislation during the period under study was undertaken by the Municipality of Tehran. In February 1941, this body issued a decree fixing wages in the building industry.[281]

Although it is difficult to evaluate the effect of these laws, it is reasonably certain that the state employees covered by the various laws benefited from them. As pointed out already above, this did not hold for the Factory Act, although here also some effect cannot be denied. However, in general working conditions continued to be as they were, bad. This was not only due to the fact that the few social laws that existed were not at all or only partially implemented, but also and more importantly, that a large part of the labor force was not covered by any social legislation at all. This held especially for the small-scale industry sector, the largest employer.

PART III. LABOR CONDITIONS

INTRODUCTION

In the last section of this chapter, some information is offered on actual working conditions in Iran. The material presented is uneven in quality, both in time and location. Therefore, the picture of labor conditions is descriptive and impressionistic rather than analytical. Nevertheless, it is a bleak picture of the lot of the worker with regard to hours, health conditions, wages, and social conditions. It also shows how ineffective labor unions had been in bringing about any change in these dismal working conditions. In fact, labor unions had hardly any, if at all, influence on changes in these conditions. This holds especially for the legislation that was passed, which was neither the result of, nor in reaction to, demands from labor unions, nor did it address the labor force's problems in practice. Where a beneficial development took place it was rather a by-product of other developments, such as the construction of modern factories. Labor had no say in or control over its own destiny, neither about the direction of the course it was on, nor about the pace at which it was to proceed.

---

278. ILO 1937b, 204.
279. ILO 1939a, 441.
280. ILO l939c. 719.
281. Monthly Labor Review 1946, 56.

WORKING HOURS

Though there is much variety in the information on the working hours of the industrial labor force in Iran in general, it can be said that ten to twelve hours per day was normal. Longer working days, of up to sixteen hours, also appear to have existed.[282] There are several difficulties with these estimates. First, there were no fixed rules where working hours were concerned, for there was no labor law fixing them. An exception to this rule was the situation of the printers who had obtained an eight-hour working day in 1918,[283] while the workers of the APOC also worked only eight hours.[284]

Second, in case of payment per unit of production, an able worker could work more than a less fortunate colleague. Or a better fed and healthy worker was able to produce more in the same time than a hungry and sick worker. These therefore could afford to work less time, it they wanted, which more often than not did not happen.[285]

Third, the length of the working day fluctuated with the seasons. In winter time the working day (from sunrise to sunset) would be shorter than in summer time.[286] Or, in case of agro-industries, when it was harvest time, the working day was longer than usual. In those cases extra time was worked, of course which brings us to the last variable: overtime. Many of the modern factories, for example, had an official working day of eight hours only. But the workers often preferred to do two hours overtime in view of their low salaries. So it would seem that their working day was ten hours, while in reality they only were obliged to work for eight hours.[287]

The average annual working week could in many cases be as short as 40 hours due to the official religious festivals. In the modern factories, however, many of these festivals were not recognized as holidays. This also held for the month of fasting, Ramadan, when fewer hours per day were worked, but people continued to work nevertheless.[288] Since workers received no wages for such holidays they did not mind to continue working on those days. It workers wanted to celebrate a festival like `eyd-e ghadir they had to compensate the employer for their absence by working on other free days. In all branches of industry Friday was not a working day.[289]

---

282. Chaqueri 1978, 29, 36, 44, 66, 71, 82, 88, Olmer 1908, 11; FO 371/9030, f.215, 218, 220.
283. see part II.
284. FO 416/112, f.114 "eight hour working day, six days per week was the rule."
285. In some professions, skilled workers had shorter working days. For example, Olmer 1908, 11, mentions that workers in the faience industry tending the oven could only work two hours per day, while in the potteries the workers only worked four to five hours per day. Ibid., 59.
286. Hours of work in the Hamadan carpet factories in 1923, for example, were "in Summer 5 a.m. to 6 p.m. with two hours off in the middle of the day i.e., eleven hours. Winter 7 am. to 5 pm. with one hour off at midday, i.e., nine hours. FO 371/9030, f.218.
287. FO 371/40222 f. 70–81; the same attitude prevailed among traditional crafts such as carpet weaving "as the head weavers are paid by piece work some of the looms may be working during part of the off hours, as the weavers do not go home at midday." FO 371/9030, f.218.
288. Chaqueri 1978, 88; FO 416/112 f.104.
289. ILO 1939, 491.

OCCUPATIONAL SAFETY AND HEALTH

Normal working conditions in Iranian industry were very bad. This was true for children as well as adults. The workers were often already in poor health before they were engaged for employment, for, even it they had not contracted one of the many endemic or contagious diseases; they were more often than not undernourished. Their working conditions contributed much to sustain this condition if to not worsen it.[290]

The buildings in which many of the industrial labor workers spent the largest part of the day had not been built with a view to providing optimal working conditions. Maintenance was badly lacking, as were the necessary repairs to walls, leaking roofs, and floors. Workers moreover were exposed to dust, steam, down and dirt, which led to all kinds of respiratory troubles. The working areas often were badly heated and very humid and it was not exceptional to see little children at work in dark humid holes, half-naked, with their feet in water under the constant supervision of the foreman or employer.[291]

Lunch, half an hour to an hour, was taken on the premises, often in the very room or hall where the workers did their normal job. There was no washing room where workers could clean themselves, except in very few establishments. Toilets were not normally provided either, and those facilities which were used for that purpose did not deserve the name of toilets. These places were not regularly cleaned, let alone disinfected. Since, more often than not, no proper ventilation existed; the air in the workshops was very insalubrious and unhealthy.[292]

Apart from washing and eating facilities, often even the provision of drinking water was lacking. If it existed, the water was often stinking and stagnant.[293] The *Vatan* textile mill (built in 1925) was reported to have only one drinking vessel for 400 persons, which was not provided by the employer, but was the private possession of the smith. Each of the 400 workers drank out of this cup - hardly a situation furthering hygienic conditions. During the summer the workers used a water melon as a drinking vessel.[294]

The working conditions in the carpet factories in Kerman have received special attention, from both native and foreign observers. This was caused by the fact that working conditions were abominable, for it was mainly child and female labor working in that branch of industry. Conditions were such that many children and women (girls rather) often became crippled for life. Apart from having to work in subterranean, often cave-like, badly-lit,

---

290. On health conditions in Iran see Neligan 1926, 635-39; see also Willem Floor, *Public Health in Qajar Iran* (Washington, DC: Mage 2006); Lingeman 1930, 37 "the endemicity of such diseases as typhoid and small-pox and the abnormally high death rate is not unnatural. Malaria, tuberculosis and affections of the eye are among the diseases commonly encountered." In 1935, Simmonds 1935, 37 stated "disease is naturally widespread and until better sanitary conditions are provided no real improvement can be expected"
291. Chaqueri 1978, 36; Olmer 1908, 11; Kechavarz 1534, 33. 53.
292. Kechavarz 1534, 33; FO 371/9030, f.215 (Tabriz 1923), "Sanitary arrangements" unknown. "Insanitary conditions abound as the work is often carried on in dark damp cellars"; Chaqueri 1978, 61.
293. Chaqueri 1978, 46; Kechavarz 1934, 53.
294. Chaqueri 1978, 46.

cold, humid, unventilated areas, the workers were seated in such a way that they always were sitting stooped. This position was often conducive to "permanent deformities of the arms and legs, and irreparable damage to general health."[295] In Kerman the girl workers were often afflicted by ankylosis of the lower abdomen. When these girls became pregnant they often died in childbirth. When a hospital was available, a craniotomy operation could be done, in up to 50 per cent of births. In the streets of Kerman the Reverend Boyland observed "one is constantly reminded of the iniquity of this child-labor by seeing deformed and stunted women, and occasionally men who are no longer able to work, as their hands are often deformed as well, and are reduced to beggary."[296]

With the establishment of the new factories, the working conditions improved. The factories were well-lit and ventilated and the buildings airy and well-constructed. Toilets and water were often available, while the surroundings of the factory were often attractive gardens.[297]

When working with machines or dangerous materials, no special protective measures were taken. This was also true of the new state and private factories established in the 1930s, which provided good working conditions in general, from the hygienic point of view. At the cement factory in Tehran, for example, the workers who filled the sacks did not have masks, so that they had nothing to keep the cement out of their lungs.[298] In private industries the situation, of course, was no different. In the fish-canning plant in Bandar 'Abbas there was no protection against the danger from the sharp spears. Since no accidents were reported the workers must have been very lucky.[299]

In case of an industrial accident, however, the employers did not bear the cost of the medical care. The same was true when a worker was ill; in that case he received no wages either. In case of death as a result of an industrial accident compensation was only rarely paid to the relatives of the deceased.[300] The adoption of the Factory Act in 1936 did not really change this situation.

---

295. Chaqueri 1978, 210–12 quoting British missionaries such as Reverend Boyland (FO 248/1343) Kirman 1921; Bishop Linton (1924). It is noteworthy that similar problems were not reported from other areas in Iran, see for example Chaqueri 1978, 205 reproducing a letter from the British consul at Soltanabad (FO 371/10131, f.140, f.14) and also the British consul at Tabriz, FO 371/9030, f.215 "At the commencement of the weaving of a carpet the operatives squat on the floor, as the work gradually rises from the ground they rise with it and sit crosslegged on planks. This is not considered a hardship for Persians as it is the posture they usually adopt when resting in their own homes. If they had chairs provided (or any other sort of comfortable seat) I doubt whether they would appreciate the innovation."
296. Chaqueri 1978, 210
297. Conolly 1935, 460; Weaver 1933, 520. However, not all observers had a favorable opinion of the new factories the American Legation reported that, "the silk factory at Chalus is doubtless a source of Imperial satisfaction, but the European foremen describe the conditions under which the women and children work as appalling, and the pay they receive as totally inadequate", Ladjevardi 1981,101 quoting James & Moose Jr. 20 July 1940 (891.00/1758) National Archives.
298. FO 371/40222, f.5.
299. FO 371/40222, f.5.
300. FO 371/40222, f.5.

WAGES AND PURCHASING POWER

Payment of wages was mostly by the day. The level of wages varied according to location, season, factory, sex, age, and skill, of course. Payment, moreover, was not so much a right as an entitlement which had to be continually enforced. When economic conditions were bad, the employer could, and in fact did, lower the wages unilaterally. It would appear that this situation improved for factory workers during the 1930's.

Most of our data on wages refer to the 1930's and more often then not are of an impressionistic nature, or are spot wages. Only in a few cases do we have disaggregated data. Because the rate of wages was also dependent on all sorts of variable conditions it is impossible, as yet, to make definitive statements on this subject, which could go beyond the level of a general observation.

In 1925 the British commercial attaché reported that minor government officials, representing 70 per cent of all those employed as clerical labor in Tehran, received a minimum wage of 32 *tumans* per month. Those doing menial work received as little as five *tumans* in the provinces. The payment of wages usually in arrears and the commercial attaché considered these wages "at all times inadequate."[301] In 1928 another British commercial attaché remarked that a laborer's wage amounted to three to four *qrans* per day. For these wages he could only buy "bread and cheese and an occasional piece of cotton cloth for his womenfolk." Artisans received more, viz. five to ten *qrans* per day.[302]

Printers were better paid than most other workers. An adult printer, around 1930, received between twelve and twenty *tumans* per month. An apprentice was paid three to six *tumans*, whilst a type-setter even received as much as 35 to 40 *tumans* per month. Printers, apart from government officials, were clearly among the best paid category of the labor force. Workers in the fisheries industry, for example, received fifteen to 20 *tumans* per month. The fact that many Russians also worked in this industry no doubt had an upward effect on the level of wages.[303]

In other industrial sectors wages were much lower. Unskilled casual labor rarely received more than two *qrans* per day. Construction workers (housing) would get two to three *qrans* per day for twelve hours of work. The railway workers received three *qrans* per day or nine *tumans* per month for a 10 to 12 hour working day.[304] In the carpet industry wages were likewise very low. For very long working days - up to sixteen hours it is reported - under very bad working conditions wages of one to three *qrans* were usual. Even in the case of an able worker not more than 3.5 *qrans* per day could be earned.[305] In 1932, an ILO mission observed that in a 'modern' factory wages for men were five riyals, for women two

---

301. Hadow 1925, 41.
302. Lingeman 1928, 30.
303. Chaqueri 1978, 75, 88.
304. Chaqueri 1978, 89.
305. Chaqueri 1978, 89. In Tabriz in 1923, wages in the carpet factoreis averaged one kran 35 cents per day, but piece workers make up to 3 krans" FO 371/9030, f.216; In Hamadan in 1923 "a ten year old learner receives a minimum of ten shahis per diem. A number of head weavers receive a daily average of six krans", Ibid., f.218

riyals, and for children 0.25 to two riyals. In another factory where wages were paid on the basis of piece-work the women and girls rarely received more than two riyals per day.[306]

In Tabriz the lowest rate was paid in the leather factories; in 1929 it amounted to two riyals per day, while in 1937 the rate was four riyals.[307]

In the *Vatan* factory the workers went on strike in 1931 because of their low wages, largely. Two different rates were in use; one for the weaving and one for the spinning section. In the weaving section wages were calculated by output, and a worker received five to seven *shahi*s per meter. Even a very able weaver could not produce more than fifteen to seventeen meters so the maximum wages to be made amounted to four to 4.5 *qran*s per day. The average workers, however, was only able to earn ten to fifteen *qran*s per week. In the spinning section wages were by the day. The minimum rate was 25 to 45 *shahi*s for unskilled labor, and semi-skilled workers received 55 *shahi*s. Women and children were paid less by fifteen *shahi*s to one *qran*.[308]

In the APOC, unskilled laborers earned between ten to fifteen *tuman*s per month in 1929, although a great many did not get more than nine *tuman*s. This wage rate was much lower than that paid in 1924, viz. fifteen to 20 *tuman*s per month. Skilled Iranian labor received between fourteen to 20 *tuman*s in 1929, but 25 to 50 *tuman*s in 1925. Wages for non-Iranian (mainly Indian) labor were much higher. English management and skilled staff received between 500 and 1500 *tuman*s per month in 1929. According to another source, the wages for unskilled labor were only two to three *qran*s per day or six to nine *tuman*s per month. The same wage also obtained in 1931 according to a letter published *Peykar* in 1931. According to a laborer from the south, the wages in 1929 amounted to a monthly average of eight to fourteen *tuman*s, whereas in 1924 they earned fifteen to 20 *tuman*s.[309]

In 1937 an enquiry was organized in 12 cotton spinning mills which yielded the following results: that the average wages per ten hour day rose from 1.53 riyals in 1934-35 to 2.07 riyals in 1936-37.[310] It is moreover striking to observe that in one year (1936-37) there could be a difference in wages between the highest and lowest paid day-laborer in different factories of nearly 300 per cent. This probably is the result of the level of productivity; unfortunately, the data did not allow the researchers to draw conclusions on that issue. Skilled wool carders and spinners, however, received higher wages, respectively 4, 5, 6 riyals and 5 to 8 riyals per day.[311]

---

306. Weaver 1933, 520.
307. FO 371/20830 f.185 (Memorandum on Economic Affairs in Azarbaijan 1936)
308. Chaqueri 1978, 43–45.
309. Chaqueri 1978, 14, 29, 74, 82 (reproducing *Peykar*, *Setareh-ye Sorkh* and *Profintern* material).
310. ILO 1938, 88.
311. ILO 1938, 88.

A ROYAL MISSTEP

On April 18, 1938 Foruhar, the Minister of Mines and Industries, addressed a circular to all spinning and weaving mills instructing their owners that the daily wages to be paid to ordinary workers and weavers should not exceed four riyals per day for a working day which should not be less than ten hours.

TABLE 2.6: Wages for Day-laborers for 10 hour Working-day (1935-1937)

Factory	1934-35	1935-36	1935-37
1	-	-	0.83
2	-	-	-
3	3.08	1.23	1.57
4	1.79	1.70	2.61
5	-	-	3.52
6	1.99	2.27	1.76
7	-	-	2.33
8	-	-	1.23
9	-	2.03	1.88
10	-	3.13	2.68
11	1.25	1.26	1.20
12	1.44	1.88	2.17
Averages	1.53	1.63	2.07

The employers were taken completely unawares by this sudden decision, for which no explanation was given, nor had any previous discussion taken place between the Government and the employers. The British Ambassador reported that "it was generally believed that the circular was drafted at the request of His Imperial Majesty, when the latter discovered that a large number of spinners and weavers from his own factory, who were receiving only four rials per diem, were deserting and leaving for Isfahan and Shiraz where more lucrative wages could be obtained."

Since the circular stated that the decision was final, the employers and workers were dismayed. The mill owners of Isfahan, in spite of the finality of the circular, lodged protests with the Governor of Isfahan and the Minister of Industry. These expressed their regrets and told the factory owners that nothing could be done in this matter. It was, however, intimated that the Ministry would not carry out the announced regular inspections on the implementation of the decree.

The situation was finally solved to the satisfaction of all parties concerned. The factory owners introduced, by common consent, various means to circumvent the circular, and avoided discussion or even reference to the document. The means employed were the promotion of a large number of workers "to be 'ostads' headmen or foremen in charge of one or two machines, laborers have been appointed to hold two jobs and get paid for each.

It is reported that most of the spinners and weavers in the various mills are now 'ostads' and that approximately 25 per cent of the unskilled labor receives 4 rials per diem." The Ministry considered the matter had settled itself in accordance with the circular and made no further investigations.[312]

Wages had increased greatly in 1941 as compared with 1937 if we take the Isfahan textile mills as an example (Table 2.7). It is difficult to compare the 1941 average in Isfahan with the 1937 data, since it is not clear whether the latter were based on the minimum or maximum wage rates. Assuming that a total average was calculated, we observe an increase of 200 per cent in average wages.

TABLE 2.7: Average Wages in Riyals in the Isfahan Textile Mills.[313]

September 1941				
Factories				
	Boys		Girls	
	min.	max.	min.	max.
Nakhtab	2.00	4.00	2.00	3.70
Pashmbaf	1.50	5.00	1.50	3.00
Risbaf	2.00	4.50	1.50	2.50
Sena'eh-ye pashm	3.50	4.50	2.00	3.0
Zayandehrud	3.20	4.70	2.00	3.20
Vatan	4.50	7.00	3.50	4.50
Shahreza	2.50	5.00	2.50	3.00
Rahimzadeh	3.00	4.50	3.00	4.50
Risandegi-e barq	2.20	4.00	2.50	5.00

Factories				
	Women		Men	
	min.	max.	min.	max.
Nakhtab	2.50	4.00	3.00	9.50
Pashmbaf	2.50	4.00	3.00	10.00
Risbaf	2.50	4.50	4.50	10.00
Sena'eh-ye pashm	2.50	4.00	6.00	10.00
Zayandehrud	2.80	4.30	3.90	8.90
Vatan	2.80	3.50	5.00	10.00
Shahreza	3.20	6.50	4.20	9.20
Rahimzadeh	3.00	4.50	5.00	8.00
Risandegi barq	2.50	4.00	3.25	7.50

---

312. FO 371/18231.
313. FO 371/40222, f.33.

TABLE 2.8: Daily Expenditure of a Family of Four in Khuzestan 1931 [314]

Sugar	5 *shahis*
Bread	12
Meat	10
Tobacco	4
Kerosene	3
Rent	3
Washing, soap, clothes, etc.	14
Total	51 *shahis*

What did these wages mean in terms of the cost of living? Unfortunately data are lacking. Household Food Consumption surveys were made in 1937, but these were restricted to middle-income families.[315] The majority of the labor force did not fall within this range, so the results of that survey cannot help. A contemporary impressionistic report reveals the data in Table 2.8. According to the same source these were the minimum requirements of a family of four, viz. two *qrans* and eleven *shahis* (51 *shahis*). A normal wage rate for an unskilled laborer would be three *qrans* per day, so that the family could save nine *shahis*. However, most workers could not even afford these expenditures. They hardly ever had meat, their daily diet consisted mainly of bread and dates. Cheese was a luxury. So it would look as it the minimum requirements were a wish rather than a reality.

TABLE 2.9: Prices of Necessities of Life Consumed by the Lower Classes in Isfahan [316]

Wheat	2 riyals per kg. Tea per packet	45.00 per kg	
Bread	2	Barley	1.15
Rice	4.15	Straw	0.35
Sugar, moist	26,70	Kerosene	1.50
Sugar, loaf	26.70	Firewood	0.35
Mutton	4.30	Charcoal	1.00
Ghee	21.65	Milk	1.70
Fowls each	10.00	Eggs each	0.25

Using the Isfahan data for 1941 (Table 2.9) as a yard-stick, together with a list of prices referring to the situation in October 1941 we may calculate the level of purchasing power. Since we have no idea what the dietary pattern was in Isfahan at that time, I have used the data of a typically dietary pattern in urban south Iran (Fars province) for the

---

314. Chaqueri 1978, 71–72
315. ILO 1937, 881–84.
316. FO 371/40222, f. 37

years 1962-68 which was the closest reliable data available on this subject.[317] From Table 2.10 we see that a few necessities such as fuel and tea are not included. We furthermore notice that, among the list of goods of 1941, pulses, fruits, and vegetables are missing. We may safely assume that all these omitted goods, from one or another Table, were used by the working class in Isfahan at that time. The five goods items for which we have been able to calculate the expenditure per person per day result in a minimum requirement per family of four persons of 5.68 riyals per day excluding fuel, tea, fruit, vegetables and pulses, goods which it is impossible they could have done without. In only three out of nine textile mills did the men earn a minimum wage sufficient to afford this expenditure. Unless they earned more, they had to starve. A similar situation existed in Azerbaijan in 1936 using the relevant data for Azerbaijan for 1962–68.

TABLE 2.10: Typical Dietary Pattern in Urban Iran/Fars Province 1962-68.

Food group	Price 1941 per kg	*Possible diets in grams per caput per diem			Expenditure
		I	II	III	
Bread	2.00 *riyals*	400	462	391	0.782 riyals
Sugar	26.70	57	84	37	0.320
Mutton	4.30	40	48	32	0.137
Ghee	21.65	11	17	4	0.086
Milk	1.70	34	154	55	0.093
Potatoes	-	46	34	12	
Pulses	-	27	25	6	
Vegetables	-	66	103	39	
Fruits	-	115	17	90	
Total calories		2210	2200	1796	1.4201 riyals
% of requirement		96	96	78	

*Possible diets made up of different amounts (grams, per caput, per diem) of comestibles listed in the Table are represented by columns I, II & III.

---

317. Based on Sen Gupta 1968. Column I refers to the data of Azarbaijan, II to that of Isfahan, and III of Fars.

TABLE 2.11: Prices of Articles Of Prime Necessity in Tabriz[318]

Group	Unit	Prices in riyals	
		Dec. 1935	Dec. 1936
Charcoal	Batman	2.40	2.40
Wood	Kharvar	70.00	95.00
Rice(Rasht)	Batman	9.00	1200
Rice(local)	do.	4.00	5.60
Bread	do.	2.00	240
Ghee	do.	32.00	44.00
Split peas	do.	7.00	4.60
Cheese (local)	do.	11.00	14.00
Beans	do.	3.40	4.00
Yarma (millet)	do.	3.00	3.00
Cotton cloth	meter	2.40	4.00
Woolen cloth	do.	30.00	42.00
Shoes	pair	40.00	50.00
Soap	batman	16.00	22.00
Sugar	do.	15.00	12.20
Tea	girvanka	10.00	22.00
Eggs	each	0.15	00.125
Chickens	do.	3.00	4.00
Meat	batman	10.40	13.00

Another alternative was not to marry, or if married, to leave one's family in the village, or if in town, to have wife and children work as well.[319]

The bleak picture offered by these data tallies with a report by the American legation on living conditions of workers in August 1941.

> Wages are certainly for more than bare existence, amounting for the common laborer to four to ten rials a day. It may be said that it will purchase a loaf of white bread or that a worker must pay from three to seven rials a day for his food. Thus it will be seen that the wage is insufficient even for food for a family and most workers have a starvation diet consisting of tea, (not white) bread, cheese and onions, with occasional greens and grapes and infrequent rice and cheap meat. It is not possible to buy as adequate clothing or even to dream of luxuries such as education of the children. Sometimes the workers' one or more wives and the children work to bring in additional skilled income to make possible a slightly higher standard of workers living.[320]

---

318. FO 371/20830, f.206.
319. Chaqueri 1978, 36.
320. Ladjevardi 1981, 103 quoting Harold B. Minor, 12 August 1941 (891.00/1816) US National Archives.

This low level of wages also explains why workers were so eager to do overtime. All British observers note that "for the great bulk of the population the standard of living remains very low,"[321] and that, as in the case of Isfahan, the workers were exploited. In Azerbaijan the British Consul in 1936 was more optimistic, for "the new industries paid better wages than are paid at present … and shortage rather than excess, of labor is likely to be the embarrassment of the future."[322] However, it is quite unlikely that he would have made the same remark by 1941 when the rise in industrialization was a thing of the past, and taxes, inflation, and unemployment were the bane of the working class.

Although data are lacking, it is unlikely that the standard of living of the working class improved much, for Iran had a serious bout of inflation over the period of 1933-1943. Nominal wages increased, as we have seen in the case of Isfahan, but the cost of living index rose as well. For example, from 1937, when the index was 8.0, it rose to 16.0 in 1941. In this way the 200 per cent rise in wages in Isfahan in that same period was completely annulled by inflation.[323] According to the American legation:

> The cost of living in Iran had increased to the point where the *tuman* (10 rials) has about the same purchasing power as the rial had twenty years ago. Wages have increased during the last twenty years about five to seven fold, so that there has been indeed a severe decline in real income.[324]

SOCIAL CONDITIONS

Working conditions resembled slavery according to a British observer,[325] while an American report states that "forced labor amounting to almost slavery, exists on some properties."[326] That this was not exaggerated is borne out by actual practice. The recruitment of labor for the state silk factory in Chalus in 1933 shows this clearly. Since in Mazandaran itself insufficient skilled labor was available locally, the government wanted Yazdi workers, who

---

321. Simmonds 1935, 36.
322. FO 371/20830, f. 179; his colleague In Kermanshah stated for example that "the same poverty and misery is to be found both in the country and in the town now, just as it existed fifteen years ago" and he only noted a slight improvement for government officials. FO 371/21900, f. 112.
323. Bharier 1971, 49.
324. Ladjevardi 1981, 103 quoting Harold B. Minor, 12 August 1941 (891.00/1816) US National Archives.
325. Simmonds 1935, 36.
326. Ladjevardi 1981, 103 quoting Harold B. Minor 12 August 1941 (891.00/1816) US National Archives. In the carpet industry for example, "where the boys have neither parents nor guardians they are frequently given advances until, like the pearl divers in the Persian Gulf, they find themselves hopelessly in debt, completely in the hands of their employers and are practically 'slaves'," FO 371/9030, f.216 (Tabriz, 1923) see also Kechavarz 1934, 30, 49–52.

were very skilled in silk weaving, to migrate to Chalus. When these proved to be unwilling to do so, the police were ordered to take care of the recruitment.

> All persons known to be silk workers have been arrested; and as soon as a truck load had been assembled in the police station they were shipped off to Mazandaran to tend the Shah's looms. ... Much of the silk weaving in Yazd is home industry, and the police have made house to house searches to locate looms and ferret out the weavers. Persons who were taken into police custody and who denied that they could operate a loom were beaten unmercifully by the police until either they confessed or the police were convinced that they were not weavers. No less than 350 men have been deported, and the search merrily continues.[327]

Although normal recruitment did not take place in this manner, it nevertheless is an indication of the Government's attitude towards workers, an attitude which of course was reflected by that of the other employers as shown by their treatment of their own labor force.

The laborers were under constant supervision by their foremen, who swore at them and even went so far as to beat them, the bastinado not excluded. In one case a young worker was even killed by his employers, who only had to pay blood money in accordance with the precepts of Islam.[328]

If late on the job, workers were fined. The fact in itself is acceptable, but if we may believe the available data, the fines were anything but just. A worker five to fifteen minutes late had to pay a fine which was twice his daily wage.[329] Workers of the APOC could be suspended, i.e., kept officially on the workforce, but without pay until work was found within the Company. "This method was also used for purposes of discipline, a common penalty for misconduct being a few days' suspension."[330]

Another abuse which appears to have existed during the pre-1925 years in the APOC area was the fact that Iranian workers were forced to buy their necessities of life in shops owned by Sheikh Khaz'al. Farmers bringing foodstuffs into Abadan either had to sell these to his shops or pay extra taxes on them.[331]

Payment of wages was not regular. The workers had to ask for their money and were often paid a few days or a week later. Workers could not protest for there was no one to turn to. They could, when in need of money, borrow from their employer and thus never get their total wages and become indebted to their employer. In the *Vatan* factory in

---

327. Bharier 1971, 49.
328. Chaqueri 1978, 15.
329. Lahuti n.d., 44.
330. Ellwell-Sutton 1955, 90.
331. Chaqueri 1978, 41.

Isfahan every Thursday night workers had to beg the pay-master ro give them their wages. Even then he did not pay them immediately, but made them wait hours for it while he showered them with a hail of vilifications. His fund of bad language was proverbial and only after the proper submissive attitude had been shown would the workers finally get their due. In practice, wages seemed not to be the workers' right but rather the employer's liberal gesture after he deigned to notice the workers.[332]

Although in this respect the situation in the APOC was much better, here (Iranian) workers were exposed to another abuse. The discrimination between APOC workers was considerable, for there was a difference between European, Indian and Iranian employees. Further cutting across this horizontal layer was the fact that there was a further division among the Iranians between those who were salaried staff, wage earners, and contract labor.[333]

The social amenities provided by the APOC were not available to all these groups, however, or to the same extent. Housing, for example, was granted on the basis of the length of service and the rate of pay. This meant that contract labor did not even qualify for housing. In Abadan the percentage of contract labor was between fifteen and 20 per cent, whilst, in the fields it was over 50 per cent.[334] In the latter case, a considerable proportion of the contracted laborers were local villagers, for whom the problem of housing did not arise. In Abadan, however, it was a serious problem.

TABLE 2.12: Houses Built by the APOC at Abadan[335]

	Houses for married salaried staff	Rooms for bachelor salaried staff	Houses for married wage earners	Rooms for bachelor wage earners
before 1934	476	774	28	33
1936–40	875	54	1995	709
Total	1351	828	2023	742

From the data available on the APOC labor force it is clear that the supply of housing just did not suffice for effective demand. It would appear that housing for salaried employees was more or less taken care of by 1941, at least the number of employees and the number of houses roughly tally. From the available data, it is impossible to see whether married and bachelor workers were employed in the same composition as their corresponding houses, but it seems unlikely. Nevertheless, their situation looks much better than that of

---

332. Chaqueri 1978, 45; Kechavarz 1934, 32–33.
333. Chaqueri, 1978, 14
334. ILO 1950, 29.
335. ILO 1950, 33, Table IX.

the wage earners who numbered 7,641 with only 2,023 houses available for married workers and 742 spaces for bachelors. Since the level of wages was more important than length of service this situation was especially resented by badly paid wage earners.[336] The privileges of housing were lost on termination of employment. The housing situation was worse in the Fields, which was partly caused by the uncertainty as to whether a certain area would be taken into production and for how long. Although construction materials were very difficult to obtain locally - a special cement factory had to be built - the APOC clearly intended to spend as little money as possible.[337] For, even in 1935, the available housing was quite inadequate compared with the number of people employed. In view of the complaints voiced by Indian workers in 1920, 1924, 1926 and the 1929 scuffle, one would have expected the APOC to deal with these problems properly. The more so, since according to Iranian data the APOC "did not build a single house, shack or shelter for the Iranian worker from 1920 to 1933."[338] By 1941 the Company had improved its performance by having built 1,552 houses for a labor force of more than 15,000.

TABLE 2.13 Iranian and Foreign Workers Employed by the APOC at Abadan[339]

	salaried		artisans		skilled	
	Iranian	Foreign	Iranian	Foreign	Iranian	Foreign
1935	495	919	2175	405	2838	42
1936	505	948	2435	510	3017	19
1937	632	869	2386	460	3034	2
1938	791	928	3055	442	3380	-
1939	1007	1260	4924	839	4452	-
1940	1008	1103	3356	701	4318	-
1941	908	1010	2757	804	4189	-

Similar remarks can be made about the difference in treatment of Iranian and foreign labor in the field of such amenities as water, electricity, food supply, recreation and medical services.[340] One can of course maintain that one cannot blame the APOC for not doing what the Iranian Government should have done. The only hospital in Abadan was that of the APOC; the Company in 1936 also undertook to supply Abadan with adequate amounts of water and electricity; all these activities should have been the Government of Iran's business. However, the Company had taken a few of these tasks upon itself and it should have executed them properly, but did not. One can also make the excuse that the APOC's record compared favorably with the record of the Iranian government, and that

---

336. ILO 1950, 33–34; what made it worse was the fact that "a wife cannot join her husband in a permanent home until he has served seven years which had bad results" PRO, LAB 13/39.
337. On housing problems and the attitude of the APOC see also Ellwell-Sutton 1955, 94–5.
338. Government of Iran 1952, 14.
339. ILO 1950, 155, Table IX.
340. Government of Iran 1952, 15 ff; ILO, 1950, 32 ff; Ellwell-Sutton 1955, 88 ff.

compared with Iranian employers, the APOC was a much better employer, but at best, the APOC was the best of a bad lot. What was worse, however, was its policy of discrimination on racial grounds and the tendency prevalent among the British staff to treat the Iranians as an inferior race.[341]

---

341. Ellwell-Sutton, 1958

FIGURE 1.3: One of the new factories built in 1935, in this case the exterior of a cotton mill in Isfahan.

FIGURE 1.4: The cotton spinning machinery inside the Isfahan mill.

CHAPTER THREE

INDUSTRIALIZATION IN IRAN 1900-1941

INTRODUCTION

Iran in 1900 was a non-industrial country, i.e., less than ten per cent of its Gross Domestic Product (GDP) was formed by industry. In 1925, when Reza Shah set Iran on a new course, this situation had not changed. In 1941 an industrial base had come into being, granted at high cost, but Iran was on the way to becoming an industrializing country, i.e., ten to 20 per cent of its GDP was formed by industry. Between 1925 and 1941 an economic policy had been developed and implemented which had made this possible. This policy was based "on four points: government assumption of the country's economic direction; reorganization of the factors of production; a balance between consumption of imported goods and national purchasing power; and expansion of the purchasing power. The industrial policy was envisaged as a system in which the government was a prime mover rather than deliberate etatism. Private enterprise was to be encouraged by import duty protection, industrial credits, and facilities for the importation of productive equipment."[1] The credit for this policy, which is given to either Reza Shah or Teymurtash his Minister of Court, must be laid at the door of a group of reform-minded people, who were in favor of a strong centralizing government to bring security and self-reliance to Iran, and for which the group provided both the ideology and political backing as well as the personnel to execute and realize these ideas. The activities of these reformers had been a recurrent pattern in Iranian politics since the mid-nineteenth century. In the field of industrialization their purpose was to achieve national self-reliance and diversification; the means chosen to promote that objective was import-substitution. To meet the needs of the industrialization program, the government of Iran had to create a social and technological infrastructure from scratch. Iran lacked an adequate transport system, while new financial institutions were needed to encourage entrepreneurial initiative. Roads were built, the trans-Iranian railway was constructed, a national bank was founded, soon followed by others, and

---

1. Grunwald and Ronall 1960, 21.

schools at all levels were started, while technical and managerial needs were satisfied by sending students abroad to receive advanced training and experience.

High tariffs were introduced to protect the infant industries, which distorted the price-mechanism and the effectiveness of resource allocation. Consequently, the unit costs of the production were very high, but this was inevitable to create and sustain these industries. Although profitability and employment generation did not receive much attention, the notions were not absent from the objectives of the new economic policy, and in fact a great many jobs were created. However, many of the industries could only survive because they were protected and enjoyed a quasi-monopolistic position. As a result of this, only specific groups within the country benefitted from the economic policy, which moreover inhibited the motivation of industrialists to export. Small private traders, artisans, industrial labor and peasants had to foot the bill for the high price which Iran had to pay for its industrialization program. Although there was considerable waste, it is difficult to say whether the industrialization program really could have been executed at lower cost. There was also considerable pride within Iran that the country had made a leap forward under its own steam, without foreign capital. Reza Shah and his supporters had in fact been able to realize almost all objectives formulated by Iran's nineteenth century reformers, and thus had fulfilled an age-old dream. The opponents and critics of Reza Shah did not disagree with the objectives of his economic policy, but about the distribution of its effects. Although a failure from the point of view of the distribution of development benefits, the industrialization policy was successful in transforming Iranian society and its economy, and formed "the most interesting example in the Middle East of a state-directed effort at economic organization."[2]

THE LABOR FORCE PRIOR TO 1914

INTRODUCTION

During the period under study the population of Iran increased from 9.29 million in 1901 to 14.55 million in 1940. The urban share of the population hardly changed during this period, although urbanization slightly increased as is shown in Table 3. 1.[3] This is also borne out by the estimated growth rates for this period which indicate that prior to 1934 there was no significant net rural/urban migration. After 1934, there is a change to be noted between urban and total growth rates, signifying a net rural-urban migration. An important factor for this development was probably Reza Shah's new economic policy, which resulted in an increase in manufacturing capacity and drew peasants to the urban areas.[4]

---

2. Grunwald and Ronall 1960, 21.
3. Bharier 1971 27, Table 2.
4. Millspaugh 1946, 31.

TABLE 3.1: The population of Iran and its urban-rural distribution (millions)

Year	Total	Urban	%	Rural	%
1901	9.92	2.08	21	7.84	79
1911	10.66	2.24	21	8.24	79
1921	11.47	2.41	21	9.06	79
1934	13.32	2.80	21	10.52	79
1940	14.55	3.20	22	11.35	78

According to Bairoch,[5] reasonably reliable data for the developing countries in general for the period from 1920 to 1950 indicate that the active population in the manufacturing sector dropped from 8.5 to 7.6 per cent, while the figure for the mid-nineteenth century was probably roughly about 10 per cent. These rough indications also hold for Iran. The rate of urbanization and population growth overall was slower than in Asian countries in general. However, although precise data are lacking there is the undeniable fact that the tertiary sector in Iran increased considerably after 1900 concomitant with a drop in the level of employment in the secondary sector.[6]

TABLE 3.2: Changes, by branch of activity, in the structure of the active population in developing countries with market economies, 1900–1950

Branch of activity	1900	1920	1930	1940
Agriculture	77.9	77.6	76.6	73.3
Mining	-	0.4	0.4	0.6
Manufacturing	9.8	8.5	8.5	7.6
Construction	-	1.0	1.1	1.8
Commerce, banks	-	5.4	5.4	5.8
Transport, communications	12.3	1.6	1.8	2.0
Services	-	5.5	6.1	8.9
Total	100.0	100.0	100.0	100.0

The data which are available for Iran are guestimates for the country as a whole and do not provide a sectoral and/or geographical breakdown. The most detailed guestimate for 1910 is that by Abdullaev, who, using mainly Russian archival material, gives a sectoral breakdown of selected urban economic activities (see Table 3.3). The economically active male population over ten years of age was estimated to be 3.9 million around 1910, of which 3.5 million were engaged in agriculture. This means that the active workforce in the urban areas at that time amounted to at least 400,000.[7] This figure no doubt was higher owing to the fact that boys under ten were also employed in handicrafts, services, com-

---

5. Bairoch 1976, 11, Table 3.
6. Korby 1977, 2–3, figure 3, Bharier, 1971, 59.
7. Bharier, 1971, 34.

merce and manufacturing. Moreover, quite a substantial number of women were engaged in all kinds of economic activities, especially in carpet and other weaving activities. Absent from Table 3.3 are the workers engaged in commerce, banks, transport and communication, while the figure for the services sector seems to be on the low side. We do not know how many of these workers were to be found in the urban areas of Iran, but their number must have been considerable. Data on unemployment are totally lacking, though it must have been fairly substantial.

TABLE 3.3: Employment in selected urban economic activities in Iran (circa 1910)[8]

Factories	850
Anglo-Persian Oil Company	2,460 (incl. 576 foreigners)
Mining	200
Railway employees	200
Railway workers (construction)	3,000
Road-workers (Rasht-Enzeli)	300
Printers	300
Carpet-making	65,000
Metal-working crafts	20,000
Leather crafts	900
Other handicrafts	10,000
Fisheries (Caspian)	4,200 (incl. 2,000 Russians)
Pearl fisheries (Persian Gulf)	4,000
Porters and dockers	4,000
Wood cutters	300
Leather production	3,000
Servants	5,000
Total	125,500

What is clear from Table 3.3 is that the labor force engaged in 'modern industry' was very small. Only some 6,700 workers qualify as such. The largest share was represented by the rail-way workers (45 per cent), followed by workers in the oil industry (37 per cent), while factory workers only represent some 12 per cent of this group. The traditional industries were much more important than any other industrial activity of a non-rural nature. The small workshop in which less than ten workers were employed in making and repairing products without the use of power-driven machinery was the predominant type of industrial establishment in Iran and remained so until the 1950s.

---

8. Abdullaev 1968, 212. These data provided by Abdullaev have been corrected where the labor force in factories are concerned, since he also counted those laborers working in factories which had been abandoned by 1900. For further details see: Floor 1991; Ferrier 1982, vol. 1, 154, Table 4.1 for the revised data on APOC employment in Iran.

TRADITIONAL INDUSTRIAL ACTIVITIES 1900–1925

Small industrial establishments were the main feature of the Iranian manufacturing sector. These establishments were still pre-industrial in nature and steeped in tradition. They were organized as guilds and a kind of moral responsibility between master and employees existed, the master often not being much better off than his workers. These workshops were often a family business, and usually consisted of a master assisted by one or more skilled laborers and apprentices (Table 3.6). Production was still along pre-industrial lines, i.e., specialization occurred in the product and not in the process as in modern industrial society. An artisan would often make all components of an article himself and assemble these into the final product Moreover production and sale often took place in the same establishment.[9]

However, these traditional industrial establishments were not always small-scale as is often mistakenly assumed. It is true in most cases, but towards the end of the nineteenth century a great number of large factories were established in a great many Iranian cities. A very large carpet-making factory in Tabriz employed up to 1,500 workers in 1899. Most of these large factories were to be found in the carpet industry, but they also existed in other industrial sectors such as leather preparation, preparation of opium, preparation of henna, and in mining. "The larger the workshop the further was the division of labor. The workers received only wages, and controlled neither the raw material nor the finished product."[10] Although modelled after modern factories, these factories did not achieve, in most cases, a complete break with the cottage industries out of which they had emerged, for their level of mechanization was very low and they mainly used manual labor. These industries therefore represent an intermediate stage of industrialization. The case of Tabriz is in this respect rather typical for the other 'industrial' centres in Iran such as Tehran, Qazvin, and Rasht. In addition to these factories there existed in Tabriz a great many small traditional workshops which employed a total of 22,942 persons. According to Soltanzadeh, the number of servants and unemployed laborers amounted to 30,000 persons in 1922. He did not mention the number of government employees and other category workers such as those engaged in mining and transport.

---

9. On guilds see Floor 1975.
10. Abdullaev 1963, 117; partly translated by Issawi 1971, 298.

TABLE 3.4: Number of factories and their labor force in Tabriz (1922)[11]

Type of factory	Number of employees	Number of workers	Average number of workers
Carpet factories	175	2,625	15
Spinning factory	1	150	150
Weaving mill	2	100	100
Weaving mill	10	100	10
Weaving mill	20	100	5
Weaving factory	30	300	6
Pottery making	10	50	5
Printing	8	120	15
Lithography	7	35	5
Tobacco processing	30	300	10
Cigarette making	5	50	10
Brick-making	5	30	6
Powder-making	3	30	10
Fruit-juice making	20	100	5
Dyeing factories	40	200	5
Soap-making	10	200	5
Iron and gypsum	5	50	10
Total	378	4,485	372

The predominance of the traditional type of industrial establishment was accentuated by the slow and modest rise of the development of modern, large-scale industry in Iran. The drive for the introduction of modern industry in Iran had begun in the 1850s. Apart from military reasons and the wish to become a modernized country, in the belief that Westernization was the panacea for Iran's troubles, the main incentive for the modernization of the industrial sector was import-substitution. Considerations of employment creation did not play a role, although Iran's native traditional industry was severely hit by the import of European goods.[12]

---

11. Ravasani n.d, 225; Chaqueri 1972. vol.4, Avetis Mikailian (Sultanzade) Selected Writings, 66–122 esp. 102.

	no. of employers	no. of workers
1. small artisans: eg. smiths, lock-smiths, bakeries, shoe makers	1090	4600
2 other small traders. dyers, saddlers, barbers, chandlers	470	1942
3. traders- vendors, merchants	1865	3865
4. day-labourers- water-sellers, qanat-diggers, porters, masons		5325
5. government employees	530	
6. other workers: drivers, gardeners.	2000	

12. Floor 1991, Olmer 1908; Radimsky 1909.

Bharier's statement that modern, large-scale industry, defined as comprising factories with ten or more workers, did not exist in Iran around the turn of the century is wrong.[13] In fact, notwithstanding the many obstacles modern industry had to overcome in Iran - cost of raw materials, energy, high transport rates, no protection against foreign competition, and non-economic factors - industrialization both prior to and after 1900 until World War I was considerable.[14] Between 1900 and 1914 some 30 modern large-scale factories were erected in Iran. Because there was a lack of integration in the economy as a whole, high-lighted by the absence of any industrialization policy of the Iranian government, this pre-1914 development was remarkable. There existed a Ministry of Public Works (*Favayed-e 'Ammeh*) which was charged, *inter alia*, with the management of Iran's industrial affairs. However, its budget of 150 to 200,000 *tumans* per year did not even suffice to pay for the salaries of the ministry's staff, and apart from giving out mining leases it did not do much to stimulate industry.[15] The role of government was restricted to a fiscal one in the sense that it tried to get money out of existing industries.

TABLE 3.5: large-scale factories in Iran and their labor force[16]

Type of factory	Number of workers
1890-1900	
Silk reeling factory/Amin ol-Zarb	150
Silk reeling factory/Birikadeh	20
Match factory/Tehran	50
Paper mill/Tehran	60
Sugar mill/Kahrizak	300
Glass & Porcelain/Tehran	20
Brick-making/Tehran	20
Oil-refineries/Gilan (5 plants with 272 men)	54 (average)
1900-1914	
Yarn factory/Tabriz	100
Brick factory/Urmiyeh	30
Olive-oil mill/Rudbar	20
Cotton ginning (26 factories with 416 workers)	16 (average)
Timber mill/Rasht	15
Timber mill/Talesh	15
Tobacco factory/Mashhad	20
Brick factory/Tehran	20
Soap factory/Nezafat	20

---

13. Bharier 1971, 170.
14. Bharier 1971, 170.
15. Mostowfi n.d, vol.2, 372.
16. Floor 1991, Table 3, which also gives more details on the pre-1914 industrialization effort.

Type of factory	Number of workers
Brewery/Urmiyeh	15
Brewery/Tehran	10
Arsenal/Isfahan	15

The attempt by Mozaffar al-Din Shah to stipulate that foreign investors who wanted to erect factories "to produce cotton, silk, etc."[17] had to acquire a permit from the government also must be seen in this light. Nevertheless, this new measure was in a way an innovation because the usual procedure was to sell concessions to foreign or Iranian investors to stimulate the utilization of the country's natural resources. In exchange for the monopoly of production of a certain commodity or service, the government received badly needed funds, while at the same time modern technology was introduced into the country. Examples of such 'successful' concessions are the D'Arcy oil concession, the Liazonov fisheries concession and the Indo-European Company's telegraph concession.[18] But not only foreigners obtained concessions. In 1898 an Iranian subject had obtained the concession for weaving-mills in Azarbaijan; he sold his rights in 1909 to Aqa Qazvini, who then built a weaving factory in Tabriz.[19] On May 21, 1910 the *Majles* permitted the import, free of duty, of certain machinery for the manufacture of tools and buttons to a Company which intended to undertake this production at Tabriz.[20] Although there was a strong group within the *Majles*, the so-called Democrats, who were in favor of modernizing Iran to which end the American mission under Morgan Shuster was invited to Iran, they were unable to implement these policies owing to the opposition from the conservative powers in Iran backed by Russsia and Great Britain.[21] It is noteworthy to observe that, about a decade later, a similar group (in fact an offshoot of the Democrats) had similar objectives and was more successful in realizing them, as we will see later.

The politically unstable situation of Iran, reinforced by the invasion of the neutral country by the armies of Turkey, Russia and Great Britain during the period 1914-1918, put an end to the various attempts at industrialization. The Iranian economy suffered considerably during the war, as a result of which its imports had fallen dramatically in 1920-21 as compared with 1913-14, excluding oil and invisibles, viz. from 647 million *qrans* to 482 million *qrans* or a drop of about 30 per cent. Exports had suffered likewise (from 447 to 138 million *qrans*). This situation led to a negative balance of trade and to the export of gold and silver, which the government was forced to prohibit. The reduced purchasing

---

17. Legatie Perzië, bundel 22, letter nr. 196 (see Appendix C).
18. Bharier 1971, 84.
19. Administrator-General of the Finances of Persia, Ninth Quarterly Report, (Oct-Dec, 1924).
20. FO 371/950, f369; Gielhammer 1939, 228 for the concession to Rabi`zadeh and partners entailing certain privileges, which would be revoked if foreigners participated in the venture.)
21. Abrahamian 1982, 104.

power of the population was also translated into fewer imports of both raw materials and manufactured goods,[22] as well as a reduction of employment in the urban areas.[23]

The war also had some positive consequences. For although hardly any of the earlier modern industries survived and the traditional industries were hit by a severe crisis "by sole exception there has sprung up in Persia, as a consequence of the temporary block of imports during the war, a leather-making industry, a boot-and-shoe making industry, and a button-making industry."[24] These industries were not of a modern type, however, but belonged to the traditional small-scale industries, using often pre-industrial methods and processes. Moreover, its products were not very satisfactory and its prices as high as its qualities were low. How important the traditional small-scale industries were in the 1920s is, for example, highlighted by the large number of small-scale workshops in Tehran in 1925. In 13,357 workshops, 13,260 masters employed 18,524 workers, who produced a wide range of goods. A similar situation existed in other cities in Iran at that time such as in Isfahan where 9,555 masters were engaged in various industrial activities. Unfortunately, the number of skilled workers and apprentices employed by these masters is unknown. Whether these industries were protected by the high freight rates for imported goods as Bharier has suggested needs further research.[25] According to the British commercial attaché, there were "virtually no indigenous industries to be protected or fostered against foreign competition,"[26] in the early 1920s at least. Moreover, when transport rates were reduced considerably, due to the introduction of motor transport and metalled roads, there was nevertheless an increase of these traditional industries to be observed.[27]

TABLE 3.6: Employment in Tehran in the traditional industrial sector (1925)[28]

Type of activity	No. of shops	No. of masters	No. of skilled workers	No. of apprentices
Metal working	765	822	769	535
Woodworking	574	500	506	310
Construction & ceramics	193	162	167	43

---

22. Temple 1922, 5.
23. Mani 1325/1946, 7, Matindaftari 1304/1925; Abdulllaev 1968, 60.
24. Temple 1922, 5.
25. Bharier 1971, 171.
26. Temple 1922, 5.
27. Abdullaev 1968, 60, gives a few examples of the considerable increase of the labor force employed by the traditional artisanal industries.
28. Keyhan, 1311, vol. 2, 327f.; these statistics were published earlier in: Tehran 1310/1931, 72f. the latter are more detailed and also provide data on the distribution of the guilds per city quarter. Bharier 1971, 171. n.9 is wrong (also where the page numbers are concerned) to state that there were 5,000 industrial workshops, for the services and trade sector do not quality as such. He is also wrong with regard to the number of handicrafts mentioned in the 1926 tax bill which is mentioned in the same note. The relevant bill enumerates 267 taxes, of which only 239 referred to guild taxes, the same mistake was made by Issawi 1971, 285. Tables 6 and 7 have been aggregated by me. The original source gives the data per guild.

Type of activity	No. of shops	No. of masters	No. of skilled workers	No. of apprentices
Textiles & leather	1,938	2,371	2,503	1,079
Food & agro industry	829	816	1,947	359
Transport	604	434	643	164
Services	507	477	1,097	248
Trade	7,906	7,684	6,569	1,565
Total	13,357	13,266	14,201	4,303

TABLE 3.7: Number of masters in the traditional industrial sector of Isfahan (1924)[29]

Type of activity	No. of masters
Metal working	1,183
Woodworking	220
Construction & ceramics	317
Textiles & leather	1,354
Food & agro industry	1,412
Transport	370
Services & Trade	4,784
Total	9,555

PRESSURE FOR INDUSTRIALIZATION, 1922–1940

The coup d'etat led by Reza Khan and Ziya al-Din inaugurated a new period in Iranian history. This period was characterized not only by the strengthening of central authority and increased security, but also by a growing dictatorship with the concomitant loss of political freedom of the Majles, when Reza Khan proclaimed himself Shah of Iran in 1925. The new government after the coup had great plans for Iran and, even after Ziya al-Din had been dismissed from the government, the subsequent cabinets retained some of the development spirit which had characterized the Ziya al-Din cabinet.[30] The cabinet led by Qavam al-Saltaneh (1921) had a program which, inter alia, had as its objective to start mines and mobilize other resources for the foundation of companies and the training of workers and unemployed to combat unemployment.[31] Although the government was not very successful in implementing this policy, the *Majles* in 1921 nevertheless made it compulsory for government employees and army personnel to wear only cloth made in Iran in an attempt to curtail the large share of textiles in Iran's imports and to encourage native industries in that field. Although this decision gave some impetus to the weaving

---

29. Janab 1303, 77f.
30. See on these and subsequent events, Abrahamian 1982, 118f.
31. Bahar, 1357, 123.

industries, the yarns still had to be imported from abroad. In a similar attempt to encourage native industries, the government appropriated a sum of money to hold an exhibition of Iranian crafts and industries in Tehran in order to bolster its export and manufacturing capability. At the same time, to encourage the use of modern technology by Iranian craftsmen, permission was given to organize an exhibition of foreign machinery. These initiatives led to a rise in demand for spinning and weaving machinery, both hand and power-driven, as well as to the erection of modern large-scale factories or the starting-up of idle factories.[32]

To enable the government to implement its plan and attain its objectives, it was necessary to get a better grip on the economy, to improve its infrastructure and to rationalize its finances. To that end an American Mission led by Millspaugh was retained, who was given far-reaching powers.[33] Amongst a great many things, he issued orders on November 29, 1923 to control the implementation of the government decree to wear only Iranian-made cloth.[34] In that same year, Hajji Mo`in al-Tojjar Bushehri re-opened his silk spinning factory in Rasht, which, although having been idle for about 20 years, was still in good running condition.[35] An Isfahani merchant, `Ata al-Molk, purchased machinery for a cotton-spinning weaving factory in Germany in that same year. However, by the end of 1923 he still had not been able to transport all the machines to Isfahan by the mountainous tracks from Hamadan.[36] The owner of a match factory in Tabriz ordered new machines from Germany in 1923 to expand his production capacity.[37] The government itself was also discussing plans to undertake various industrial activities such as the start up of the Kahrizak sugar mill. Millspaugh reported that "if the sugar factory resumes operation we are prepared to plant sugar beets on the public domains in order to supply the factory."[38] Furthermore, there were discussions about constructing railways and building a hydro-electric station for lighting and supplying power to Tehran and for working a tramway service to Tajrish.[39] In 1924 the Ministry of Public Works (*Favayed-e `Ammeh*) granted a concession for the period of ten years to build textile factories in the provinces of Astarabad, Shahrud, Bistam, and Damghan.[40] In that same year, the ministry also agreed to a proposal by a German entrepreneur to build spinning factories (silk and cotton) to weave cloth, and to build factories producing paper and beverages on the following conditions: the factories had to be built within one year after the agreement, while the number of foreigners working in the factories had to remain restricted. The import of machinery for the factories would be free of customs, while a tax holiday of three years was granted. After that period an income tax of 10 per cent on the net income would have to be paid. These activities

---
32. Hadow 1923, 9; Gielhammer 1939, 229 (29 Dey 1301/ January 19, 1923).
33. Millspaugh 1973.
34. Administrator-General of the Finances of Persia, 1924.
35. FO 371/9026, Rasht Diary June 23, 1923. f. 124.
36. FO 416/112, Annual Report 1923. f. 92 (p.44).
37. FO 416/112, Annual Report 1923. f. 92 (p.44).
38. Administrator-General of the Finances of Persia, 1923.
39. Administrator-General of the Finances of Persia, 1923, FO 416/112 Annual Report 1923, f. 92.
40. Administrator-General of the Finances of Persia, 1924.

are an indication of the need felt by both government and the *Majles* to attract industrial investors and to given Iran the beginnings of a modern industrial base.[41]

In 1925 a cotton-spinning and weaving mill was established in Isfahan, while an idle cotton and wool spinning mill in Tehran (Sani` al-Dowleh) was started up again.[42] The owner of a cotton-spinning mill in Tabriz also built a wool-spinning mill in his home town of Qazvin.[43] Small-scale industrial activities in the field of shoes, saddlery, socks and other consumer goods were developing rapidly as well.[44] To improve the quality of these small factories and crafts the government founded a Technical Institute (*madraseh-ye san`ati*) in 1924, where young technicians were trained by European experts.[45]

Several measures were taken to protect native industries and provide investors with incentives to start new industries. In 1925 a law was passed which exempted industrial and agricultural machinery and instruments and their component parts from import duties for a period of 10 years. The exemption was clearly biased towards large-scale industries since it did not apply to small-scale capital goods such as sewing and knitting machines.[46]

These new industries in many cases were in a shaky economic and financial position as was the modern *Vatan* factory, in Isfahan. This modern factory which turned out a good product, coarse cloth and blankets, could only survive with "strenuous Government support in the form of cash contracts and decrees which aim at forcing officials to wear home-manufactured cloth."[47] Such government support was given because there were powerful interest groups within the government that wanted to modernize Iran and make it an industrial state "as if such a transformation necessarily implied progress," the British commercial attaché commented.[48]

These interest groups were formed, inter alia, by young, Western-educated, reform-minded people, who backed Reza Khan (later Reza Shah). Apart from their education in Europe, the traumatic experience of Iran's subservience to Britain and Russia and the near break-up of the country led these reformists to back a strong central government, preferably led by a strong man such as Reza Khan.[49] The various options for the economic development of Iran (which interest us here) were hotly debated in various clubs, such as

---

41. Administrator-General of the Finances of Persia, 1924; see also Gielhammer 1939a, 229 for other activities.
42. Lingeman 1928, 24.
43. Lingeman 1928, 24.
44. Lingeman 1928, 24.
45. Pars Agency, 18–21, which provides details and pictures of the technical school; Hadow 1923, 41 "A technical school recently opened, the need for technical education is paramount, as there are today in Persia no surveyors, road engineers, architects, agricultural experts, mechanical engineers able to assist in the reorganisation of their country."
46. Bharier, 1971, 174 n.19.
47. Lingeman 1928, 24; Wilber 1975, 134, "On April 24, 1930, anniversary of the coronation, the Shah received the diplomatic corps in a uniform... that was obviously made of locally-woven material. In accordance with his recent order that all government officials must wear, clothes of domestic cloth. His senior officials were similarly attired. Reza Shah spoke cordially to the owner of the textile mill at Esfahan, remarking that his mill was the source of the uniforms."
48. Lingeman 1928, 28.
49. Abrahamian 1982, 122 f.

the Economic Association (*Majma`-ye Eqtesad*), which was founded in Tehran in 1924.[50] Davar, later Minister of Justice, but in 1923 editor of the paper *Mard-e Azad*, for instance, led a party known as the Reformists which, inter alia, wanted to bring about "an industrial and agricultural revolution with new machines" in Iran.[51] The ideas for these and other program were not only provided by their training in Europe, but also by the publication of various books, journals such as *Ayandeh, Iranshahr*, and *Farhangestan*[52] and dissertations by Iranians.[53] Many elements of the economic policy pursued in the 1930s were to be found in these books and there is no doubt that they had a profound influence on the policy-makers. An important example of such a book, if only because it was written in Persian, was the study by Ahmad Matindaftari entitled *The key of Iran's economic independence*, in which he argued for direct state control over the economy leading to development of infrastructure, and national industries which were to be protected against foreign imports, while exports of industrial products had to be promoted. To attract investors, especially foreign ones, he also advised tax holidays as one of the policies to be pursued.[54]

But even more important than the various reformist-minded associations, economic or otherwise, though closely bound up with them, was the Revival Party led by Davar, Teymurtash and Tadayyon.[55] This party, an off-shoot of the Democrats, the main defenders of the Constitutional Movement, many of the veterans of which were members, was the main channel for these ideas. The party program "called for separation of religion from politics, creation of a well-disciplined army and a well administered bureaucracy, an end to economic capitulations, industrialization, replacement of foreign capital by indigenous capital, transformation of nomads into farmers, a progressive income tax, expansion of educational facilities for all, including women, careers open to talent, and replacement of minority languages throughout Iran by Persian."[56] Most of the party program was executed during Reza Shah's reign. This is not surprising, since the party supported Reza Khan's centralist policies actively and its leaders and many of its important members joined the government as ministers, high government officials or in other capacities.[57] It is due to these men that Iran was able to make a big step forward during the 1930s.

It is true that they were unable to realize profound reforms and created an expensive government machinery and big disparities in income between urban and rural areas. However, they were able to change the face of Iran and laid the stepping-stone for the second

---

50. Matin-Daftari 1304, 30.
51. FO 371/9024, f. 160–63 has the text of the party's program. The Foreign Office commented "in the past similar so-called political parties issued these sorts of programme, quite meaningless in a country like Persia."
52. Abrahamian 1982, 123.
53. For example: Safiniya 1307; Fateh 1926; Naficy 1924; Ghadimy, 1923; Ehtechami 1930; Hechmat as Saltana 1920; a very early Mosaddeq al-Saltaneh, 1332; and Jamalzadeh, 1335.
54. Matindaftari 1304; the subtitle of this book (in French) made the purpose of the writing of the book clear "ad usum des capitalistes étrangers désirant placer leurs capitaux aux enterprises rémunératrices."
55. Abrahamian 1982, 122 f; Bahar 1357, 123 with a slightly different view.
56. Abrahamian 1982, 123.
57. Teymurtash, Davar, Tadayyon, Taqizadeh, Mostowfi al-Mamalek, Foroughi, for example all became ministers.

leap forward made in the 1950s. There is no doubt that these steps were made at high cost and the same targets could have been achieved more cheaply, but this can be ascribed to the enormous problems these people had to face, and for which they had to pay 'the costs of learning,' as John Stuart Mill put it.

Whether as a result of this policy or not, in 1931 some 230 large and small-scale modern industrial factories and establishments existed in Iran, according to a list drawn up by the Iranian Department of Labor & Industry (Appendix B). In this list no mention is made, however, of the number of workers, the installed horsepower, the invested capital or the date of erection. What is striking in this list is the large number of agro-industries, in particular the 34 cotton-ginning plants. Moreover, the list mentions 35 electric installations, which is striking indeed. For the British commercial attaché in 1928 had stated that "only the towns of Bushire, Tabriz, Enzeli and Rasht have electricity."[58] This discrepancy between the data—it is impossible that between 1928 and 1931 so much electricity-generating capacity had been imported and installed in Iran—can only be explained by either omission and lack of knowledge or, more likely, by the omission of the less important and small-scale establishments.

That this was probably the case is borne out by a statement from the British commercial report of 1930 that "no industrial development of any consequence has taken place"[59] in Iran. This observation does not tally with the list of industries drawn up by the Iranian government and may be explained by the fact that what looked modern and industrial to an Iranian was considered to be insignificant and not worth mentioning by a European.

Notwithstanding these results, the Iranian government was disappointed with the reaction of local private capital and the lack of entrepreneurship shown by Iranian capitalists in the field of modern industry. The tax holidays and subsidies provided for investors had been of no avail; the government therefore decided to take the initiative itself, if possible in co-operation with foreign investors.[60] In 1927 it had given the go-ahead for the construction of the Trans-Iranian Railway, while the building of a paper-mill was also being considered. In vain the government tried to interest foreign capital to invest in the water and power supply of Tehran.[61] The government also wanted to build the national railway with Iranian-manufactured steel. It had therefore employed a German engineer to study the feasibility of the construction of smelting works at Semnan.[62] Because there was no suitable coal available in the Semnan area, the works would be dependent on the

---

58. Lingeman 1928, 24.

59. Even in the 1930s this mentality prevailed, for although six factories existed in Shiraz the British Consul nevertheless reported "there are only four big factories," FO 371/40222 f.7531.

60. FO 416/113, Annual Report 1928, f. 58 (p.40) "the Government has at least learnt to appreciate the rashness of its erstwhile plans to industrialize Persia at all costs. It has realised that the State subsidies granted to the weaving factory in Isfahan and the match factory in Tabriz have been of no avail, and decided that it would be well advised to use its influence and apply its resources to the development of projects better calculated to succeed."

61. Lingeman 1930, 32; Ibid., 1928, 28–29.

62. The Persian text of the expert's (Martin) report has been published by Keyhan 1311, vol.3, 253–256.

coke of the Shamshak mine near Tehran. The production of this mine would also be used to supply Tehran with a cheaper fuel, where coal cost £6 a ton in winter. Furthermore, the coal would be used for the railway itself, and it was intended that the economic rentability of the project would be favorable. On August 11, 1928 the *Majles* voted 200,000 *tumans* to operate the Shamshak mine. Coal was sold at half the cost of production but, when it became known that the Direction of Mines of the Ministry of Public Works had misappropriated a considerable share of the mine's working capital, the government closed it down. The government was more fortunate in interesting a Czechoslovakian company in obtaining a concession for the construction of a sugar mill in Karaj, where trials were made with beets.[63] In order to speed up the economic development of the country, a series of measures were taken to increase the influence of the state on the economy.

THE BIG LEAP FORWARD (1930–40)

At the beginning of the Iranian year 1309 (March 1930), the government of Iran had decided to "develop new industries as a means of reducing imports and supporting the exchange."[64] Apart from these arguments, there was also the strong desire to make Iran into a self-reliant country that would be free from foreign interference and influence. To make this possible the government believed that Iranian society and economy had to be modernized. This change, it believed, had to be directed by the state through direct involvement in the economy and entrepreneurship and deliberate purposeful economic planning. The instrument chosen to implement this policy was that of import substitution, which implied interference with the allocative functions of the market and with international competition. On December 14, 1930, Reza Shah opened the eighth session of the *Majles* with the statement that "We wish this Majles to be known in the history of the country as the 'Economic Parliament' (*Majles-e eqtesadi*)."[65] This announcement inaugurated a period in which the government acted as the supreme organizer. This important step was taken by the government partly to countervail the effects of the Great Depression on the Iranian economy, and partly because the government had already been developing an economic policy aimed at improving its trade balance. To that end, the government had terminated the Capitulations of foreign states in 1928 in order to obtain full tariff and fiscal authority. The absence of this autonomy had handicapped, inter alia, industrialization attempts in Iran from its very beginnings in the 1850s. Although, as yet, no full autonomy was obtained (this was achieved in 1936) due to treaty obligations, the government of Iran nevertheless could give real protection to its economy for the first time as of 1928. The fiscal autonomy coincided with the fall in export prices of Iranian products, which led to a deterioration of Iran's terms of trade and a deficit in the balance of payments. This development provided an argent and necessary incentive for the government to find other

---

63. FO 416/113, Annual Report 1928, f. 50.
64. Lingeman 1930, 32; Wilber 1975, 190, "As far as the textile mills are concerned, I know that we should make cloth in our own country and avoid Imports and I have told this to many people, but as no one came forward I had to do it, " Reza Shah declared later.
65. Pars Agency (a), 55 which reproduces the text of the speech.

sources of income and foreign exchange. Industrialization was one of the answers to that problem; the Foreign Trade Monopoly Law of 1931 was the government's policy instrument to achieve that end.[66]

The Iranian government realized that it lacked the necessary infrastructure to develop an industrial base. The transportation system was inimical to the development of trade, while other infrastructural activities (power supply for example) were unsatisfactory. The banking and financial institutions needed to be further developed to encourage and serve industrial initiatives. Trained supervisors, managers, engineers, and skilled personnel in general at all levels were totally lacking. Without such an infrastructure, Iran would not be able to develop an industry and we observe that the government mounted a large programme to fill this need.[67]

In June 1931, the Ministry of National Economy, which up till then had been charged with the promotion of industry, was split up into three Departments, one of which was the Department of Mines and Industries (*Edareh-ye San'at va Ma'aden*).[68] The newly appointed chief, Farrokh, describes in his autobiography that the new Department did not even have offices when it started to function and so he selected the *Madraseh-ye Kamal al-Molk* for that purpose. For the Department of Mines he put in, charge engineer Zahedi, who had recently returned from France where he had received his training in mining. The new Department had no proper funds to work with and Farrokh therefore decided to start mining at Shamshak, Gajareh and Lalun and to run the Department with the proceeds of the sale of coal. In this way the Department gradually started its work It had to start slowly, not only because of its low resources, but also because it was a new organization. For Farrokh had the old staff of the Ministry of National Economy transferred to other ministries and had attracted a totally new staff.[69]

The new Departments were charged with the implementation of the new economic policy. This policy was concentrated around the Foreign Trade Monopoly Law, which gave the Iranian government a firmer control on the imports and exports, control of transactions in foreign exchange and made it possible to establish an industry geared to import-substitution, which otherwise could not have existed.[70]

---

66. For a more detailed discussion see Mazandarani, 1316 and Djazaeri, 1938.
67. Bharier 1971; Issawi 1971, 373–386.
68. Wilber 1975, 143; Bharier 1971, 174, n.19, the organization was as follows: 1900-21 Ministry of Commerce and Public Utilities, 1922-29 Ministry of Public Utilities, 1929-31 Ministry of Economy, 1932-37 Directorate General of Commerce, Agriculture and Industry, 1937-39 Ministry of Industry and Mines, 1939-41 Ministry of Arts and Crafts. For slightly different details see Pars Agency (c), (e), and (f). According to Farrokh 1347, 309, 320 (he was the first DG of Commerce, Agriculture and Industry) although the name and tasks of the Ministry (or DG) changed, this was not so much due to internal defining of boundaries, but to direct personal interference by Reza Shah. He also mentioned other cases of the Shah's personal intervention in industrial matters. For example, when Reza Shah saw timber machinery lying idle on the quay of Bandar-e Shah and heard that it was not used he ordered the Department of Industry to buy the machinery and use it. Within the year, Farrokh adds, the new plant produced timber.
69. Farrokh 1347/1968, 290.
70. Simmonds 1935, 28–29.

The selection of the types of industry was in general well conceived where the supply of raw materials and the domestic market were concerned. The policy of import quotas and import prohibitions created a situation in which the Iranian industrialist was free of external competition and could charge high prices. The tariffs were used to protect the national industry as well as to collect revenue. The system of import quotas did not work very effectively, however. It prevented the government from having good control over the level of protection of the industry, while the resulting monopolistic structures with their high administrative costs and corruption led to inefficiency and loss of foreign exchange.[71]

Because of the inward-looking economic policy, an industrial structure came into being that increasingly reflected domestic consumption patterns. Export promotion did not figure high on the government's or industrialists' list of priorities. Apart from the fact that the domestic market still offered a great many opportunities, Iran would have had difficulty in selling its manufactured goods internationally because of the lack of quality and the protective measures taken by other countries at that time. There is also the fact that the high tariffs distorted the price-mechanism. The resulting high unit cost of production only created problems for entrepreneurs who wished to sell in the international markets. The Iranian industrialist was handicapped in two ways: whether he had to import his raw materials or intermediate goods, or had to acquire them from domestic producers, in both cases his production costs were higher than for his competitors. In the first place he had to pay high import-tariffs and transportation, in the second case the domestic supplier could charge high prices because of the protection he enjoyed. The export opportunities of the Iranian industry were therefore also hampered by the high level of protection.[72]

The per unit rates of return on the domestic market were, moreover, much higher than on the international market. Industrialists therefore preferred even to reduce their output to low levels rather than to turn to export markets. This attitude is also reflected in the rather substantial amount of unutilized industrial capacity and of unutilized labor.[73] Another obstacle to export promotion was the effect of tariffs on the country's exchange rates. Because of the tariffs, imports declined relatively and so also did the total amount of foreign exchange spent on imports. The national currency tended to become overvalued, which resulted in exporters receiving less domestic currency for the same volume of exports. With the passing of the foreign exchange law in 1932 a black market came into being.[74] "In consequence some merchants, finding (international) trade operations more and more difficult and unprofitable, began to turn their attention to developing industrial production within the country."[75]

---

71. FO 371/20050, Economic Conditions In Esfahan, f.13; FO 371/20835. Economic Conditions in Fars, f.22; Bharier 1971, 87, Simmonds 1935, 23–24.
72. For some examples see FO 371/20050, f. 132.
73. When there was fear of overproduction industrialists would decrease the number of shifts and lay-off part of their labor force, see for example FO 371/200835, f.21–23; Aderholt 1938, 87–88.
74. Bharier 1971, 123.
75. Simmonds 1935, 53. When visiting the industrial exhibition in Shiraz in 1937, Reza Shah said "No more spinning mills are needed. You should not all pursue the same lines of endeavour. It is perfectly proper if the yarn produced by the spinning mills is turned into

As a result of the government's policy, a great many new factories were built in Iran over the next decade. As is clear from Appendix B, the most important industries were sugar, cotton and woolen textiles, matches and cement factories. A number of smaller factories —chemicals, other textiles, soap, oil processing, glass works, hosiery, leather works, rice milling, tea processing, flour mills, beer and wines - were also erected in various parts of the country, mainly by private investors. Appendix B shows that between 1934 and 1938 the industrialization wave was at its peak. The number of workers employed by these new factories showed an increase of some 250 per cent above the previous employment offered by the industrial sector.[76]

In October 1934, the Department of Industries and Mines issued a notice that all future applicants for the installation of industrial plants must first obtain a license from the Department[77] in order to prevent wasteful competition, which is an indication that by that time the government's policy was successful. For, although no ordered plan of industrial development existed, investors found it increasingly rewarding to jump on the industrial bandwagon. The government had spearheaded the industrial wave with the erection of the sugar mills but it was private enterprise and capital which provided the main thrust for development and capital.[78] Especially in the Isfahan area, the response had been very positive, for "nearly every section of the population of Isfahan and its districts has invested some, it not all of its savings.""[79] Such widespread support and such a broad investment base were facilitated by the fact that shares were issued in small denominations of 1,000 riyals. The money invested had in most cases been in ready cash and was not the proceeds of sales of fixed assets such as land.[80]

In Azarbayjan, the merchant class was more cautious in reacting to the government's policy, but by 1936 investors there were making up for lost time through a rapid development of new factories. "Even those who in face of diminished opportunities for investment in private trade, were disposed to hoard their capital, are now being persuaded by the success so far of certain pioneer factories, and their inability to convert funds into safer foreign currencies, to participate in industrial development."[81]

---

cloth to meet our internal requirements. but it would be detrimental to the country if the number of spinning mills was increased." Wilber 1975, 179.
76. Bharier 1971, 172.
77. Simmonds 1935, 29.
78. See Table 13.
79. FO 371/20050, Report on Economic Conditions of Esfahan in October 1936, f. 129.
80. FO 371/20050, Report on Economic Conditions of Esfahan in October 1936, f. 129, for a list of the principal investors see Ibid., f.137–143.
81. FO 371/20838. A Memorandum an Economic Affairs in Azarbaijan (Tabriz, December 31, 1936), f. 179; in the South investors continued to show considerable lack of enthusiasm, although "Governors continue to exhort people to form Companies or subscribe to those in the North, but beyond this nothing is done," FO 371/20050, Annual Commercial Report for Khorramshahr and Abadan ending March 20, 1936, f. 72; nevertheless in 1935 a cotton spinning and weaving mill was started in Ahvaz. Ibid., f. 71 which had to operate under disadvantageous conditions and therefore did not do much to provide capitalists with the incentive to invest in industry, see e.g. FO 416/95, f.75. When Reza Shah visited the mill at Ahvaz in 1937, the owner asked the Shah for cheaper cotton, for the mill worked at considerable disadvantage because the cotton had to be imported largely from the north, while the finished yarn had to be sent north for sale. Cost of transport made the Ahvaz

Since a proper public credit market did not exist in Iran, the government decided to stimulate private capital by making bank loans and trade credits available to industrialists. The National Bank founded in 1927, played an important role in co-financing many industrial investments. To attract private investors, the bank charged very low rates of interest of only 5 to 6 per cent This stood in contrast to the high rates of interest prevailing in the non-market sector of the economy which the National Bank failed to penetrate. The same also holds for the Agricultural Bank founded in 1933.[82] The distribution of the benefits of economic development between urban and rural areas was in this way heavily in favour of the urban areas. Urban investments were clearly favoured over rural ones, a policy which contributed to the drift of workers from rural to urban areas, resulting in slums and unemployment. Moreover, within urban areas large-scale industry was preferred to small-scale industry and we observe that the traditional artisan industries did not receive much attention as a means to combat unemployment and poverty.[83]

From what we know about the rates of return or rather about the dividends paid by factories in Shiraz and Isfahan to shareholders, these indeed looked very promising. The Fars Manufacturing Company declared a dividend of 20 per cent in 1934, of 80 per cent in 1935, and of 66 per cent in 1936. The dividends were all paid in cash.[84] This was undoubtedly also due to the fact that the locally-produced cottons were very much in demand all over Iran. The British commercial attaché observed that "in order to cope with demand the factories which are actually in operation are working at full pressure."[85] Both import prohibitions for some goods as well as high prices for many others encouraged national entrepreneurs to produce these goods or their substitutes. In either case, of course, the consumer was presented with the bill for an article which in most cases was more expensive than those previously imported and of lower quality. This became especially true when new tariffs were introduced on May 22, 1936 which increased the level of duties on almost all imports.[86]

Notwithstanding the high profits for investors and the government control on permits to start new factories since 1934, it became clear in 1936 that the danger of overproduction loomed large. After 1938, the incentive to start new industries diminished due to the

---

mills product very expensive. The Shah replied that the supply of local-grown cotton would soon be sufficient and he added "you should import a weaving plant in order to avoid the necessity of sending the yarn north." The Ahvaz plant was not the only mill having difficulties with the supply of cotton. See also FO 371/20050, f.74.

82. Soheily 1950, 40.

83. Simmonds 1935, 23, FO 371/2900 (Kermanshah 1938) f.114–15; Ibid (Khorramshahr), f.151; FO 371/20048 (Mashhad), f. 175–77.

84. FO 371/20835, f. 22, "this is not surprising, since the price they formerly got for their yarn was three times the cost of Japanese yarn of the same quality c.i.f. Bushire;" FO 371/20052, f.214; FO 371/20834, f. 180; Gielhammer 1939, 229 mentions profits of 40 to 50 percent, on p. 263 he mentions average profits for 80% of the textile industry between 1934–1937 of 20, 36, 34 and 21 per cent. According to the Government, dividends paid by industrial companies averaged 22.3% between 1931 and 1937, see Banque Mellié Iran 1939 a, in particular, p. 812 and Table 4.

85. FO 371/20050, f. 130 (Esfahan, 1936).

86. Gray 1937, 7.

real fear of overproduction and governmental attempts to limit profits.[87] Already in 1936 there were indications that investors believed that there were too many factories or too large a production capacity in some sectors, such as textile mills and tanneries. In Tabriz the Khosrovi tannery was saved by army orders from its financial difficulties.[88] In Shiraz, the Dehqan brothers did not use their 1936 permit to erect a new weaving mill. In the same town the Fars Manufacturing Company cancelled orders for spinning machinery in 1938, although the factory building had already been constructed. Other textile mills cut down the number of shifts to lower their output.[89]

The diminished interest of private capital in investment in industry is also indicated by an increasing tendency towards financial participation by the National Bank (*Bank-e Melli*) and the Agricultural Bank in new ventures. Towards the end of the 1930s, we also observe that the government increasingly took the initiative again in starting a number of industrial establishments, owing to the reluctance of private capital to start new industries. This reluctance, which had always existed, increased after 1937 when opportunities to buy crown lands were opened up due to the government's need for money. This became an important outlet for private capital, the more so since new regulations drawn up by the Department of Industries in August 1936 also made it more difficult to start or organize a factory easily and freely.[90]

To show how modern and successful Iran had become in the field of industry, an exhibition of Iranian industrial and agricultural products was held in 1934 in Tehran. This exhibition was repeated in 1937 and in subsequent years. Similar provincial exhibitions were held in Mashhad, Tabriz, Isfahan and other cities. According to the British commercial attaché, the exhibitions showed that the products were of good quality and that each year improvements were to be noted compared with the previous years.[91]

Although the issue of employment-generation was not an objective per se for Iranian industrialization policy, at that time no government excelled in that respect, the effect of the policy was a quite considerable increase in employment. The economically active male population over ten years of age in 1940 amounted to some 4.9 million, of which about 3.75 million were engaged in agriculture. The active male workforce in the urban areas therefore amounted to some 1.2 million at that time.[92] How many women were engaged in urban industrial activities at that time is not known, but their number probably would not have exceeded the figure of 80,000.

Abdullaev's estimate of the size of the urban industrial labor force (Table 3.8) is on the low side. He underestimated for example the sizeable labor force in small-scale industries.[93]

---

87. Bharier 1971, 174; Aderholt 1938, 88 mentions an increase of the working hours per number of spindles from 24,699 hours in 1313/1923 to 59,404 hours in 1315/1936.
88. FO 371/20835, Memorandum, f. 180.
89. FO 371/20835, Report on Shiraz, f. 21–22.
90. Simmonds 1935, 31; Avery 1965, 309, 313, 325.
91. Simmonds 1935, 22; FO 371/18995, f.129; Pars Agency (f), 141 (part two) which has a picture of the stand of the Khollar wine factory in Shiraz; Ettela'at newspaper, 1329/1950, 126, 134.
92. Bharier 1971, 34.
93. Abdullaev 1968, 84.

TABLE 3.8: Employment in selected urban economic activities in Iran, 1940

Oil industry	31,500
Textile & hosiery industry	25,000
Food industry	8,000
Mining	3,000
Fishing	3,000
Chemical industry	2,000
Military industry	1,500
Matches + electricity	1,600
Cotton-ginning & building materials	1,500
Building materials workers	5,700
Railroad workers	14,5000
Car transport workers	20,000
Construction workers (roads/housing)	60,000
Tanneries	3,000
Various factories	4,000
Carpet industry	60,000
Shawls & other weaving	5,000
Other urban crafts	10,000
Total	260,100

Another Russian (military) estimate puts the Iranian industrial labor force at 525,000, which is also too low, for it still falls short of the 1.2 million active male work force and the considerable female workforce, the size of which is unknown. Moreover, this military estimate gives too high a number for the size of the labor force in the railway industry, as well as for the carpet industry, of which only 60,000 can be classified as urban.

TABLE 3.9: Composition of the industrial labor force in Iran 1940 (military) estimate [94]

Railway industry	60,000
Textile industry	30,000
Wool & rice cleaning	25,000
Railway & road construction	55,000
Carpet industry	180,000
Fishing industry	15,000
Dockers, etc.	10,000
Cottage industries	30,000
Unemployed	30,000
Total	525,000

---

94. Mahrad 1978, 207.

Unfortunately, we lack sufficient information to form a complete picture of the composition of the urban labor force. The size of traditional crafts and trades, for example, is totally unknown, and probably would have amounted to some 250,000 by 1940. The number of unemployed or that of other gainfully employed is totally unknown as well. On the basis of the information presented, the best guestimate for selected urban industrial activities is given in Table 3.10.

TABLE 3.10: Employment in selected urban industrial activities (1940)

Oil industry	31,500
Textile industry	30,000
Food industry	9,500
Railways	14,500
Transport/roads	20,000
Construction	60,000
Fisheries	15,000
Dockers	10,000
Mining	3,000
Chemical/military/Tanneries/matches	9,500
Carpet industry	6,000
Sub-Total	263,000
Traditional crafts	250,000
Total	513,000

The differences which nevertheless exist with regard to the various industrial subsector or even per factory are due to the fact that the data are as yet incomplete. Another variable factor is the date of observation; for example, the cement factory in Tehran had only 360 workers in 1936, but after its expansion in 1939 it boasted of 1,000 workers.[95] Similar examples can also be indicated for other factories. Finally, the fact whether one bases one's estimate on peak season or off-season labor demand, makes quite a difference for the size of the labor force, due to the existence of many agro-industries in Iran.

The oil industry constituted the most concentrated form of industry in Iran as far as both geography and ownership was concerned. It dominated the Khuzestan province as regards industrial labor and the national budget as regards revenues in other areas also. The oil industry had an important impact. It was the only industry that provided training for Iranians in the fields of crafts, technology and management. This experience did not remain restricted to the APOC, for many Iranian staff members preferred to work elsewhere in Iran under more benign climatological conditions, taking their know-how and experience with them.[96]

---

95. FO 371/20839 Intelligence Summary nr. 28, October 23. 1937, f.30, the cement factory was also shown an Iranian stamps issued in 1935 (see stamp on back cover).
96. Bharier 1971, 150–69.

TABLE 3.11: Growth of the labor force in modern industry per sector 1914-1939[97]

Sector	1914	1920-30	1939
Oil industry (APOC)	7-8,000	24-30,000	31,500
Textile industry	1,000	1,000	24,500
Electricity sector	100	200	600
Cotton-ginning	416	800	1,500
Construction/road	3,300	-	60,000
Mining	200	-	3,000
Car transport	Non-existent	12,000	20,000

Although this figure is too low, the data for the individual sectors of economic activities are good estimates. The labor force for the sector 'servants and government officials' is higher, however, for in Tehran alone 23,261 government officials were employed in 1928.[98]

The textile industry was one of the old branches of industry, in fact, the first modern European-type factory being established in Iran in the 1850s.[99] Although since that time textiles continued to play an important role in the Iranian economy, this branch of industry was still dominated by cottage industrial production. Even the spectacular growth of new factories in the 1930s could not change this. Between 1931 and 1938, not less than 29 large-scale textile mills were erected in Iran, both by state and private capital. The textile town of Iran was Isfahan with eight mills (5,372 workers), followed by Yazd with two (1,074) and Kerman (696) and Shahi (3,396) with one mill each.[100]

---

97. Abdullaev 1968, 87. His data for 1930 need correction, however. See e.g. Ferrier. 1982, 401, Table 10.4. According to the newspaper *Setareh-ye Sorkh*, (published in Germany) nr. 7, April 8, 1930, Chaqueri 1979, 290 the labor force in 1930 was composed of the following selected groups:

Oil-industry	39,000
Fisheries (seasonal)	3,000
Textile industry	2,000
Carpet factories	100,000
Dockers/ports North & South Iran	2,000
Rail and road construction	15,000
Drivers & assistants	15,000
Tobacco, tannery, chemical (dyeing) industry	4,400
Printers	1,000
Servants & government officials	15,000
Total	180,000

98. See Tehran Municipality 1310, 72.
99. See Floor 1991; Issawi 1971, chapter Industry.
100. Abdullaev 1968, 79; according to Mahrad 1978, 234 there were 37 textile mills in 1940; according to Korby there were 41 textile mills in 1941, Korby 1977, 60.

Related industries such as the hosiery, wool-cleaning and cotton-ginning industry also experienced great expansion of their production capacity and labor force. In the 1930s, a total of 32 smaller hosiery factories were established with a total labor force of 1,584 workers.[101] In the same period, 12 small wool cleaning factories were erected with 225 workers. The cotton-ginning industry, which had already flourished at the beginning of the 20th century, was mainly concentrated in Khorasan, the main producer of cotton. By 1931 there were already 26 factories in Iran with an average labor force of not less than 25 workers per plant.[102] By 1940 the number of cotton-ginning plants had become as high as 76 factories with a labor force of about 1,500 workers.[103]

After the failure of the sugar mill at Kahrizak at the end of the 19th century,[104] the government of Iran in 1930 decided to retro-fit this plant.[105] The promising results led to the construction of seven other sugar-mills which during the sugar season employed an average of 400 workers per plant; and 50 workers during the off-season. The total labor force of this sub-sector therefore amounted to 3,200 workers.[106]

Other agro- and food industries such as rice-cleaning, distilleries, flour-mills, soap-works, vegetable oil-pressing, paper-mills and tea-mills also came into being during the 1930s and provided employment for some 5,500 workers.[107] The grain silos built by the government to maintain a reasonable level of food security provided another 1,112 jobs.[108]

A new phenomenon was the chemical industry, which employed 2,044 workers,[109] while the military industry offered jobs to 1,500 workers.[110] There were 11 big tanneries in Iran which offered, according to Abdullaev, 3,000 jobs.[111] However, in 1941 the four big Tabriz tanneries alone gave employment to 5,000 workers,[112] so Abdullaev must have relied on earlier data when this industry was still in its infancy. Six match factories employed 1,000 workers by 1940.[113]

Quite spectacular was the rise in employment in the modern transport sector, both in the railways and in car transport. Neither of the two had existed in Iran before 1914.[114] Between 1935 and 1940, the railways doubled their labor force from 3,900 to 14,500. The car transport sector, which at the and of the 1920s employed some 12,000 drivers and

---

101. Abdullaev 1968, 79.
102. Abdullaev 1968, 79-90.
103. Abdullaev 1968, 80; Mahrad 1977, 224.
104. Issawi 1971, 307.
105. Salnameh 1314, 149.
106. Abdullaev 1968, 80, see also annex B.
107. Abdulleav 1968, 81.
108. Abdulleav 1968, 81, Mahrad 1978, 224.
109. Abdullaev 1968, 81.
110. Abdullaev 1968, 81.
111. Abdullaev 1968, 83.
112. FO 371/27249 (October 2, 1941). According to Abdullaev 1968, 83 only some 600 men were working in the tannery factories in Tabriz.
113. Abdullaev 1968, 82.
114. This statement is not completely true. There were two small railways In Iran, one from Tehran to Shah `Abdol-`Azim (nine miles) and another between Mahmudabad and Amol. Olson 1981; Millspaugh 1973, 277.

helpers for a car park of 8,600, had grown by 1939 to a size of 20,000 workers with a car park of 15,000.[115]

All these industrial activities required power, which was provided by diesel-engines. Nevertheless electricity also played an increasing role and 40 electricity plants employed 600 workers at the end of the 1930s.[116] Quite spectacular was the development of the railways, roads, factories and houses. From a mere 3,300 prior to 1914 this sector grew into one of the biggest employers of Iranian labor by 1939 with 60,000 jobs.[117]

Nevertheless, small-scale industries, and especially the carpet industry, continued to be the biggest source of employment. With the growth of industry the importance of this sector appears to have diminished in some cities, where workers preferred the higher wages in industry. In the rural areas, however, carpet weaving continued to play a dominant role until recent times. If we assume that four persons were working per loom,[118] the figure of 180,000 given by the Russian military estimate is still too low, the more so if we include the designers, master weavers and other ancillary operatives. An American estimate puts the number of the labor force in the carpet industry in 1940 at 250,000.[119]

In view of the fact that more than 50 per cent of the imports of Iran consisted of sugar, textiles, tea, and cement, it is not surprising that the thrust of the country's industrial development was in those areas. Why the government concentrated, for example, on the sugar industry, while private capital mainly invested in textiles is difficult to tell. It may have to do with the fact that the government had already owned a sugar-mill since 1891, while private investors already had experience with textile production. At all events, the government played an important role in the development of industry and allocated 20.9 per cent of its general budget to industry in 1941.[120] This was in line with the increased participation of the state in the economy in general shown by Table 3.12

TABLE 3.12: Number of looms in the carpet industry (urban and rural) 1940[121]

Town/area	Total number of looms	Town
Qom	1,000	1,000
Tabriz	1,000	1,000
Heriz	2,250	-
Hamadan	30,000	-
Malayer	2,500	100

---

115. Abdullaev 1968, 78.
116. Abdullaev 1968, 76.
117. Abdullaev 1968, 83.
118. Edwards 1949, 99; "Weaving is organised in the factories as follows: each loom has its ostad or head-weaver, who is expected to bring her own nakcheh nevis (lit. design writer) and shagirds or apprentices. A good ostad with her nakcheh nevis and two shagirds tie about 25.000 knots a day."
119. Ladjevardi 1981, 99 quoting R.Hare, December 12, 1935 (891.655/30) US National Archives.
120. Soheily 1950, 49.
121. Based on Edwards 1949.

Town/area	Total number of looms	Town
Bijar	1,000	-
Arak	10,000	1,500
Mashhad	3,000	2,000
Berjand	1,000	-
Kerman	3,950	1,745
Yazd	30	30
Isfahan	2,500	2,000
Kashan	12,000	4,000
Total	70,230	12,275

The state also represented about one-third of all investments in industry by 1941, which at that time was estimated to amount to some $ 260 million, over half of which had been invested by private capital.[122]

TABLE 3.13: Budget allocation per sector (million riyals)[123]

	1309/1930	%	1317/1938	%	1320/1941	%
National economy	78	19	702	46	1725	64
Defense	124	31	354	23	124	16
Administration	201	50	471	31	963	30

Table 3.14 shows that the number of registered companies increased from 93 in 1931 to 1,735 in 1940, while the corresponding numbers for industrial companies are 38 in 1931 and 460 in 1940. Although the number of industrial companies in Tehran was larger than those in the provinces (251 against 209) the level of investment per company was higher in the provinces. From Appendix B it is clear that light industries prevailed in Iran and that agro-industries prevailed in the provinces due to the need to be near the source of raw materials.[124] Market dependent industries were mainly concentrated in and around Tehran.

---

122. Issawi 1971, 379.

123. Soheily 1950, 48-49. It was only in April 1937 that the Council of Ministers decided to constitute an "Economic Council for the solution of the economic problems of the empire." In this council three non-official persons versed in economic affairs were included. FO 416/95, Seymour to Eden, April 24, 1937, f.72 (see also *Journal du Téhéran* of April 16, 1937 annexed to Ibid).

124. Many industries were also established because of the desire to bring industry and progress into the provinces. Apart from the case of Ahvaz mentioned above in note 80 there was, for example, the factory in Yazd where there was no cotton at all to spin or weave. *"elle ne doit son activité dans cette branche qu'à la force de l'atavisme et à l'esprit d'enterprise de ses habitants."* Alami 1939, 121; this attitude led the British embassy to make the following comment: "When the Shah orders a railway, a harbour or factory, one has the feeling that he does so, not because the estimates of the experts show that it will be profitable, but simply because he feels that every respected country had a railway &c.,

TABLE 3.14: Iran general and industrial companies registered (capital in thousand *riyals*)* [125]

	Teheran		Provinces		Total		Average Capital		
	No.	**Capital**	**No.**	**Capital**	**No.**	**Capital**	**Tehran**	**Provinces**	**Country**
1931/32	63	116,994	30	26,015	93	143,009	1,857	867	1,537
thereof industry	24	30,405	14	17,441	38	47,846	1,267	1,246	1,258
1935/36	377	570,296	504	275,763	881	846,059	1,512	547	960
thereof industry	151	92,100	111	135,634	262	227,734	610	1,222	869
1939/40	685	101,194	1,060	772,790	1,735	1,863,984	1,593	736	1,080
thereof industry	251	204,984	209	322,112	460	527,097	817	1,541	1,146
1944/45	1,101	2,347,883	1,194	1,507,449	2,195	3,855,331	2,346	1,263	1,756
thereof industry	378	725,442	257	779,891	635	1,505,334	1,191	3,035	2,370

The rates of exchange were: 1932: 1 dollar=29.60 riyals; 1936: 16.96 riyals; 1940: 18.34; 1945: 32.50

Although light industries prevailed, the government wanted to develop a heavy industry as well in connection with the construction of the trans-Iranian railway.

THE IRON WORKS

In 1927, plans had already been drawn up for a scheme to establish smelting works in the north to produce rails locally in connection with the go-ahead given by the *Majles* to start the construction of a railway between Khor Musa and Mohammareh. Out of the railway budget 4.5 million *tumans* were earmarked for this purpose and a German expert was engaged to make a feasibility study. Suitable iron had been found near Semnan, but no

---

and because it gives him an inferiority complex not to possess one also." FO 416/94, Butler to Eden. June 26, 1936, f. 97.
125. Grundwald and Ronall 1960, 213, Table; see also Soheily 1950, 43.

coal. The works would be dependent on the Shamshak coal mine, which was about 100 miles away, a special railway would have to be built between the mine and the works and, moreover, it was feared that the ore deposits at Semnan would be exhausted in 15 years, if the works were to operate at full capacity; so the project fell through at the end of 1928. In the beginning of that year, bids had actually been invited, despite the fact that the feasibility study had estimated the costs to be twice the amount which the *Majles* had earmarked, while Krupp even estimated the costs at 13 millions *tumans*.[126]

Although the government shelved the project for the moment it did not forget about it. In 1938 an agreement was reached, after much study and preparation, between Iran and a German consortium for the construction of two blast-furnaces with a daily production of 150 tons, a steel factory, a rolling-mill, a wire-drawing mill, a foundry, a wrought ironworks, a coke crusher, a power plant and the usual ancillary industries such as a lime plant, ammonia and benzol plan, and a tar distillation plant. The works had to be completed in three and a half years time and would employ 1,200 workers when working at full capacity. The original site was planned to be south of Tehran near the cement works, but Karaj was chosen instead, because of its more suitable water supply. A disadvantage, however, was that coal supplies for the power plant and the blast furnaces had to be transported from Shamshak and Zirab at about 35 miles distance.[127] In 1939 Reza Shah laid the first foundation stone,[128] and although work proceeded as planned the works were still unfinished in 1941 when the Allies invaded Iran. This meant, of course, that the whole project was jeopardized, for all relations with Germany were cut, which led to the demise of the project.[129]

Another area of activities which also received increasing attention was the power sector, the development of which was needed to energize the various industrial products.[130]

Conclusion

One cannot but be impressed by the progress made in Iran during one decade, the period between 1930 and 1941. A country which hardly possessed any industry had realized a $260 million industrial program by 1941 and a similar amount had been invested in its railways. It is true that the gap with countries like Egypt and Turkey had not been closed, but a big leap forward had been made.[131] Although the cost for this big leap had been high, both in economic and social terms, it is difficult to see how Iran could have made such progress at a lower price. The burden of this price had to be borne by the mass of the population, a burden which could not be off-set by the great number of new jobs that had been

---

126. FO 416/113, Annual Report 1928, f. 58.
127. Gielhammer 1940b, 122.
128. Farrokh 1347/1968, 416-16, 423-26 (picture on 425), 434-44.
129. Bharier 1971, 176, note 22.
130. See for further details Banque Mellié Iran. 1939 b.
131. See Issawi 1971, 379.

created.¹³² Although the majority of the population did not share the benefits of development which gave rise to criticism from the ranks of the intelligentsia,¹³³ nevertheless, there was, at the same time, pride in the fact that Iran had achieved that much progress under its own steam without foreign capital.¹³⁴ Although Reza Shah's regime stands out as the epitome of all that is bad in the works of later and present-day critics, he had, ironically, been able to realize many social-economic objectives of 19th-century reformers as well as those formulated by the Democrats in the first two decades of the 20th century.

---

132. "The condition of the laboring class has (and this is becoming rapidly more evident) deteriorated under crushing taxation on every necessity of life," FO 371/20048, f.177 (report by Daly on the situation in Eastern Persia; and Floor 1985a).

133. "A rising generation of young men who feel that these changes ought to bring them prosperity, but that they are not doing so, and therefore something is wrong." FO 371/20048, Butler to Eden, July 10, 1939, f. 175; see also Abrahamian 1982, 136f. on this subject in general.

134. "Complaints are heard against the government from time to time. These are the inevitable result of measures to secure increased revenue for the need of the fighting services and of the civil administratior.The merchant class in general is dissatisfied with the restrictions on trade and the interventions of Government as a trader. But as individuals many recognise that they are paying in taxation no more than before and that they are now living under more favourable conditions of security. And all educated classes realize with pride that the work of progress has been carried out without binding the country with foreign loans" FO 371/20048, Hoyland to Butler. Shiraz, April 15, 1936, f.136.

CHAPTER FOUR

FINANCE AND FOREIGN EXCHANGE FOR INDUSTRIALIZATION IN IRAN. 1310–1319 (1931/2-1940/1)[1]

PATRICK CLAWSON & WILLEM FLOOR

INTRODUCTION

Since the 1820s, Iranian policy-makers and reformists wanted to modernize the economic base of Iran and thus enable it to withstand and complete success fully with the European powers that encroached upon the country's economic and political independence. During the nineteenth century, various efforts were undertaken to achieve this objective. However, all these endeavors failed to achieve the desired result, owing to the weakness of the government, ignorance, lack of infrastructure, and the inability of the government to protect its nascent industry. With the advent of a strong, nationalist government after 1921 headed by Reza Khan, the drive to establish a modern industrial base, which would enable Iran to become more self-reliant, increased considerably.

In 1931, the government, disappointed by the lack of response by both national and foreign investors towards modern industrial development in Iran, decided to develop new industries as a means of reducing imports and supporting the foreign exchange position. This decision was further influenced by concern over deterioration in Iran's terms of trade due to a fall in export prices, and over decreasing availability of foreign exchange to pay for necessary imports. Industrialization was seen as a partial answer to those problems.[2] Although Iran's economic development in the 1930s was not based on an articulated central plan, there was nevertheless the conviction that economic development could only be

---

1 The views expressed herein are purely personal and do not necessarily represent the positions of the Institutions with which the authors are affiliated (the IMF and the World Bank, respectively).
2 See Floor 1984b, reprinted as chapter 3 here, for other sources used for this paper.

achieved through a compulsory rise in the share of national income withheld from consumption for investment purposes. Iran was partly successful in realizing its economic policy objectives, and in pulling itself up by its bootstraps; however, owing to the failure to grow proportionately through an increase in management effectiveness, better education of labor, better health and nutrition, and better political and social organization, Iran did not manage to accomplish a take-off into self-sustaining growth.

This article discusses two aspects of the Iranian development program of the decade beginning in 1310 (1931/32–1940/41) first, the extent of industrial development and the means by which the investments were financed and, second, the mechanisms for securing the foreign exchange needed for the investment program.

INDUSTRIAL DEVELOPMENT AND ITS FINANCING

While many new industries were created in this decade, the industrialization effort was not without its problems. These can partly be ascribed to start-up problems, partly to the lack of competition, but in general to the low level of development of the country. For example, the sugar industry had to face a shortage of beets and a low sugar content in the beets that were available. The result was a short milling season, such that the plants were utilized at a rate sometimes as low as ten per cent of the year. Underutilization explains why, in spite of duties on imported sugar, which amounted to over 200 per cent of the c.i.f. price, and the very low price of beets in relation to sugar prices, no profits were made. In 1936, the British consul in Shiraz estimated that the Marvdasht mill produced sugar at a cost which was 200 per cent higher than imported sugar.[3] The annual loss on sugar production therefore was substantial, amounting to 50-70 million riyals per annum between 1938 and 1941.[4] However, the growing demand for sugar during the 1930s was increasingly met by internal production. By 1940, 20 per cent of the total sugar consumption was met by national production as compared with only five per cent in 1933.[5]

A similar development can be observed in other industries. Iran had seven match factories by 1935; these factories produced some 85 per cent of total demand by the end of the 1930s, as compared with only 48 per cent in 1933. The cement factory supplied about 20 per cent of the national consumption.[6] The textile industry which was larger than that of Hungary or Yugoslavia by the end of the 1930s, was able to reduce the import of cotton yarn from 24 million kg to about 300,000 kg. Although less successful than with yarns, this branch of industry was also able to reduce the imports of textile fabrics by some 25 per cent during the same period. Another factor of importance was the development of the power sector in Iran.[7] In 1930 there was an installed capacity of about 600 kilowatts, while in 1939

---

3   PRO/FO 371/20834, f. 180 and PRO/FO 371/21900, f. 94–96.
4   Bharier 1969, 176
5   Gielhammer 1940, 22–23. Gielhammer was a director of the *Bank-e Melli* from about 1929 to 1936.
6   Gielhammer 1941, 27–29.
7   Gielhammer 1939, 263.

this had been increased to about 19,000 kilowatts. The total investment costs amounted to Rls. 77 million which were invested in almost equal parts by the state and private financiers.[8]

The single most important investment in the period was the construction of the trans-Iranian railroad, which played an important role in reducing transport costs and thereby encouraging production for distant markets, internal or external. The total cost of construction was about Rls 2,565 million (Table 4.1). Most of the financing came from the revenue produced by the monopolies on sugar and tea, including taxes of both domestic and imported sugar and tea. Reflecting the cautious character of public finance in this era, the government began collecting these taxes in 1925/26, well before construction on the railroad began; the unspent balance was accumulated in a fund which was not exhausted until 1935.[9] However, about twelve per cent of the railroad financing came from oil revenues, about sixteen per cent from the general government budget, and about fifteen per cent from bank borrowing.

TABLE 4.1: Iran: railroad construction finances 1925-39 (in millions of riyals)

Income:		2565
	Monopoly over sugar and tea	1405
	Government contribution in riyals	449
	Government contribution in sterling (1)	310
	Loans from domestic banks	370
	Other income	30
Expenses:		2554
	"Works"	2149
	Other	405
Deficit:		10

Source: *Bank-e Melli* Bulletin, May-November 1940.
(1) 3,846,681 pounds sterling.

Since public credit did not exist in Iran, the government took the initiative in stimulating private capital to invest in industrial development by facilitating the procurement of bank loans. Moreover, since foreign trade was becoming less profitable owing to exchange regulations and government monopolies, capitalists turned to industrial developments. As a result of a policy of import quotas and steep tariffs, Iranian industry faced reduced external competition and could therefore charge high prices. The profitability of industrial investment was therefore a significant inducement to expansion of industry. Profit rates as high as 80 per cent were reported; however, in general the profit rates reported to official sources were much lower. According to a survey conducted by the *Bank-e Melli* during the period 1313–16, the average rate of return on capital was 27 per cent for the 293 companies surveyed.[10] Although profits in trade were higher, averaging 34.5 per cent, this was not considered a serious obstacle to encouraging industrial development.

---

8 Bulletin November 1939, 536-537.
9 Moghadem 1956.
10 Government borrowing from banks injects liquidity into the economy; the assets of the banks rise by the amount lent to the government and so liabilities must rise by an equal amount. Liabilities are principally deposits, which are part of the money supply, but also include bank capital and some other items. Government expenditures financed by bank borrowing would be a pure 'inflation tax' in a perfectly functioning market economy.

The state not only took the initiative in spearheading industrial development; it was also the main investor in industries such as the sugar industry, silk-spinning industry, cement industry, chemical industry, and a metal/steel industry. As shown in Table 4.2 during the period 1310–19 the government invested a total of Rls 2,099 million in industry, of which Rls 1,857 million were in state industries. Private investors also followed suit, attracted by the profitable returns (Table 4.3). Most of the private money invested appears to have come from re-invested earnings and hoards of ready cash, rather than proceeds of sales of fixed assets such as land; however, there are few data to confirm this general impression. Thus, of a total of about Rls 2,800 million invested in industry during the 1930s, the state took the lion's share.

One method of financing industrial development is through government expenditure by increasing the money supply, that is, the government borrows from banks and the money supply rises by nearly the same amount. During the Reza Shah period, the Iranian government made use of the railway construction and of industrial development to do so.

Prior to the establishment of the *Bank-e Melli* in 1928, the ability of the Iranian government to finance its operations through bank borrowing was severely limited because the government had effectively no control over the money supply. The money supply consisted of: (a) silver coins whose face value approximated their silver content[11] and (b) paper notes issued by the Imperial Bank of Persia against backing in metal or hard foreign currencies.[12] Under such conditions, the money supply and the price level in Iran were heavily influenced by the fluctuations in the world price of silver. Since decisions about the issue of bank notes were made by a private bank based on commercial considerations alone, the Government was unable to manage monetary policy in a manner to promote economic development. While the initial motivation for the establishment of the *Bank-e Melli* was primarily nationalistic, the Government soon became aware of the now Bank's potential for

---

However, to the extent that the expansion of the money supply contributes to an increase in real economic activity as well as an increase in prices, the expenditure financed by the bank borrowing is an increase in prices, the expenditure financed by the bank borrowing is a Keynesian free lunch: government spending rises and no one's income must fall to pay for it.

11 Indeed, the function of the Mint was to melt coins for those who wished to realize their metal content or to stamp coins for those who provided the metal, as described in Yanegani 1935, chapter four.

12 The percentage of metallic backing required rose in steps with the amount of currency issued, from a minimum of one-third to a maximum of 100 per cent. The amount issued –Rls 163,3 million at the start of 1930/31- was generally below the level that required 100 per cent backing, owing to the conservative character of the Bank management, which was concerned about runs of the Bank (thanks to G. Jones for information on this subject).

financing development by expanding the money supply.[13] By the end of 1319, the currency outstanding was Rls 1,212 million and the gold and silver cover was Rls 720 million.[14]

TABLE 4.2: Iran: budget for investment by government in industry, 1310–1319 (in millions of riyals)

	1310	1311	1312	1313	1314	1315	1316	1317	1318	1319
Budget for investment in capital or private firms										
Annual	11	11	4	11	35	11	2	16	63	60
Cumulative	11	22	26	37	72	83	85	101	164	224
Ministry of Industry and Mines Budget										
Annual	-	16	23	20	66	73	145	315	454	745
Cumulative	-	16	39	59	125	198	343	658	1112	1857
Memorandum Items:										
General budget expenditures: (1)	373	481	509	903	1154	1300	1639	1528	2613	3111
Ministry of War	179	186	215	239	256	275	319	388	415	520
Transportation, communications	1	1	1	280	424	479	646	147	854	999
Industrial Investment	11	27	27	31	101	84	147	331	517	805
Other	182	267	266	353	373	462	527	662	827	787
General budget revenue (2)	373	500	508	712	831	1100	1360	1528	1930	3094
Public undertakings	33	41	43	53	69	71	142	181	256	435
Tobacco, opium, cotton goods	98	127	92	115	166	235	285	347	347	835
Tariffs, sugar, tea	103	108	151	261	261	400	473	422	502	508
Other	139	224	222	283	335	394	460	578	825	1316

Sources: League of Nations, 1938, and United Nations, 1951.
Note that data are not actual revenue and expenditures, only the budgeted levels. (1) Including extra budgetary expenditures on roads and railroads for 1313–16; excluding all other extra budgetary expenditures, which evidently included considerable military allocations. (2) Including the sugar and tea monopolies for 1313–16 when these were extra budgetary; excluding other extra budgetary revenue, which came primarily from oil income and a road tax.

---

13 The Law of 31 May 1930 ratified the accord of 13 May 1930 under which the Imperial Bank surrendered its right to issue bank notes in return for compensation of 200,000 pounds. Under the law of 13 March 1932, the *Bank-e Melli* was empowered to issue notes against 100 per cent cover, which it began to do on 21 March 1933. The cover requirement was changed to 60 per cent on 11 September 1934. The amount of notes issued was also governed by a ceiling set by law, raised roughly annually. The best description of these legal developments is by Pour Homayoun 1937, Part II. At the same time that the *Bank-e Melli* took over the note issue, the name of the currency was changed from the *qran* to the riyal; for simplicity, the new name is used throughout this article.

14 The currency outstanding includes currency in commercial bank vaults which is not part of the money supply; the foreign exchange figure includes metal held outside the country, which evidently was excluded by law from the currency cover. Both figures are from the Banque Mellie Bulletin.

TABLE 4.3: Iran: Increase in Share Capital in Private Industrial Firms, 1314–19
(in millions of riyals)

	1314	1315	1316	1317	1318	1319
Paid-in capital of existing firms	227.7	706.6	441.6	464.8	527.1	624.6
Increase in capital	-	-	20.9	22.7	33.2	57.3
Reduction in capital	-	-	-	2.4	3.8	2.5
Firms dissolved	-	-	330.6	33.6	17.4	25.2
Other (residual)	-	-	-	36.5	50.3	67.9

Source: *Bank-e Melli* Bulletin, annual article on "sociétés enregistrées." The reasons for the large movements in 1315 and 1316 are not known.

The exact magnitude of the Iranian government's borrowing from domestic banks in the 1930s is difficult to measure. For one thing, the concept of "government borrowing" is not clear-cut in countries such as Iran where the government owns many productive economic enterprises. To some extent credit to such an enterprise may be considered as comparable with commercial credit extended on the same basis as any other bank loan. However, banks may be motivated or pressured to lend to parastatal enterprises on implicit guarantee from the government, in which case the lending is essentially to finance government-sanctioned expenditure. Since most of the bank loans to parastatals in Iran in the 1930s went for long-term industrial finance of a sort the banks were not making available to other borrowers, that financing can best be considered to be lending to the government. The problem then arises of measuring bank lending to the government, including the parastatals. Unfortunately, in the 1930s, many of the modern concepts of macroeconomic analysis had not yet been developed, such that no country kept what are now known as monetary accounts. Furthermore, in Iran, the information available about the balance sheets of the banking system are rather fragmentary. Some information is available about the balance sheet of each of the major banks (Table 4.4), but these data do not provide details of government borrowing.[15]

The Iranian government evidently had no loans from domestic banks outstanding at the start of 1310 (March 1931). Data for the end of 1319 on the basis of modern concepts are available and indicate that, for the *Bank-e Melli*, net credit to government was Rls 480 million at the end of 1319, while credit to official entities was Rls 480 million.[16] To this can certainly be added the Rls 70 million loan for the railroad from the Agricultural and Industrial Bank. Lacking other data - on, for instance, loans to the government by other banks - let us take the sum of Rls 1,400 million as the increase in government borrowing during the decade 1310-1319.

---

15 Note how heavily-capitalized was the Imperial Bank, an indication of cautious management. Similarly conservative was the asset portfolio, which consisted largely of cash, foreign goods, and foreign securities. This was not the sort of bank that would willingly finance industrial expansion.

16 International Monetary Fund, International Financial Statistics, February 1950.

TABLE 4.4: Iran: Balance Sheet of Major Banks, 1933 (in millions of riyals)

	Total	Bank-e Melli	Imperial bank	Pahlavi Bank	Russo-Persian Bank
Assets:	1480.9	673.6	626.7	62.1	118.5
Cash, precious metals	558.8	422.0	109.2	15.6	12.0
Foreign securities	365.2	-	365.2	-	-
Loans	513.1	229.3	135.0	42.1	105.7
Other	43.8	22.3	16.3	4.4	0.8
Debits:	1480.9	673.6	626.7	62.1	118.5
Currency notes	195.0	195.0	-	-	-
Deposits	966.8	451.3	441.1	37.9	36.5
Capital and reserves	283.2	21.4	160.7	20.4	80.7
Other	35.9	5.9	24.9	3.8	1.3

Source: Malikpour, A. (1935) *Die Wirtschaftsverfassung Irans*, p. 94.

Such a sum can be compared with the railway construction cost of Rls 2,555 million and with the Government's total spending during the decade on the Ministry of Agriculture and Industry, as well as capital invested in firms, of Rls 2,081 million. Taking such sums as the proxy for the Government's physical development efforts, we would conclude that the government bank borrowing financed about 30 per cent of that effort.

ACQUIRING FOREIGN EXCHANGE FOR DEVELOPMENT

A major problem facing any less-developed country that wishes to embark on an ambitious industrial development program is the need to acquire foreign exchange. The capital goods required to establish now industries must in general be imported, as often must at least some of the inputs in the production process of the new industry. At the same time, the spending on the industrial development program creates jobs and increases incomes, such that consumers have more disposable income, which translates into more demand for all sorts of goods. While local products may be able to satisfy part of the extra demand, some of that demand is for imports, which further adds to the import requirements. Acquiring the foreign exchange for the extra import needs posits difficulties. The new industries under construction are of no use in generating foreign exchange until completed. In order to meet the expanded import needs, industrial development programs usually require some combination of foreign investment, foreign loans, reduction in the country's foreign exchange reserves and intensification of the export effort.

TABLE 4.5: Iran: Composition of imports. 1310–19 (1) (in millions of riyals)

	1310	1311	1312	1313	1314	1315	1316	1317	1318	1319	Total
Machinery	24	38	46	96	81	69	90	41	21	33	539
Metal goods	26	40	82	54	88	143	190	94	92	171	980
Vehicles	47	61	66	82	98	92	80	90	29	32	677
Cotton cloth	231	169	143	134	163	127	183	54	103	127	1434
Other	303	303	268	282	373	539	427	416	367	502	3780
Total	631	611	605	648	803	970	970	695	612	865	7410

Source: L'administration générale des douanes, *Statistique du commerce de l'Iran avec les pays étrangers*, various issues.

(1) Excluding monetary gold and non-dutiable imports.

Iran's industrialization during 1310–1319 (1931/32–40/41) was no exception to this general pattern. Imports rose from an annual average of Rls 616 million in 1310-12 to Rls 970 million annually in 1315-16 at the height of the railroad construction, declining to Rls 724 million in the last three years of the decade (Table 4.5), however, owing to some possible shortcomings in the data, caution must be used in interpretation.[17] The increase was particularly dramatic for metal goods, the category which included nearly all the railroad construction material. From an average of Rls 50 million in the first three years of the decade, metal goods imports rose to Rls 165 million in 1315-16, finishing off the decade at an annual average of Rls 119 million. In the same period, machinery rose from Rls 33 million to Rls 80 million before settling back to Rls 32 million. To some extent the increased imports for industrialization were compensated for by reduced imports of consumer goods produced by the new industries; in particular, the import of cotton goods fell from an average of Rls 132 million in the first three years of the decade to Rls 107 million in the last three years of the 1310s. However, the substantial rise in the overall import bill meant that Iran had to acquire considerably more foreign exchange than had been its wont - no small task in the midst of a world-wide depression that saw world trade fall about 80 per cent from its pre-depression peak.

The process by which Iran acquired the foreign exchange for its industrialization effort can be studied from two angles. First is the macroeconomic approach, namely, the overall pattern and direction of exports and finance, which shows what commodities Iran exported and to whom, and what amounts it borrowed and from whom. Second is the microeco-

---

17 Moghadem 1956, 86 and Khosropour 1956, 65 suggest that the Customs Service may have changed its method of valuing imports after 1936/37 in such a manner as to understate imports thereafter. Exports and imports through 1936/37 were valued at Iranian domestic wholesale prices, imports after 1936/37 were, according to these two, valued at the foreign price converted at the official exchange rate excluding the cost of the exchange certificate. However, the alternative data offered by Khosropour from bank sales of foreign exchange show the same trend as the Customs data, as does the Customs series on the volume of imports (corrected for price changes). Note that inflation, which may have become noticeable by the end of the decade, affects the data. All data on composition and direction of trade are for dutiable goods only, excluding imports for APOC, the government, and some exempt companies. Some customs data are, for 1311-15, for a fiscal year beginning June 22, most data, however, are available for the Iranian calendar year (the solar Hejri year) beginning March 22.

nomic approach, namely, the inducements that led businessmen to increase exports and economize on imports. These two topics will be considered in turn below.

THE PATTERN AND DIRECTION OF EXPORTS AND FINANCE

The additional foreign exchange for industrial development could come from several sources, which can be grouped into two basic categories: larger export earnings (the 'bootstrap' method) or foreign capital (the borrowing method). In order to determine whence the foreign exchange to meet the increased bill for imports came, information is needed on the balance of payments. Unfortunately, few data are available, partly because the very concept of a 'balance of payments' had not been developed by economists at this time, and the data that would be needed to construct the balance of payments were not collected. One particularly thorough scholar[18] made estimates for 1307 of many detailed items that permit presentation of a balance of payments along modern lines (Table 4.6), but nothing similar exists for any year between 1310 and 1319.

With regard to the oil sector, the Customs Service collected data on exports and imports of goods, but little is publicly available about profit remittances or the imports of services. The best way to estimate the net contribution of the oil sector is to add two elements: (i) direct payments to the Iranian government of about 33 million pounds or, converting at the official exchange rate for the applicable year, Rls 2,600 million; and (ii) purchase of goods and services in Iran, to the extent these were not met with riyals generated from the sale of petroleum products in the local market. Widely different estimates of such purchases are available;[19] a lower-bound figure would appear to be about Rls 600 million.

Non-oil trade data are available from the Customs Service, including figures on non-dutiable imports by diplomats, the government, and some industries. However, in addition to the qualifications noted earlier, further complications exist in that certain categories of goods were excluded from the Customs data,[20] particularly caviar exports and arms imports. There may have been some imbalance in the smuggled trade as well. For those reasons, caution indicates one should include Rls 100 million for net unrecorded trade.

The capital and services account are more difficult to measure. Service expenditures were evidently rising during this period, owing to increased employment of foreign consultants and to more Iranians studying abroad. Other elements in the services account included profit remittances by the Imperial Bank, pilgrimage costs and, on the income side, remittances, e.g., from Iranians in Kuwait. Anecdotal evidence suggests that the gov-

---

18 Doevel 1933.
19 Adli 1960, cites data from banks to suggest APOC purchases of riyals in the five years 1335–39 were Rls 385 million. Moghadem 1956, uses data on the labor force and on the volume of petroleum sold locally to estimate APOC's indirect contribution of foreign exchange as the equivalent of Rls 1213 million for 1930-39.
20 Bulletin June 1958, estimating caviar sales in 1311-17 as Rls 85 million per annum. Gray 1938, 4, cites arms sales of 3 million pounds (about Rls 240 million) in 1934-36, which was evidently the main period of arms purchase.

ernment effectively restricted the flow of funds out of the country,[21] so the imbalance on the services account may have been contained to a relatively modest Rls 400 million. The balances on the bilateral accounts with Germany and the USSR can be derived from the trade data, adjusted in Germany's case to include the hard currency payments made by Iran in 1938/39. The government capital account reflects the repayment in 1933 of a 490,000 pound loan from the British Indian government made during World War I.[22] The government appears to have made no reduction in its other outstanding foreign loans (from 1911 for 1.125 million pounds) nor to have borrowed abroad. With regard to private capital, the *Bank-e Melli* estimated that during the 1934 crisis alone, Rls 200 million in unrecorded silver left the country.[23] As for foreign exchange reserves, Iran began the decade with about Rls 500 million in reserves (2 million pounds sterling in gold in London and the rest in silver in Iran) and ended with about Rls 1,200 million (Rls 311 million in gold, Rls 409 million in silver and US$30 million in foreign exchange).[24]

TABLE 4.6: Iran. Balance of payments. 1307 (1928/29) (In millions of riyals)

Oil sector:		79
	Exports	1038
	Imports	-80
	Services, profit remittances (1)	-879
Non-oil trade:		-119
	Exports-recorded	477
	-unrecorded (net)	81
	Imports	-671
Services and transfers (net):		1
	Diplomatic missions in Iran	10
	Iran's expenditure for diplomats and students	-13
	Travel (net)	-3
	Debt service	-3
	Remittances	15
	Other (net)	-5
	Current account	-39

21 Mahrad 1979, 453, reprints a letter from the British Legation discussing inter alia the difficulty of sending money out of Iran.

22 The foreign debt is discussed in League of Nations, Economic Intelligence Service 1938, 43, and United Nations 1951, *Public Finance Information Papers,* No.4, 52; see also Simmonds 1935, 7. The 1911 loan was from the Imperial Bank of Persia, but from the London office, and so it was a foreign loan. In addition, the Imperial Bank may have lent to the Iranian government in foreign exchange, which is similar to a foreign loan.

23 Bulletin March 1937.

24 Bulletin various issues, and, for foreign exchange holdings in 1940, IMF, International Financial Statistics. February 1950.

Capital account:		15
	Foreign investment	15
Overall balance:		-24
Financing:		24
	Deposits in the UK of AIOC payments	-29
	Exports of gold and currency	3
	Imports of gold and currency (2)	-63
	Drawdown of railroad reserve	52
	Other (residual)	61

Source: Doevel, H. (1933) *Persiens auswärtige Wirtschaftsbeziehungen*. Hamburg: Friedrichsen, de Gruyter, und Co., pp. 63–64.

Putting together the information cited above, a balance of payments for the decade 1310-19 can be produced (Table 4.7). The picture that emerges is that Iran's relatively high import bill in this period was met by export earnings, not by foreign capital, and that furthermore the contribution of the oil sector was somewhat limited. Iran's export earnings during the 1930s were remarkable in the context of a worldwide contraction in trade that reduced the volume of goods traded by some 60 per cent.[25] The decade began with trade shrinking on the same pattern as for other countries: the value of exports fell from Rls 702 million in 1310 to Rls 522 million in 1311, and Rls 466 million in 1312. Then the turn-around began, with exports rising to Rls 513 million in 1313 and averaging Rls 660 million in 1314-17, before closing out the decade at Rls 804 million in 1318 and Rls 925 million in 1319.

The reasons for the growth in Iran's exports after 1933/34 (1312) are not hard to find (Table 4.8). Trade with Germany grew rapidly, from 1313 until 1319, the average annual growth rate in exports to Germany was 47 per cent; however, the trade data may overstate the growth in trade somewhat.[26] Exports to Germany went from less than nine per cent of Iran's global exports to 48 per cent, despite the difficulties of transportation owing to the war in 1319 (1940/41). Furthermore, the increase in exports to Germany seems to have been largely a net addition to the total export bill, not a diversion of products that otherwise would have found a different market. Exports to Germany were primarily fruits (especially raisins) and wool, not cotton and carpets; the new German market allowed Iran

---

25 World imports in constant prices went from 100 in 1929 to 57.4 in 1931 and 40.6 in 1938, League of Nations, Monthly Bulletin of Statistics, May 1940.

26 Prior to 1935, merchants had little incentive to pay much attention to the destination or origin listed on the customs forms, and some goods shipped between Iran and Germany through the USSR may have been listed as trade with that country; on the other hand, the German government was concerned that the Soviets were falsely claiming some Soviet exports were of Persian origin, evidently to receive payment in hard currency rather than under the Soviet-German payments agreement (Mahrad 1979, 44). Comparison of Iranian and German trade data is difficult for all the reasons that usually afflict such numbers: timing, classification, treatment of freight costs, etc. After 1935, it is not clear by what method the Customs Service valued goods in German-Iranian trade, use of the official exchange rate would have considerably overstated the trade.

to expand its wool exports from under Rls 30 million per annum. In the first four years of the decade to an average Rls 140 million in the last two years.

TABLE 4.7: Iran: Balance of Payments, 1310–19 (1931/32–1940/41) (in millions of riyals)

Oil sector:		3200
	Exports	14300
	Imports	-2100
	Other foreign currency costs, including profits	-9000
Non-oil trade:		-1300
	Exports	6600
	Imports – dutiable	-7400
	-non-dutiable	-400
	Net unrecorded trade	-100
Services and capital:		-1200
	Services (net)	-400
	Account with Germany	-350
	Account with USSR	300
	Official capital (net)	-50
	Private capital (net) (1)	-700
Change in reserves:		700

Source: *L'administration générale des douanes, Statistique du commerce de l'Iran avec les pays étrangers,* various issues. (1) Excluding petroleum and caviar.

TABLE 4.8: Iran: Direction of Exports, 1310-19 (1)

	1310	1311	1312	1313	1314	1315	1316	1317	1318	1319	Total
Germany	63	43	66	44	83	138	199	290	393	442	1762
USSR	251	117	90	203	186	270	235	37	-	117	1506
Other	338	362	310	266	377	269	237	323	411	365	3308
Total	702	522	466	513	646	677	671	650	804	925	6576

Source: *L'administration générale des douanes, Statistique du commerce de l'Iran avec les pays étrangers,* various issues. Excluding petroleum and caviar.

Similarly, fruit exports (mostly raisins and dates) averaged under Rls 70 million per year in 1310-13, but over Rls 170 million in 1318–19. Germany was the destination for 67 per cent of the fruit and 74 per cent of the wool exported in 1318–19. Germany's motivation for the expansion of trade with Iran was primarily the need to secure access to markets for her industrial output and guaranteed sources of raw materials, in the context of the enormous barriers to free trade erected in the 1930s and in view of Germany's lack of colonies. In each year's negotiations with the Iranians under the trade agreement in the late 1930s, the German side was eager to see a considerable all-round expansion of trade. The German government had adopted Schacht's *Neue Plan* in September 1934, under which German foreign trade was to be expanded through bilateral trading agreements, in view of the difficulties of access to the world market. The *Neue Plan* was in many ways an extension of the statist approaches to development which had long been popular in German academic and political circles. Within this context, Germany and Iran entered into a bilateral trading agreement in October 1935, replacing the unilateral bilateralism imposed by Germany in July 1934.[27] Under the bilateral agreements, any excess of exports over imports by one country (Iran or its trading partners, Germany and the Soviet Union) was deposited in a special account and could not be used for any purpose other than imports from the country with a deficit. Indeed, it was this feature of the arrangements that made them into clearing agreements, quite different from the sort of bilateral trade accords so frequently signed now by Eastern and Third World countries, which simply specify a target for trade and may entail some procedures to encourage reaching the target. After the signing of the German-Iranian trade agreement the German government explicitly re-oriented trade from hard currency countries to Iran; for instance, Germany shifted its purchase of dried fruits from California, Iraq and Southern Europe to Iran.[28]

The bilateral agreement with the USSR - signed in 1931 and renewed in 1935 - also aided the expansion of Iran's export, but nowhere near as much as the accord with Germany.[29] For one thing, the USSR had long been a major trading partner of Iran, so the bilateral agreement did not open up a new market for Iran, although of course the Soviet Union during the 1930s was turning firmly away from foreign trade and towards an autarchic policy that would have led to a sharp decline in trade with Iran had there been no bilateral agreement. In addition, exports to the USSR essentially halted in 1317-18; indeed, in the latter year, total trade with the Soviet Union (exports and imports) was Rls 7 million. Furthermore, the commodities exported to the USSR were to a larger extent than with Germany, goods that might have had a reasonable market elsewhere. For instance, Iran's cotton exports went entirely to the USSR in 1315, while in 1316, the Soviets took Rls 84 million out of the Rls 93 million total.

In so far as Iran ran a deficit under the agreements, Iran was effectively financing imports with a loan, that is, using foreign capital to meet the import needs created by the industrialization program. During the years of peak railway construction, 1314-16, Iran used this mechanism to finance part of its record import bill. The total import bill in this period was Rls 2,743 million, while exports earned Rls 1,994 million, or 27 per cent less. Over one-third of the Rls 749 million gap was made up by deficits in the clearing account with Germany for Rls 136 million and with the USSR for Rls 142 million. In addition, Iran appears to have used the bilateral payments account to pay for some services from Germany, in that the reported imbalance in October 1938 had reached RM 34 million, or somewhat over Rls 230 million.[30]

---

27 From July 1934, non-oil trade with Iran largely had to be conducted through ASKIs (*Ausländersonderkonten für Inlandzahlungen*), a system under which each firm that exported to Iran received credits it could use to finance imports from Iran. The effect was to create great difficulties for Iranian exporters, in that those German firms which sold to Iran were not necessarily in a line of trade that would lead them to want Iranian goods. See Mahrad 1979, 54–55, and Glaesner 1976, 213–28.
28 Mahrad 1979, 47.
29 Khosropour 1956, 30.
30 Floury 1977, 243.

The imbalance in the account with the USSR was not corrected before the war, owing in part to the breakdown in the trade agreements in 1938/39-1939/40 (Table 4.9). On the other hand after 1937 Germany became intensely concerned about the imbalance in trade, and Iran was subject to increasing pressure to address the issue. Beginning during the visit of *Reichsbank* President Schacht to Iran in November 1936, discussions were held about a large loan to the Iranian government; however, the Iranian side saw this loan as a means of financing additional imports of industrial equipment, not settling the existing imbalance.[31] After negotiations with Ripken from the Foreign Ministry in April and October 1938, Iran agreed to pay 800,000 pounds to settle RM 25 million of the deficit in the payments account.[32] Since 800,000 pounds was equivalent at the official rate of exchange to only RM 9.3 million, Germany in effect agreed to a discount in order to obtain hard currency.

TABLE 4.9: Iran: Foreign Trade in 1310–19 (1931/32–1940/41) (in millions of riyals)

	Germany	USSR	US	UK	Other	Total
Exports except oil:	1762	1506	766	669	1873	6576
Carpets	187	-	522	241	399	1349
Cotton	233	492	-	-	138	863
Fruits	500	492	-	93	371	1090
Wool	338	681	244	335	916	2680
Other	504	681	244	335	916	2680
Imports subj. to duty:	1569	1844	614	693	2690	7410
Tea	-	-	-	-	587	587
Sugar	-	416	-	-	329	745
Cotton cloth	76	629	6	199	524	1434
Machinery	249	42	5	58	185	539
Metal goods	392	226	72	83	207	980
Vehicles	135	28	371	68	75	677
Other	717	503	160	285	783	2448
Balance:	193	-338	152	-24	-817	-834
Memorandum items:						
Oil export	195	10	3	7361	5704	14339
Non-dutiable imports	-	-	-	-	-	2450

Source: *L'administration générale des douanes, Statistique du commmerce de l'Iran avec les pays étrangers,* various issues.

From the material relating to the negotiations of 1937-39, the clear impression emerges that Reza Shah was eager to expand and deepen ties with Germany in order to secure arms and industrial equipment, particularly a steel mill. He evidently saw the railroad construction as only the first stage in an all-round development effort - an effort which

---

31 The first proposal was for a loan of RM *(Reich Mark)* 10 million, later proposals were for larger sums. See Fleury 1977, 241-43, and Glaesner 1976, 265–85.
32 Glaesner 1976, 265–85. The payment was in two installments: October 1938 and January 1939.

would require continuing high import levels, financed through expansion of exports, but also through loans and/or imbalance in bilateral trading agreements. The Iranian government arranged for a loan to pay for much of the cost of construction of a steel mill by the German firm *Demag*; that is, the imports would not be billed to the payments agreement.[33] The German government was not pleased either by the construction contract or the financing mechanism; it was clearly concerned about the effect on the preparations for war. Germany pushed hard for increased exports from Iran to Germany while holding back on shipments from Germany, particularly of arms and equipment for the steel mill.[34] The effort was so successful that Iran built up significant positive balances in the payments account: RM 40 million, or about Rls 290 million by November 1939.[35] The result was frustration of Reza Shah's plans for industrial development.

Despite the problems in trade at the end of the decade, much of Iran's industrial development utilized German machinery, although the Soviets report that 90 per cent of the new industrial installations were of German origin may be exaggerated.[36] For example, most of the match factories were of German make, while in the power sector, some 70 per cent of the equipment was German, although the largest plant with 32 per cent of the installed rapacity was produced in Czechoslovakia.[37] The cement plant was completely equipped with German machinery.[38] The grain silos, however, were all Russian-made and the modern cotton ginneries were of US origin.[39] In the most important industry, textiles, 60 per cent of the spindles were of German origin and the remainder was supplied from UK sources.[40] At the end of 1933, four of the five cotton mills were of German origin and none British. By the end of 1936, a further ten mills had been built of which two used German equipment and seven British. In the next two years (1937–38), an additional nine mills were built; six with German equipment and three with British. At the end of 1938, Iran then had 24 mills, of which twelve had German equipment and ten British.

In addition to its importance as a trading partner, Germany also had a considerable impact on policy formation. The first and second directors of the *Bank-e Melli*, Dr. Lindenblatt and Mr. Gielhammer, were German; the Bank employed 50 Germans.[41] The impact of German advisers and German étatist concepts was said to be particularly great on Ali Akbar Davar, who held several ministerial posts over time, including that of Minister of Finance.[42]

---

33 Mahrad 1979, 87-106. After the outbreak of the war, the British counter-offered with loans of up to 5 million pounds; nothing came of this proposal either.
34 Mahrad 1979, 111.
35 Moghadem 1956, 209-11. The trade data roughly agree, if the hard currency payment of Rls 168 million is added to the trade deficit for the decade of Rls 136 million.
36 Fleury 1977, 249.
37 Gielhammer 1941, 28; Bulletin November 1939, 542–43, 549.
38 Gielhammer 1941, 27.
39 Gielhammer 1940, 24.
40 Gielhammer 1939, 263.
41 Fleury 1977, 213-14, Mahrad 1979, 248ff. and Glaesner 1976, 202.
42 Fleury 1977, 230. However, owing to the relative unfamiliarity with the German language, only 142 of the 1,523 students in 1932 were in Germany, compared with 1,031 in France, Fleury 1977, 215.

INDUCING BUSINESS TO EXPORT AND ECONOMIZE ON IMPORTS

The three principal policy tools available to a government that wishes to induce business to export and to economize on imports are: to go into business itself, to establish a system of controls that restrict imports and/or compel exports, and to adopt policies (exchange rate and tax policies, especially) that make exports profitable and imports expensive. Further research is needed to establish the relative importance of each of these instruments in Iran during 1310–1319. The preliminary evidence available suggests that the main effect came from the pricing policies with an important contribution from the government-run enterprises.

The Iranian government during the 1930s established a variety of enterprises to encourage exports. In particular, the government arrogated to itself the right to export opium, caviar, rice, and some other commodities including, for a period in the mid-l930s, rugs and dried fruits.[43] It is unclear to what extent such government-owned monopolies served to increase export earnings. Indeed, the experience of other countries suggests that sometimes government monopolies reduce exports, in part because the monopolies are not always particularly efficient. The casual impression is that the Iranian export monopolies may have increased government revenue, but they seem not to have had a major impact on stimulating exports, except in the case of some non-traditional exports.[44] With regard to import substitution, the record of the newly-established government enterprises is unclear, again because of the general inefficiency of the operations.

Besides entering into production itself, the Iranian government also used direct controls to regulate foreign trade. Direct controls should be distinguished from exchange rate regulations that raised the prices of foreign exchange. The former involved import quotas for each category of goods established at the beginning of the year, with merchants having to apply to the Ministry of Commerce for licenses which were counted against the quotas. The latter entailed requirements, described below, about the purchase of foreign exchange which raised its price. If the operative constraint were the direct controls, then merchants would direct their energies primarily towards securing licenses rather than foreign exchange. All the dissertations and UK economic reports consulted described the process in quite the opposite terms: merchants were principally concerned with acquiring the necessary foreign exchange. Indeed, one long-time employee of the *Bank-e Melli* suggests, "issue of import licenses by the Ministry of National Economy appeared superfluous."[45] However, one effect of the controls was to give a considerable advantage to merchants in Tehran, who were able to pursue applications much more easily than could their provincial colleagues.[46] Even setting aside 20 per cent of the import licenses for the

---

43 Bulletin February 1938, 1-45 and March 1938, 28-63; also Alami 1939.

44 E.g., the monopoly on dried fruit may have helped introduce modern packing methods and stricter quality control (Adli 1960, 63, and Bulletin May and June 1939).

45 Khosropour 1956, 55. While import licenses may not have been particularly significant another form of direct controls may have been more important, namely, direct government orders to parastatals (especially government owned firms with monopoly rights on imports of some goods) to limit imports.

46 Khosropour 1956, 281, and PRO/FO 371/21889, f. 269.

merchants from outside Tehran, the 1310s evidently witnessed a considerable migration of merchants to Tehran.

With regard to the use of the price mechanism to limit imports, one element of the government's policy was the increase in tariffs. The proclamation of tariff autonomy was more than an expression of nationalism; it was also a major economic initiative. While there are no easy means to compare the average rates under two different sets of tariffs, the *Bank-e Melli* estimated that on average the new customs rates were 20 per cent above the old.[47] The effect on revenue from import duties was dramatic (Table 4.10). In the period 1310-14, customs duties averaged 21 per cent of durable impost while in the period 1315-19, they averaged 38 per cent - an effective fourteen per cent price increase.

Unfortunately, little information is available on the revenue from different imports. For 1319, the Customs Administration reported that Rls 193 million out of the total import duties of Rls 325 million came from sugar, a truly astounding percentage. Since total imports of sugar were only Rls 87 million, this figure implies that the effective tariff rate on sugar was 222 per cent. Such a high tax rate is evidence that the domestic sugar industry needed a great deal of protection and was not very efficient, as suggested earlier. In addition, the government levied a heavy tax on sugar, which applied to domestic and imported sugar alike, with the result that the consumers were paying a price well in excess of the world market level.

TABLE 4.10: Iran: Import Duties, 1310–19 (1931/32 - 1940/41) (1)

	1310	1311	1312	1313	1314	1315	1316	1317	1318	1319
In millions of riyals	101.9	144.1	130.6	148.5	170.9	263.0	340.7	288.4	289.8	324.7
As percent of imports	16.1	23.6	21.6	22.9	21.3	27.1	35.1	41.5	47.4	37.5

Source: *L'administration générale des douanes, Statistique du commerce de l'Iran avec les pays étrangers,* various issues. (1) Import duties are *"droits d'entrée"* only; imports are dutiable imports only.

Besides taxes, the other major price mechanism which discouraged imports was the exchange rate. Through 1929, a freely fluctuating market determined the value of the riyal, primarily on the basis of its silver content. In response to the collapse of silver prices in the fall of 1929, the Government established an official exchange rate.[48] Despite periodic adjustment, the official exchange rate remained generally out of line with market forces during the decade of the 1310s. The official rate was primarily used for government transactions, meaning mostly royalty payments by the Anglo-Iranian Oil Company and imports for the government. The bulk of trade, however, was conducted at more depreciated exchange rates. The regulations governing private trade underwent frequent major changes, suggesting that the government was never entirely satisfied with the limited

---

47 Bulletin August 1936, 59.
48 Yaganegi 1935, 48.

control it was able to exercise over private imports.⁴⁹ As established by the law of 11 March 1931, implementing the government 'monopoly' on foreign trade, the essence of the system was a free market in foreign exchange, in which the price readily adjusted.⁵⁰ The free market in foreign exchange generally took the form of a system of exchange certificates: while exporters had to surrender their foreign exchange, exports earned certificates which would then be sold to importers, who could use the certificates to purchase foreign exchange at the official rate from banks. The free market exchange rate was then the sum of the official rate and the premium for the export certificates. At times, the government attempted to control the price of the certificates - which basically had the effect of driving the market in certificates into illegality.⁵¹ Generally, the government allowed exporters of certain categories of goods (non-traditional exports which the government wanted to encourage) to keep a higher percentage of their export proceeds, which they could then sell directly rather than through the indirect mechanism of the market in certificates.⁵²

Table 4.11 gives the evolution of the official and the free market exchange rates. The riyal appreciated somewhat in the first part of the decade, in part because the price of silver (the main backing for the riyal) increased from 17.3 pence per standard ounce in 1311 to 27.8 pence in 1314, before dropping back to about 20 pence in 1315, where it remained for the rest of the decade. As the government's development expenditures rose sharply in 1315-16, the exchange rate came under pressure, with about a year's lag. Between 1314 and 1317, the value of the riyal was slashed in half, which must have been a not inconsiderable inducement to import restraint. However, it is not clear what effect the free market exchange rate had on the trade under the bilateral agreements with Germany and the USSR. It seems that, overall, the German mark was overvalued relative to the riyal, such that Iranian producers had a strong incentive to export to Germany, while Iranian importers would take advantage of imports from Germany only in so far as marks were available at the official rate without having to pay the premium for export certificates needed for trade with other countries.⁵³

---

49 This period is described in Yanegani 1935, Chapter 4.

50 While the regulations are set out in successive issues of the Banque Mellie Bulletin, the best summary is in Khosropour 1956, 9-29 and 36-73.

51 After attempting to set the price of exchange certificates from July 1934 onwards, the government set up a system of exchange certificates in January 1938. Since certificates, which traded freely at a fluctuating rate, were required for imports, the new system mirrored the old (Khosropour 1956, 48-56).

52 The depressing effect of the less attractive exchange rate on traditional exports is set forth vigorously in Moghadem 1956, 165-67.

53 The evidence for the relative overvaluation of the mark comes from the exchange rate of 20 riyals per mark which prevailed in 1929 when both currencies were freely convertible. By contrast, the exchange rate specified under the bilateral accords was between 6 and 7 riyals per mark. Such a rate could have been economically justifiable if inflation in Germany in the 1930s had been much higher than in Iran; however, there is no evidence this was the case.

TABLE 4.11: Iran: Exchange Rates, 1310-19 (1931/32 – 1940/41) (in riyals per pound sterling)

	1310	1311	1312	1313	1314	1315	1316	1317	1318	1319
Official exchange rate	90.00	103.00	84.50	78.67	83.31	80.50	80.50	80.50	77.20	65.64
Free market rate	100.00	103.00	84.50	78.67	83.31	97.50	120.00	168.60	179.90	172.48

Sources: Bank Melli Bulletin, various issues, and Khosropour, 1956. Dr. Khosropour, who cites no source, was a long-time employee of the Bank Melli and its Vice- Governor in 1950-51.

CONCLUSION

The financing for Iran's large-scale industrialization and development effort in the 1310s would appear to have come primarily from domestic sources, although this conclusion must remain tentative. A major component of the financing was the inflation tax, made possible by the active monetary policy followed by the *Bank-e Melli*. In addition, the government increased its revenue through substantial increases in tariff rates and through the pricing policy followed by the sugar and tea distribution monopolies. To some extent financing may have come from re-invested earnings; however, in public enterprises, unlike private ones, the rate of profit was quite low during the period. In addition, during the peak years of railroad construction, some of the financing for the development effort came from overseas in the form of negative balances in the payments agreements with the USSR and Germany.

The foreign exchange requirements for the development effort were heavy, as the new industries and the rail road required large-scale imports of capital equipment. The principal source for the necessary increase in foreign exchange came from greater exports, not from controls on consumer imports nor from foreign loans. The growth in export earning, which went against the strong trend towards contracting world trade during the decade, came largely in the trade with the Soviet Union and Germany and seems to have been due to bilateral payments agreements with those to countries. The principal encouragement to businessmen to increase exports and economize imports, both with regard to the hard currency countries and to the USSR and Germany, seems to have been the exchange rate, operating through the system of export certificates.

Appendix A

List of existing factories in Iran (1311/1932)

Location	Type	Owner/Founder
Tehran	Spinning mill	Sani` al-Dowleh
	Leather/tannery Baghshah	Amir Monazzam
	Gunpowder Parchin	State
	Gunpowder Shemran	State
	Arsenal	State
	Mint	State
	Electricity	Hajji Hoseyn Aqa Mahdavi
	Majles printing office	State
	Soap making	Hajji Rabi` Aqa
	Soap making	Gholam Reza Darugar
	Soap making	Deli Company
	Shoe making	Raghibiyan, Kazeruni
	Paint making	State
	Repair plant	Tramway & Railway Comp.
	Car repair plant	State
	Glass making	Hajji Mehdi Zajjaji
	Glass making Chaleh Hesar	Hajji Moh. `Ali `Arab
	Cloth making (hand)	Mohtasham al-Saltaneh
	Cloth making (hand)	Aqa Moh. Kashi
	Hosiery	Qods Jorrabafi Comp.
	Hosiery	Meshkvat Jorabchi
	Hosiery	Mirza `Ali Akbar Omidvar
	Hosiery	Mirza Moh. Soheyli
	Wheat & lime mill	Karim Khan Amir Khosrovi
	Lime pounding	Mirza `Abdollah Nezami
	Steam mill	Esma`il Khan; Moh. Aqa Khorram; Mirza `Ali Khan
	Tannery	Mr. Kentjens
	Tannery	Arbab Shahryar Jamshidi
	Sugar mill Kahrizak	State
	Match factory	Hajji Moh. Rahim; Hajji Moh. Baqer Khoy'i
	Twining	Hajji Yusof Aqa Qazvini; Hajji Reza Tobi
	Cloth making	Karbala'i Hoseyn Aaqa Tabrizi

Location	Type	Owner/Founder
	Wool spinning	Hajji Taqi Jorabchi
	Wool carding & steam mill	`Abdollahzadeh
	idem	Mashhadi `Ali Aqa Jurabchi
	Tannery Iran	Ramazani va Qolipur
	Wool spinning	Hajji `Ali Moh. & Hajji Moh. Baqer
	Steam mill	Hajji Hoseyn Ghaji
	Wool spinning	Hajji `Abbasqoli Hanifehzadeh
	Glass making	Shafraru
	Hosiery	Mirza `Abdol-Rahim; Rahim Aqa
	Hosiery Shams	`Ali Aqa Mashinchi; Shams & Bros.
	Cigarette paper	Hajji `Ali Asghar
	Soap & cigarette *Mir*	Shahgeldiyan c.s.
	Almond oil press	Jabril Shakiyan Salmasi
	Electricity	Private company
Ardabil	Electricity	Private company
Yazd	Wool weaving	Ostad Gholam San`ati
	Hosiery/clothes making	Akhavan Gorji
	Hosiery/rice mill	Hajji `Abo'l-Qasem Gorji; Rasuli
Shiraz	Paint	State
	Carpentry plant	State
	Smithery	State
	Electricity	Private company
Isfahan	Spinning & weaving mill	Hajji Mohammad Hoseyn Kazeruni
	Electricity	Mirza Fazlollah Khan Dehdashti
	Tobacco & cigarette factory	Mirza Hasan Khateybi
	Cigarette factory	Aqa Moh. Qasem Rashti
	Cigarette factory	Khajik
	Cigarette factory	Sayyed Moh. Javad Kasa'i
	Cigarette factory	Shams Comp.
Qazvin	Motor mill	Tasevanderuni Yunani
	Electricity/iron plant	Hajji Rahim Aqa Qazvini
	Yarns, hosiery, soap	E`temad Comp.; Kuros
	Oil press	Ghaffari Bros.
	Wool washing & weaving	Not specified
Bandar Lengeh	Steam flour mill	Hajji `Abbas `Ali Moqim Lengeh
	Water lifting (wind)	Hajji Moh. Rashid Fekri
	Lemonade and soda	Hajji Moh. `Abdollah Boluki

Location	Type	Owner/Founder
	Steam flour mill	Ostad Moh. Kazeruni
	Water lifting (steam)	Aqa Sayyed Moh. Kamel
	Lemonade and soda	Sina Azari
Naseri	Electricity	Mirza Hoseyn Khan Movaqqer
	Oil-press & soap making	Hajji Aqa Mashallah Dezfuli
	Ice-making, 5 plants	Various persons
	Steam mills, 12	Various persons
Bandar `Abbas	Electricity & ice-making	Hajji Sheikh Ahmad Gallehdari
Jask	Electricity	Telegraph Office
	Electricity	Wireless
Mohammareh	Electricity	Hajji Jasem Bohrani
	Ice making	David Mark + Aqa Asadollah Badi`
	Ice making	Hajji Jasem Bohrani
	Motor mill	`Abud Molla Ahmad + Hajji Sa`d Me`mar
	Motor mill	David Mark
	Motor mill	Hajji Jasem Bohrani
	Motor mill	Mirza Jalal Movaqqar
Bushire	Wheat mill	Aqa Hasan
	Wheat mill	Hoseyn + Habib Dehdashti
	Wheat mill	Sayyed `Ali
	Wheat mill	Hajji Gholam Reza
	Wheat mill	Karbala'i `Ali
	Wheat mill	Karbala'i Abol-Khabbaz
	Wheat mill	Karbala'i Ahmad
	Wheat mill	Sayyed Kazem Dehdashti
	Electricity & ice making	Private company
	Ice making	Haygi Mekzad
Abadan	Steam mill	Hajji Hasan
	Steam mill	Hajji Abul
	Steam mill	Hajji Mostafa
	Electricity	Mlrza Hoseyn Movaqqar
	Ice making	Ostad Da'ud + Badi`
Dezful	Rice cleaning	Sayyed Moh. Khan Vesal & Comp.
Fallahiyeh	Steam mill	Hajji Masjed
Hendiyan	Steam mill	Karbala'i Mandani + Hajji Ra'is al-Tojjar Deylami
Nishapur	Electricity	Malek Qasem Mirza'i
	Electricity	Municipality

Location	Type	Owner/Founder
	Cotton ginning	Hajji `Abdollah Bros.
	Cotton ginning	Hambarsom & Co.
	Cotton ginning	`Aliyof
	Cotton ginning	Haqq Nazariyan
Torbat	Electricity & Cotton ginning	Aqa-ye Farshi
Quchan	Alcohol	Hasan Aqa Kashaneski & Co.
	Electricity	Municipality + M. Hartavaniyan
Mashhad	Electricity	Shrine
	Cigarette making	Kuzehkonani
Rasht	Soap making	`Alibandeh Qolipur
	Soap making	Ebrahim Ghaffarzadeh & Comp.
	Rice cleaning	Mashhadi Moh. Hoseyn Mikhchi
	Ice making	Hajji Rostam Badkubehi & Hamzavi
	Ice making	Yusof Gushfil
	Ice making	Mr. Das Kupikes
	Silk weaving	Hajji Mo`in al-Tojjar + Russians
	Silk weaving	Russian
	Electricity	Mo`en al-Mamalek & Co.
	Hosiery	Hoseyn Aqa Esteqamat
	Hosiery	`Abbas Jurabchi + Moh. Ebrahim San`at
Lahejan	Electricity	Arbab Keykhosrow
	Rice cleaning	Darakub Biliris
	Rice drying, 9 plants	Various persons
	Tea factory	State
	Tea factory, 5 plants	Various persons
Pahlavi	Wheat mill	Abrishomi Comp.
	Timber	Tata'os & Co.
	Ice making	Idem
	Electricity	Not specified
Lengerud	Cotton dryers, 8 plants	Various persons
Soltanabad	Electricity	Seham al-Soltan Bayat & Co.
	Paint, dyeing, soap making	Tavtanjiyan
Bandar-e Gaz	Timber	Simun
	Cotton cleaning & electricity	`Abdollah Qasemiyan
	Cotton cleaning, soap making, cotton seed press, timber	Karbala'i Moh. Hoseyn Akhvin
	Cotton cleaning	Russian state

Location	Type	Owner/Founder
Shahrud	Electricity (for cinema, mill, and lemonade making)	Hajji `Ali Akbar Sadeq & Co.
	Cotton cleaning	Messrs. Ikhyani
	Cotton ginning in Jajarm district	Idem
Lurestan	Electricity	Hajji `Abdol-Karim Amini, Sayyed Mojtabi
	Electricity	Soltan Hesam al-Dim Raghebiyan
Astarabad	Electricity	Bagrad Martaniyana
	Cotton ginning (water)	Hajji Sayyed Kazem Hoseyni
Kord Mahalleh	Cotton ginning (water) 14 small plants	N.N.
Gemesh Tepeh	Motor mills, 4 plants	N.N.
Hamadan	Electricity	Hajji Naser al-Mamalek Sharif & Co.
	Match factory	Hajji Hasan Partavi
Kashan	Electricity	Keykhosrow Jampur Parsi & Co.
	Cotton ginning	Hajji Taqi Aqa-ye Taqavi
Qom	Electricity Astaneh	Shrine
	Cotton ginning	Russian Cotton Company
	Electricity Bozorg	State (for the Shrine)
`Aliabad	Silk factory	Qannad + Municipality
Sari	Electricity	Qannad + Municipality
Babol	Cotton ginning Barforush, 6 plants – one idle; the rest operate 4 months per year	Various persons
	Electricity	Qannad + Municipality
	Oil pressing, soap making	Qannad + Mirza Gholam Hoseyn Chitsazi & Co.
	Electricity	Qannad + Municipality
Mashhad-e Sar	Electricity	Fisheries Comp.
	Cotton ginning	Qannad

APPENDIX B

List of factories in Iran in 1940.

TABRIZ				
Name/owner	Type of factory	Date of erection	No. of workers	Source
Khosrovi	Leather, tannery	Before 1931	n.a.	FO 371/20830
Omid	Idem	Idem	5,000	Idem
Iran	Idem	Idem	n.a.	FO 371/27249
Vahabzadeh Bros.	Idem	1936	n.a.	Pars Agency (e) 217
Vahabzadeh Bros.	Skin pickling	Before 1931	n.a.	Idem
Khoy'i	Matches	Idem	n.a.	Idem
Qazvini	Cotton spinning	Idem	400	Idem
Khoy'i Calcuttachi	Idem	Idem	n.a.	Idem; Mahrad 1978, 258
Idem	Wool spinning	Idem	n.a.	Pars Agency (e) 217
Idem	Wool weaving	1936	n.a.	Idem
Qazvini	Wool spinning & weaving	1936	n.a.	Idem
Jurabchi	Idem	Before 1931	300	Idem; Mahrad 1978, 258
Idem	Wool carding	Idem	n.a.	Pars Agency (e) 217
Sahakiyan	Idem	Idem	183	Idem; Abdullaev 1968, 97
Khoy'i Calcuttachi	Idem	Idem	n.a.	Pars Agency (e) 217
Bavaria	Beer brewery	Idem	n.a.	Idem
Sahakiyan	Idem	Idem	90	Idem; Abdullaev 1968, 79
Idem	Box making	After 1931	n.a.	Pars Agency (e) 217
Idem	Flour mill	Before 1931	n.a.	Idem
Rafi`	Idem	After 1931	n.a.	Pars Agency (e) 217
Sahakiyan	Soap making	Before 1931	n.a.	Idem
Mir	Idem	Idem	n.a.	Idem
Rashidi	Idem	Idem	n.a.	Idem
Yusofi	Idem	Idem	n.a.	Idem

Eqdam	Idem	Idem	n.a.	Idem
Minu	Idem	1936	n.a.	Pars Agency (e) 216
Private	Hosiery, 7 plants	?	670	Abdullaev 1968, 79
Idem	Glass making	1934	n.a.	FO 371/18995, f. 129
Idem	Saw-mill	?	n.a.	Mahrad 1979, 225
State	Grain silo	After 1936	n.a.	Idem, 224
Private	Rice-mill	Idem	n.a.	Idem, 256
Idem	Cotton-ginning 8 plants	?	n.a.	Idem
Idem	Knitted goods	?	70	Idem
	Oil-mill	?	8	Idem
Idem	Tricotage 4 plants	1936	n.a.	Pars Agency (e) 216
ZANJAN				
Sa`adat	Matches	After 1932	n.a.	FO 371/20830, f. 206; Abdullaev 1978, 82
State	Sugar-mill	1936	n.a.	Zahedi 1325, 44; FO 371/20830, f. 206
Lekvani	Flour-mill	After 1932	n.a.	Idem
MARAGHEH				
Bodhaghiyan	Fruit cleaning	Before 1931	n.a.	FO 371/20830, f. 206; Mahrad 1978, 258
REZAYEH				
Unknown	Hemp-mill	1936	n.a.	FO 371/20830, f. 206
MASHHAD				
Private	Leather, tannery	1935	n.a.	Mahrad 1978, 309
State/Ab-e kuh	Sugar-mill	1936	n.a.	Idem
Khosrovi	Cotton spinning	1936	900	Idem; FO 371/27249, f. 375
Private	Flour-mill 3 plants	?		Mahrad 1978, 309
Idem	Oil-press	?	n.a.	Idem
Idem	Papyrus-mill	?	n.a.	Idem
Idem	Cotton weaving	?	n.a.	Idem
Idem	Woll spinning	1932	n.a.	Gielhammer 1939c, 292
Idem	Candy	-	n.a.	Idem
Idem	Chocolate	-	n.a.	Idem
Idem	Furniture	-	n.a.	Idem
Idem	Fruit canning	-	n.a.	Idem
Idem	Alcohol	-	n.a.	Idem
Idem	Cotton-ginning	-	n.a.	Idem

Idem	Saw-mill	-	n.a.	Idem, 225
State	Grain	-	n.a.	Idem, 224
SEMNAN				
Private	Cotton spinning	1932	n.a.	Zahedi 1325, 33; Gielhammer 1939a, 231; Pars Agency (e) 213
VARIOUS				
Kermanshah/ State	Oil-refinery	1935	269	FO 371/20052, f. 213; Korby 1977, 60
Idem	Sugar-mill	1935	700	Zahedi 1325, 44; FO 371/44222, f. 700
Idem	Grain silo	-	n.a.	Mahrad 1978, 225
Kermanshah/ private	tricotage (several)	-	n.a.	Pars Agency (e) 216
Hamadan/Yanegi	Leather, tannery	-	n.a.	FO 371/21900; Mahrad 1978, 225
Hamadan/private	Matches	-	n.a.	Idem
Hamadan/Hakim	Yarn spinning	-	10	Gielhammer 1939c, 294
Ahvaz/private	Cotton spinning & weaving	1935	700	FO 371/20050, f. 2; Gielhammer 1939b, 259
Ahvaz/State	Grain silo	-	n.a.	Mahrad 1978, 224
Bushire/ Etmadiyeh	Cotton spinning & weaving	1936	1,028	FO 371/40222, f. 41
Qom/private	Cotton spinning	1936	n.a.	Pars Agency (e) 214; Gielhammer 1939b, 262
Perskhlopkom	Cotton cleaning	1925	1,500	FO 416/78, Intel Summary nr. 30, 13
Bandar `Abbas/ Khonji	Cotton spinning	1935	n.a.	Pars Agency (e) 213; Gielhammer 1939b, 262
KERMAN				
Private	Cotton spinning	1937	n.a.	Gielhammer 1939b, 262; Abdullaev 1968, 97
Private	Wool carding, 3	?	32	Idem; FO 371/20040, f. 186
YAZD				
Eqbal/private	Cotton spinning	1939	1,074	Abdullaev 1968, 79; FO 371/18995; Gielhammer 1939b, 259; Pars Agency (e) 213
Herati/private	Wool spinning	1935	250	Gielhammer 1939b, 259; Pars Agency (e) 219
Derakhshan/ private	Wool spinning	1933	n.a.	Pars Agency (e) 215
Private	Tricotage (several)	?	n.a.	Pars Agency (e) 216
KASHAN				
Private	Wool carding	1934	10	Abdullaev 1968, 79; Pars Agency (e) 215

Private	Yarn spinning	?	n.a.	Pars Agency (e) 213; Gielhammer 1939b, 262
QAZVIN				
Private	Cotton spinning & weaving	1935	400	Mahrad 1978, 282; Golriz 1326
Private	Wool spinning	1935	400	Mahrad 1978, 282; Golriz 1326, 702 has 320 workers
Private	Flour mill (3)	1932-34	n.a.	Mahrad 1978, 282; Golriz 1326, 705
Private	Wool carding	1939	n.a.	Golriz 1326, 707
Private	Distillery	1933	35	Idem 708
Private	Cotton ginning	1935	30	Idem 713
Private	Leather, tannery	1939	80	Idem 713-14
Private	Oil-mill	1936	32	Mahrad 1978, 282
Private	Soap-works	1937	n.a.	Golriz 1326, 714
Private	Carpet weaving	1939	132	Idem
Private/Qorughli	Wool spinning & weaving	1929	200	Gielhammer 1939c, 292
ISFAHAN				
Vatan/private	Cotton spinning	1923	2,400	FO 371/20050, f. 137
Risbaf/private	Idem	1934	1,100	Idem
Zayandehrud	Idem	1935	1,400	Idem
`Ata al-Molk	Idem	1935	400	Idem
Maktab	Idem	1936	n.a.	Idem
Chit	Idem	1935	n.a.	Idem
Shah Reza	Idem	1935	n.a.	idem
Risandegi-ye pashm	Wool spinning	1936	-	Idem
San`eh-ye pashm	Wool spinning	1936	1,000	Idem
Kaghadh-e Iran	Paper mill	1936	80	Idem; Abdullaev 1968, 85
Private	Paper mill	?	70	Abdullaev 1968, 85
Ettehad-e Shah Reza	Cotton spinning	1936	n.a.	FO 371/20050, f. 137
Katva ?	Idem	1936	n.a.	Idem
Private	Matches	?	n.a.	Abdullaev 1968, 82
Private	Hosiery	?	89	Idem 79
State	Grain silo	?	n.a.	Mahrad 1978, 224
Private	Boot factory	193?	n.a.	FO 371/20050, f. 128
Private ?	Weaving mill	1940		Soheyli 1950, 83
Private ?	Spinning factory	1938	n.a.	Kia 1939, 142; Gielhammer 1939a, 230; Idem 1939b, 259; 1939c, 292

MAZANDARAN & GILAN				
Private	Hosiery (3)	?	54	Mahrad 1978, 224; Abdullaev 1968, 79; Pars Agency (e) 216, 216
State	Jute factory	1933	600	Zahedi 1325, 40; Mahrad 1978, 224; Gielhammer 1939c, 295
Private	Flour mill	?	n.a.	Mahrad 1978, 224
Private	Brewery	?	n.a.	Idem
Private	Saw mill	?	n.a.	Abdullaev 1868, 82
Private	Glass works	?	n.a.	Mahrad 1978, 225
Private	Silk reeling (several)	?	n.a.	Gupta 1947, 74; Kia 1939, 143
ENZELI				
Private	Saw mill	?	n.a.	Mahrad 1978, 225
State	Shipyard	1938	n.a.	Gupta 1947, 76
BABOL				
Private	Leather, tannery	?	n.a.	Mahrad 1978, 225; Abdullaev 1968, 83 says it is in Barforush
Private	Glassworks	?	n.a.	Mahrad 1978, 225
Private	Weaving	?	150	Idem, 295
Private	Oil mill	1935	20	Idem; Pars Agency (e), 218
Private	Soap works	?	n.a.	Pars Agency (e), 152
SHAHI				
State	Cotton spinning	1932	900	Mahrad 1978, 295; Abdullaev 1968, 79 lists 3,396 workers
Private	Fruit canning	?	146	Abdullaev 1968, 81
State	Sugar mill	1933	1,000	Pars Agency (e), 211; Gupta 1947, 73
State	Jute-mill	?	n.a.	Gupta 1947, 74
VARIOUS				
Ashraf/State	Cotton spinning	1935	1,000	Mahrad 1978, 295
Bandar-e Khaz	Oil-mill	?	55	Idem
Bandar-e Khaz	Rice-mill	?	25	Idem
Chalus	Silk weaving	1935	n.a.	Pars Agency (s) 150
Shahrud	Matches	?	n.a.	Abdullaev 1968, 82
Unknown	Rice-cleaning (16)	?	n.a.	Mahrad 1978, 225, 295
Unknown	Tea factories (9)	?	450	Abdullaev 1968, 82
State/Shirgah	Saw-mill	1934	n.a.	Idem; Pars Agency (e), 212
TEHRAN				
Private	Hosiery (17)	?	771	Mahrad 1978, 224; Abdullaev 1968, 79

Private	Flour mills	?	n.a.	Mahrad 1978, 224
State	Grain silo	?	n.a.	Mahrad 1978, 224
Private	Tobacco	1937	1,750	Idem 225; Abdullaev 1968, 81; FO 371/20833, f. 23
Private	Brewery	1934	n.a.	Mahrad 1978, 225; FO 371/18995, f. 129
Private	Leather, tannery (4)	?	n.a.	Mahrad 1978, 225
Private	Matches	?	n.a.	Idem; Abdullaev 1968, 82
State/`Abdol-`Azim	Cement	1934	1,000	Ibid; Mahrad 1978, 225; FO 371/20833
?	Glass-works	1939	520	Mahrad 1978, 225; Abdullaev 1968, 82
State	Silicate	-	n.a.	Mahrad 1978, 225
Private	Saw-mill (3)	-	n.a.	Idem
State/Rey	Glycerine, soap	1940	450	Abdullaev 1968, 81
State	Soda	-	1,024	Idem
Karaj	Chemicals	-	500	Idem
State	Amonia	1936	200	Idem
State	Salt	-	80	Idem
State	Vaccines	-	40	Idem
State	Electrolite	-	200	Idem
State/Vanak	Gas masks	1940	400	Idem
State	Gunpowder	-	500	Idem
State/Karaj	Sugar-mill	1932	n.a.	Pars Agency (e), 149
State/Kahrizak	Sugar-mill	1931	n.a.	Idem
State/Veramin	Sugar-mill	1934	n.a.	Zahedi 1325, 46
Sani` al-Dowleh	Cotton spinning	1904	n.a.	Gielhammer 1939a, 230
Jurabchi	Yarn spinning	1936	n.a.	Pars Agency (e), 214
Private/Qorughli	Yarn spinning	1933	n.a.	Idem; Gielhammer 1939c, 292
Private/Darugar	Soap works	-	n.a.	Pars Agency (e), 216
Private/Meshkat	Cotton spinning	1936	n.a.	Gielhammer 1939c, 262
SHIRAZ				
Stock Company	Cotton spinning & weaving	1929	630	FO 371/40222
Stock Company Fars	Idem	1934	630	Idem; FO 371/20885 & 371/20834 states 3 shifts of 200
State/Marvdasht	Sugar-mill	1935	200 permanent 800 seasonal	FO 371/40222
Dehqan Bros.	Cotton spinning	1939	180	FO 371/20835, f. 22 in one shift

| Khollar Comp. | Spirits & wine | - | n.a. | FO 371/20835, f. 23 |
| State | Grain silo | - | n.a. | Mahrad 1978, 224; Pars Agency (e), 213; Gielhammer 1939b, 258, 262 |

APPENDIX C

Official note that foreigners need to get permission to establish a factory

وزارت امور خارجه

Téhéran
le 29 Djamadi ol san 1322
(10 septembre 1904)

Monsieur le Ministre

Des rapports reçus par le gouvernement mentionnent que des sujets étrangers ont l'intention d'établir des fabriques pour manipuler le coton, les cocons de soie etc. Ces sujets étrangers n'ont pas demandé jusqu'à présent l'autorisation nécessaire du gouvernement Persan.

J'ai l'honneur de Vous prier de bien vouloir faire savoir aux sujets de Votre gouvernement que sans l'autorisation du gouv.t. Persan aucun sujet étranger a le droit de construire des fabriques. Pour obtenir cette autorisation ils doivent s'adresser au ministère des Affaires Étrangères afin

Appendix D

Programme of the Ranjbaran (workmen's) Party of Persia

As a religion is composed of orders and rules which God had conveyed through His innocent Prophet to His people who were in need of it for their training, and to express His kindness towards them, so that they under shadow of their belief and by living in accordance with those rules should attain to those things which are necessary for leading a just life and should eventually succeed to their real aim in the next world which is life eternal: Similarly principles consist of complete rules which show the way to achieve certain ends such as freedom of the press and of thought, and the right of assembly which are essential for the removal of the defects of human life. In order to achieve these needs of life two things are essential:

Object

Organization and principle

If the National Government of Persia can take advantage of the geographical importance which is attached to Persia being situated in Central Asia, her political and economic relations with foreign powers will increase: whereas if she ignores the existence of these advantages she will find her Government enmeshed in the policies of foreigners and life will be eternal death for her. Therefore the object of the Workman's Party of Persia (especially at the present time when efforts are being made for the establishment of International peace and political and economic relations) is to gather themselves under one political party and work diligently, without imitation and after seizing the reins of power, to lay the foundations of a Government which shall work in accordance with modern requirements, shall safeguard the country from becoming economically a besieged state and protects her from foreign encroachments. In order to attain these objects it is essential that every honourable and patriotic man, who wishes to safeguard the freedom and independence of Persia and to see her progressive and prosperous and has also in view the maintenance of her historical dignity, should at once join the Workman's Party and without hesitation should follow freely and courageously the caravan of the seekers of justice of the present time. He should devote all his energies to help Persia along the path of progress. The Workman's Party has been organized solely for this purpose. This party is organized under the protection of the 12th Imam and under the shadow of the real union of workmen who form the majority of people of this country. This party expects every member to be honest and upright and to adhere to the principles of Islam.

Fundamental.

The objects of the Workman's Party of Persia are: (*a*) to protect the right of the people to govern themselves by choosing their Government in general elections, (*b*) the cancellation of concessions, (*c*) to uproot the power and pride of the aristocracy, (*d*) to ensure the reward of merit, (*e*) to uphold religion.

Organisation of the Government.

1. To frame special laws is the right of Parliament which is the source of power Government.
2. The Legislative, Judicial, and Executive departments of the National Government should be kept separate from each other.
3. Ministers should be selected from Parliamentary Deputies who are the representatives of the nation.
4. Ministers should be responsible to the National Parliament.
5. Ministers should be responsible for each other's honesty.
6. Laws should only be recognized when they are passed by Parliament.
7. Equality of all persons under the law.
8. Freedom of thought, of the press, of occupation, of residence, and of travel; right of assembly and right to strike.
9. Protection of life, property, and residence.
10. Elections should be public, uniform, secret, and direct.
11. Every person over the age of 15 should have the right to vote. Any person above the age of 30 should be eligible for election.
12. As the *ulema* are deputed to publish and enforce the religious laws of Islam and are the guardians of the rights of the nation, and are considered to be instruments for the carrying out of the orders of the Government they should be brought under departmental control.
13. Primary education should be free and compulsory.
14. Special attention should be paid to female education.
15. Education should be conducted in the national and religious languages.
16. In levying taxes preference should always be given to direct revenues over indirect revenues.
17. Indirect revenues are essential and should be used for introducing improvements of the arts and crafts, to facilitate trade, and to increase the population.
18. Taxation should be levied according to income.
19. Freedom of sale of all foodstuffs.

20. Abolition of all illegal pensions.
21. All religious endowments should be brought under Government control.
22. The income which is derived from religious endowments and in not intended for special purposes should be spent on public education and charitable works.
23. Action should be taken to ensure the circulation of wealth among the nation generally.
24. Rivers, forests, grazing, and mines should be the property of the Government.
25. The employment and labour of boys under the age of 15 should be discouraged.
26. Working hours for workers should be fixed at 8 hours per day.
27. In addition to other public holidays Friday should be understood as an official holiday.
28. National resources should be exploited and agriculture should be encouraged.
29. The cornering of grain should be prohibited.
30. The dealings of the Government with villagers and labourers should be on a just basis.
31. Enforcement of laws by Government on the public should be uniform.
32. Abolition of forced labour demanded by landlords from agriculture and villagers.
33. Abolition of the rights of landlords over the villagers.

Military.

1. Military service should be compulsory for all.
2. All persons of good health should serve for two years with the colours.

Justice.

1. Court proceedings generally should be free of cost, and their actions should be prompt and uniform for every body.
2. The cause of arrest should be declared promptly to prisoners.

Printed at the 'Tus' Press, Sarshur Bazar (Meshed)
Source: FO 371/7821, f. 59.

BIBLIOGRAPHY

Transcripts of Crown-copyright records in the Public Records Office (PRO) appear by permission of the Controller of Her Majesty's Stationary Office.

Abdullaev, A. 1963. *Promyshlennost i Zarozhdenie Rabochecego Klassa v kontse XIX nachala XX*. Baku: Nauka.

Abdullaev, A. 1968. *Formirovanie Rabochego Klass Iran*. Baku: Nauka.

Abrahamian, E. 1982. *Iran between two Revolutions*. Princeton: Princeton Univ. Press.

Adamiyyat, Fereydun. 1348/1969. *Amir Kabir va Iran*. Tehran: Amir Kabir. Accounts and Papers, House of Commons, Parliamentary Papers.

———. 1351/1972. *Andisheh-ye Taraqqi va Hokumat-e Qanun-e `Asr-e Sepahsalar*. Tehran.

——— & Natiq, Homa. 1356/1977 *Afkar-e ejtema`i va siyasi va eqtesadi dar athar-e montasher nashodeh-ye dowran-e Qajar*. Tehran: Amir Kabir.

Aderholt. K. 1938. "Der Aufbau einer Iranischen Textilindustrie." *Orient Nachrichten* 1. January: 86-89.

Adli, A. 1960. *Aussenhandel und Aussenwirtschaftspolitik des Iran*. Berlin: Druckner und Humblot.

Administrator-General of the Finances of Persia. 1923. *Fifth Quarterly Report*, October-December. Tehran.

———. 1924. *Ninth Quarterly Report*, October-December. Tehran.

Alami, E.K. 1939. "Le redressement économique en Perse." Ph. D. diss. University of Paris, Law Faculty

Algar, H. 1969. *Religion and State in Iran 1785-1906*. Berkeley: University of California Press.

Anon. 1946. "Isfahan," *Royal Central Asiatic Journal* 33.

———. 1973. *Die Kommunistische Bewegung Irans*. Munich: Verlag 20 Mai

Ardakani, Hosein Mahbubi. 1353/1974. *Tarikh-e mo'assasat-e tamaddoni-ye jadid dar Iran*. 3 vols. Tehran: Daneshgah.

Ashraf, Ahmad. 1359/1980. *Mavane`-ye tarikhi-ye roshd-i sarmayehdari dar Iran*. Tehran: Payam.

Avery, P. 1965. *Modern Iran*. London : Benn.

Bahar, Malek al-Sho`ara. 1357/1978. *Tarikh-e mokhtasar-e ahzab-e siyasi-ye Iran*. Tehran: Amir Kabir, 2nd edition.

Bairoch. P. 1976. *Urban unemployment in Developing Countries*. Geneva: ILO.

Bakhash, Shaul. 1978. *Iran: Bureaucracy & Reform under the Qajars: 1858-1896*. London: Ithaca.

Banque Mellie Iran (1939a) "Le Rendement des Sociétés Anonymes en Iran" *Bulletin* 32, 802–14.

Banque Mellie Iran (1939b) "L'éclairage électrique en Iran" *Bulletin*, 41, Novembre, 535–549.

Bashkirov, A. 1948. *Rabotsee Profsoyuznoe Dvizhenie v Irana*. Moscow: Nauka.

Berichte über Handel und Industrie. Band 14, Heft 7, Juni 1910.

Bharier, Julian. 1969. "Capital Formation in Iran 1900–1965." Ph. D. thesis London University, Economics Dept.

———. 1971. *The Economic Development of Iran: 1900–1970*. Oxford: Oxford Univ. Press.

Browne E.G. 1909. *The Persian Revolution*. Cambridge. Cambridge UP.

Bulletin, Banque Mellie Iran (various issues).

Chaqueri, C. (1972) *Historical Documents On the Labour Movement in Iran*. Florence : Mazdak. 7 vols. Vol. 4 Avetis Mikailian (Sultanzade) Selected writings

———. ed. 1974–1978. *Historical Documents on the Labour Movement in Iran*. 7 volumues. Vol. 4 Avetis Mikailian (Sultanzade) Selected writings. Florence: Mazdak.

———. ed. 1978. *The Condition of the Working Class*. Florence: Mazdak.

———. ed. 1979a. *Le Mouvement communiste en Iran : articles et documents*. Florence : Mazdak, Histoire du mouvement ouvrier et révolutionnaire en Iran. vol. 2

———. ed. 1979b. *The Revolutionary Movement in Iran versus Great Britain*. Florence: Mazdak.

———. ed. 1359/1980. "Asnad-e Tarikhi-ye jonbesh-e sendika'i," *Ketab-e Jom`eh*. Ordibehesht 33.

Conolly, V. 1936. "The Industialization of Persia," *RCAJ*, 22-45.

Curzon, G. 1892. *Persia and the Persian Question*. 2 vols. London: Longmans, Green & Co.

d'Erp, Baron. 1893 "Rapport concernant l'établissement d'une sucrerie en Perse." Bruxelles.

DCR or Diplomatic and Consular Deports: Annual Series: DCR, no. 1376, Isfahan, 1892-93; DCR no. 1662, Isfahan, 1894-95.

Djazaeri, Chams-ed-Dine. 1938. *La crise économique mondiale at ses répercussions en Iran*. Paris.

Doevel, H. 1933. *Persiens auswärtige Wirtschaftsbeziehungen*. Hamburg: Friedrichsen, de Gruyter & Co.

Donboli, `Abd al-Razzaq. 1351/1972. *Ma'ather-e Soltaniyeh*. ed. Gholam Hosein Sadri Afshar. Tehran: Ebn Sina.

Dowlatabadi, Yahya. n.d. *Hayat-e Yahya*. 4 vols. Tehran: Ebn Sina.

Eastwick, E. B. "Report" [on the trade of Persia]. *Accounts and Papers* 63 (1863), 70–71

Edwards, A. C. 1949. *The Persian Carpet, a survey of the carpet weaving industry of Persia.* London: Duckworth.

Ehtechami, H. 1930. *La situation économique de la Perse*. Montpellier.

Ellwell-Sutton 1958. *Persian Oil. A Study in Power Politics*. London.

Entner, Marvin L. 1956. *Russo-Persian Commercial Relations, 1828-1914*. Gainsville: Univ. of Florida Press.

Ettehadiyeh, Mansureh. 1361/1982. *Maramnamehha va Nezamnamehha-ye Ahzab-e siyasi-ye Iran dar dovvomin dowreh-ye Majles-e shura-ye melli*. Tehran: Tarikh.

Ettela`at Newspaper. 1329/1950. *Ettela`at dar yek rob` qarn*. Tehran.

———. 1329/1950. *Ettela`at dar yek rob` qarn*. Tehran: Ettela`at.

E`temad al-Saltaneh (Sani` al-Dowleh), Mirza Mohammad Hasan Khan. 1298-1300/1880-83. *Montazam-e Naseri*. 3 vols. Tehran (lithograph).

———. 1301-03/1884-86. *Matla` al-Shams*. 3 vols. Tehran 1301–03 (lithograph).

———. 1345/1967. *Ruznameh-ye Khaterat*. ed. Iraj Afshar. Tehran: Amir Kabir.

———. 1357/1978. *Sadr al-Tavarikh*. ed. Mohammad Moshiri. Tehran.

Farmanfarmayan, Hafez. 1968. "The Forces of Modernization in Nineteenth Century Iran." In: *Beginnings of Modernization in the Middle East*, 119-154 edited by W.R. Polk & R.L. Chambers, Chicago: Univ. Chicago Press.

Farrokh, M. 1347/1968. Mo`tasam al-Saltaneh, *Khaterat-e Farrokh*. Tehran: Amir Kabir.

Fatemi, N. S. 1952. *Diplomatic History of Iran, 1917-1923*. New York.

Ferrier. R.W. 1982. *The History of the British Petroleum Company*. London: Cambridge UP, Volume 1.

Fleury, A. 1977. "La Politique Allemande au Moyen Orient 1919–1939." Ph.D. diss. University of Geneva Institute of Advanced International Studies.

Floor, W. M. 1975. "The Guilds in Iran - an Overview from the earliest Beginnings till 1972" *Zeitschrift der Deutschen Morgenländische Gesellschaft* 125, 99–116.

———. 1976. "The merchants (*tujjar*) in Qajar Iran." *Zeitschrift der Deutschen Morgenländische Gesellschaft*, 126, 101-135.

———. 1981. "The Political Role of the Lutis in Iran," In: *Modern Iran, the Dialectics of Continuity and Change*, edited by M.E. Bonine and N.R. Keddie, 83–95. Albany: SUNY.

———. 1984a. "Guilds and Futuvvat in Iran," *Zeitschrift der Deutschen Morgenländische Gesellschaft* 134, 106-114.

———. 1984b. *Industrialization in Iran 1900–1941*. Durham Centre for Middle Eastern and Islamic Studies, Occasional Paper No 23.

———. 1985 a. *Labour Unions, Law & Conditions In Iran: 1900–1941*, Durham : Centre for Middle Eastern & Islamic Studies.

———. 1987. "Asnaf," *Encyclopedia Iranica*.

———. 1991. "Traditional handicrafts and modern industry in Iran: 1800–1914." *Zeitschrift der Deutschen Morgenländische Gesellschaft* 141, pp. 317-52.

———. 1999b. *The Persian Textile Industry, Its Products and Their Use (1500-1925)*. Paris: L'Harmattan.

———. 2001. The Economic Role of the ʿUlama in Qajar Persia, in Linda Walbridge ed. *The Most Learned of the Shiʿa*. New York: OUP, pp. 53-81.

———. 2003. *The Traditional Crafts of Qajar Iran*. Costa Mesa: Mazda.

Foreign Office Files. Public Record Office, London (transcripts of Crown copy-right records in the PRO appear by permission of Her Majesty's Stationary Office), 248/906, 1030, 1072, 1259, 1278, 6450, 7829, 10131, 18995, 21900

———. 371/902, 950, 7809, 7819, 7821, 7823, 7828, 7836, 9024, 9026 (Resht Diary), 9027, 9030, 9034, 9035, 9506, 13783, 13784, 18995, 20046, 20050, 20830, 20834, 20835, 20839, 21900, 27249, 40222

———. 416/70, 72, 73, 74. 75, 76, 77, 78, 79, 80, 81, 82, 83, 84, 95, 112(Annual report, 1923), 113 (Annual report, 1928), 194.

Fraser, J.B. 1826. *Travels and Adventures in the Persian Provinces on the banks of the Caspian Sea*. London: Longman, Rees, Orme, Brown, and Green.

Ghadimy. M. 1923. *Les finances publiques de la Perse*. Paris.

Gielhammer, L. 1939a. "Der Aufbau einer Industrie in Iran I" *Orient Nachrichten* 15, August, 228–231.

———. 1939b "Der Aufbau einer Industrie in Iran II" *Orient Nachrichten* 15, August, 258–63.

———. 1939c. "Der Aufbau einer Industrie in Iran III" *Orient Nachrichten*, 18/19, October, 292–96.

———. 1940a. "Zum Aufbau einer Industrie in Iran (I)" *Der Nahe Osten*, 22–25, 122.

———. 1940b. "Zum Aufbau einer Industrie in Iran (II)" *Der Nahe Osten*. 1, 7, 122.

———. 1941. "Wichtige iranische Industrie Zweige" *Der Nahe Osten*, 27–29.

Gilbar, Gad. 1976. "Demographic Developments in Late Qajar Persia, 1870-1906." *Asian and African Studies* 11, 125-56.

———. 1978. "The Persian Economy in the mid-19th century." *Welt des Islams* 29, 177-211.

Glaesner, H. 1976. "Das Dritte Reich und des Mittlere Osten." Ph. D. diss. Univ. of Würzburg.

Golriz, M.A. 1326/1947. *Minudar ya Bab al-Jennah-ye Qazvin*. Tehran: Daneshgah.

Government of Iran. 1952. *Some Documents on the Conditions of the Iranian Wokers under the Ex-Anglo Iranian Oil Co.*

Government of the Netherlands, 1893. Ministerie van Waterstaat, Handel en Nijverheid, *Verzameling van Consulaire en andere Verslagen en Berichten* (Legatie Teheran. Jaarverslag over 1892), no. 125 (1893).

Gray, F. A. 1937. *Report on Economic and Commercial Conditions in Iran during 1937.* London : HMSO.

———. 1938. *Economic and Commercial Conditions In Iran Report.* London: HMSO.

Grunwald, K. & Ronall. J.O. 1960. *Industrialization in the Middle East.* New York: Council for Middle Eastern Affairs.

Gupta, Raj Narain. 1947. *Iran, an economic study.* New Delhi: Indian Institute of International Affairs.

Hadow. R.H. 1925. *Report on the Trade and Industry of Persia.* London: HMSO.

Ha'eri. A.H. 1977. *Shi'ism and Constitutionalism in Iran.* Leiden: Brill.

Hechmat al-Salatana, S.K. 1920. *La Perse économique.* Paris.

Hedayat, Mehdiqoli. 1344/1965. *Khaterat va Khatarat.* Tehran : Zavvar.

Hedayat, Mehdiqoli Mokhber al-Saltaneh. 1363/1984. *Gozaresh-e Iran.* 4 vols. Reprint Tehran: Noqreh.

Hezb-e Tudeh. 1349/1970. *Salnameh-ye Tudeh.* n.p.

Hushyar, M. ed. 1330/1951. *Enqelab-e mashru`iyat-e Iran va rishehha-ye ejtema`i va eqtesadi-ye an.* Tehran.

IMF, *International Financial Statistics.* February 1950

ILO or International Labour Organisation:

1928a (note 262) *Informations Sociales* 10, Avril-Juin 109-110

1928b (note 256) idem   10, Avril-Juin 381-382

1932 (note 268) idem   41, Janvier-Mars 135

1933a (note 270) idem   47, Juillet-Septembre 335

1933b (note 271) idem   48, Octobre-Décembre 11

1934 (note 272) idem   50, Avril-Juin 185-86

1936a (note 277) idem   58, Avril-Juin 32

1936b (note 274) idem   59, Juillet-Septembre 222

1937a (note 277) idem   63, Juillet-Septembre 342

1937b (note 278) idem   64, Octobre- Décembre 204

1937c "Récentes enquêtes en Iran." *Revue Internationale du Travail*, 36, 881-884.

1938 "L'Industrie cotonière." *Revue Internationale du Travail*, 37

1939a (note 280) *Informations Sociales*, 69, Janvier-Mars, 441

1939b (note 289) idem 70, Avril-Juin, 491

1939c (note 279)idem 72 Octobre-Décembre, 719

1950. *Labour Conditions in the Oil Industry in Iran*. Geneva: ILO

Issawi, C. 1971. *The Economic History of Iran 1800–1914*. Chicago: Chicago UP.

Ivanov, M.S. 1356/1977. *Tarikh-e Novin-e Iran*. Stockholm: Hezb-e Tudeh-ye Iran.

Jamalzadeh, Mohammad 'Ali. 1335/1916. *Ganj- e Shayegan*. Berlin: Kaveh.

Janab, Aqa Mir Sayyed 'Ali. 1303/1924. *Ketab al-Esfahan*. Isfahan (lithograph).

Kambakhsh 1972. *Nazari beh Jonbesh-e Kargari va Komunisti dar Iran*. Strassfurt: Hezb-e Tudeh-ye Iran.

Kechavarz, K. 1934. "La Protection du Travail des Femmes et des Enfants en Perse." Ph. D. thesis., Univ. of Toulouse.

Kedourie, E. & Haim. S.G. eds. 1961. *Towards a modern Iran*. London : Cass.

Keyhan, Mas'ud. 1311/1932. *Joghrafya-ye mofassal-e Iran*. Tehran. Ebn Sina. 3 vols.

Khosropour. A. 1956. "Le Contrôle des Changes en Iran depuis 1930 jusqu'à la fin 1955." Ph.D. diss. University of Paris. Law Faculty.

Kia, Abbas Chamseddine. 1939. "Essai sur l'histoire industrielle de l'Iran." Ph.D. diss. University of Paris.

Korby, W. 1977. *Probleme der industriellen Entwicklung und Konzentration in Iran*. Wiesbaden: Reichert.

Kuznetsova. N. A. 1358/1978. *Owza`-ye Siyasi va Eqtesadi - Ejtema`i-ye Iran [Ocherki novoi istorii Irana xix- nachalo xx vv*, Moscow 1978] tr. Sirus Izadi. Tehran.

Ladjevardi, H. 1981. "Politics and Labour in Iran: 1941–49." Ph.D. diss. Oxford university. (Also published under the same title in 1981 by Syracuse UP, but quotes are from the dissertation).

Lahuti A. n.d *Zendegani-ye man*. Tehran.

Lambton. A.K.S. 1954. *Islamic Society In Persia*. London.

———. 1970. "Persian Trade Under the early Qajars." In: *Islam and the Trade of Asia*, 215-44 edited by D.S. Richards. Oxford: Cassirer & Univ. Pennsylvania Press.

League of Nations, Economic Intelligence Service 1938, *Public Finance 1928-1937* Volume LVII: Iran. Geneva.

League of Nations, *Monthly Bulletin of Statistics*, May 1940. Geneva.

Letter August 17, 1907. Record Group B 993, Ministerie van Buitenlandse Zaken, den Haag (the Netherlands)[these records have been transferred to the Algemeen Rijks Archief around 1990, probably to record group Legatie Perzië]

Lenczowski. G. 1968. *Russia and the West in Iran*. New York: Greenwood Press.

Lingeman, F. R. 1928. *Report on the Finance & Commerce of Persia 1925–1927*. London: HMSO.

———. 1930. *Economic Conditions in Persia*. London: HMSO.

MacLean, H.W. 1904. *Report on the Conditions and Prospects of British Trade in Persia*. Accounts and Papers: HMSO.

Mahrad, A. ed. 1978. *Iran am Vorabend des II. Weltkrieges, Ein Materialsammlung deutscher, britischer und sowjetischer Geheimberichte*. Osnabrück: Eigen Verlag.

———. 1979. *Die Wirtschafts- und Handelsbeziehungen zwischen Iran und dem nationalsozialistichen Dritten Reich*. Anzali : Gilan Publikation

Majd al-Islam Kermani, Ahmad. 1350/1971. *Tarikh-e enqelab-e mashrutiyyat-e Iran*. 3 vols. ed. Mahmud Khalilpur. Isfahan: Daneshgah.

Majles-e Shura-ye Melli. n.d. (1924?) *Modhakerat-e Majles*, 4th Session. Tehran. Now also digitally available, see [http://www.yadashena.com/]

———. *Majmu'eh-ye Qavanin-e Mozu'eh va Mosubat-e dowreh-ye panjom-e taqniniyeh*. Tehran: Majles Printing Office.

Malcolm, John. 1820. *The History of Persia from the early period to the present time*. 2 vols. London: John Murray.

Malek, Rahim Rezazadehi. 1357/1978. "Nakhostin tajalliyat-e nahzat-e kargari dar Iran," *Naqd va Tahqiq* 4, 53-70.

Malekzadeh, M. 1328–38/1949–56. *Tarikh-e enqelab-e mashrutiyat-e Iran*, Tehran: Soqrat. 6 vols.

Mani. S. 1325/1946. *Tarikhcheh-ye Nahzat-e Kargari dar Iran*. Tehran: Taban.

Matindaftari, A. 1304/1925. *Kelid-e esteqlal-e eqtesadi-ye Iran*. Tehran: Majles.

Mazandarani, Gh.Vahid. 1316/1937. *Eqtesad-e melli va siyasat-e Iran*. Tehran: Ja'fari.

Migeod, Heinz-Georg. *Die persische Gesellschaft under Nasiru'd-Din Shah (1848-96)*. Berlin: Klaus Schwarz.

Millspaugh, A. C. 1926. *The Financial and Economic Situation of Persia, 1926*. New York.

———. 1946. *Americans in Persia*. Washington DC: Brookings

———. 1925. *The American Task in Persia*. New York: The Century.

Moghadem, G. 1956. "Iran's Foreign Trade Policy and Economic Development in the Interwar Period." Ph.D. diss. Stamford University, Economics Department.

Monthly Labour Review 1946. US Government.

Morgan, J. de 1905. *Histoire et Travaux de la Délégation en Perse*. Paris.

Mosaddeq al-Saltaneh, Mohammad 1332Q/1913. *Kapitulasiyon va Iran*. Tehran.

Mostowfi, 'Abdollah. n.d. *Sharh-e Zendegani-ye man*. Tehran: Zavvar, 2nd edition.

NA, (National Archives, The Hague, the Netherlands) Legatie Perzië, bundel 22, letter nr. 96, note verbale September 10, 1902.

Naficy, H. 1924. *L'impôt et la vie économique et sociale en Iran*. Paris.

Neligan, A.R. 1926. "Public health in Persia." *The Lancet* 20 March, 635–39.

Olmer, U. 1906. "L'Industrie Persane," *Nouvelles Archives des*

Missions Scientifiques et Littéraires, 16, 1-110.

Ossetrov V. 1922. "Rabochee professional'noe dvizhenie v Persii," *Novii Vostok*, 2.

Ovanessiyan, A. 1974. "Khaterati dar bareh-ye fe`aliyat-e sazman-e hezb-e komunist dar Iran," In *Historical Documents on the Labour Movement in Iran*, edited by C. Chaqueri. Florence: Mazdak. vol. 1.

Pars Agency 1929.	*Salnameh* 1308/1929
Pars Agency (a)	*Salnameh* 1309/1930
Pars Agency (b)	*Salnameh* 1311/1932
Pars Agency (c)	*Salnameh* 1312/1933
Pars Agency (d)	*Salnameh* 1314/1935
Pars Agency (e)	*Salnameh* 1315/1936
Pars Agency (f)	*Salnameh* 1319/1940

Polak, J.E. 1865. *Persien, das Land und seine Bewohner*. 2 vols. Leipzig: F.A. Brockhaus.

Pour Homayoun. A. 1937. "La Banque Nationale de l'Iran et son Rôle dans le Développement du Pays." Ph.D. diss. University of Paris, Law Faculty.

Rabino, H.L. 1352/1973. *Mashruteh-ye Gilan*. Resht: Ta`ati. Edited by M. Roshan. Tehran: Tahhuri.

Radimsky, W. 1909. *Industrie und Gewerbe Verhältnisse im Persien*. Wien.

Ravasani, S. n.d. *Sowjetrepublik Gilan. Die sozialistischen Bewegung in Iran seit Ende des 19 Jhdt bis 1922*. Berlin: Basis.

Rezun, M. 1981. *The Soviet Union and Iran*. Alphen aan de Rijn: Sijthoff & Noordhoff.

RMM or *Revue du Monde Musulman*, Paris.

Safa'i, Ebrahim. 1344/1965. *Rahbaran-e mashruteh*. Tehran.

Safiniya, R. 1307/1928. *Kelid-e Esteqlali-ye gomroki-ye Iran*. Tehran: Ferdousi.

Seidov, R.A. 1974. *Iranskaja Burzhuazja v kontse XIX nachala XX veka*. Moscow: Nauka.

Sen Gupta, P.N. 1968. "Food Policy and Planning Based on Household Food Consumption & Nutrition Survey - Report to the Government of Iran." Rome, FAO (mimeo).

Setareh-ye Sorkh 7, April 8 1960 (published in Germany).

Shaje`i, Zahra. 1344/1965. *Namayandegan-e Majles-e Shura-ye Melli dar bist va yek dowreh-ye qanungodhari*. Tehran: Daneshgah.

Shidfar, Z. 1339/1960. *Hoquq-e Kar va San`at*. Tehran: Daneshgah. 3 vols.

Simmonds, S. 1935. *Economic Conditions in Iran*. London: HMSO.

Soheily. K. 1950. "Essai sur l'industriallsation de l'Iran." Dissertation University of Neuchâtel, Law Faculty. Montreux.

Some Documents on the Conditions of the Iranian Workers under the Ex-Anglo Iranian Oil Co. Tehran. Government of Iran. 1952.

Stolze F. & Andreas, F.C. 1885. "Die Handelsverhältnisse Persiens." In *Petermanns Mitteilungen* Erg.-Band. 17, no. 77.

Tahvildar, Mirza Mohammad Hoseyn Khan. 1341/1962. *Joghrafiya-ye Isfahan*. Ed. M. Setudeh. Tehran: Daneshgah.

Tehran Municipality. 1310/1931. *Second Statistical Yearbook of the City of Tehran, 1925–29*. Tehran: Majles. or Baladiyeh-ye Tehran (Servis-e Ma'aref va Ehsa'iyeh va Nashiriyat), *Dovvomin Salnameh-ye Ehsa'iyeh-ye Shahr-e Tehran* (Tehran 1310/1931).

Temple, B. 1922. *Report on the Trade and Transport Conditions in Persia to January 1922*. London: HMSO.

Thompson, R.F. 1864. "Report [on the trade of Persia]." UK Government, Parliamentary Paper, *Accounts and Papers* 30-2, LXI 2 (3392).

United Nations 1951. *Public Finance Information Papers*, No.4. New York.

US Government. 1946. *Monthly Labor Review*. 63, 56.

Vambery, A. 1884. *His life and adventures*. London.

Vaziri, Ahmad `Ali Khan. 1346/1967. *Joghrafiya-ye Kerman*. ed. Bastani Parizi, Tehran: Farhang Iran Zamin.

Waterfield, G. 1973. *Professional Diplomat 1880–1961*. London.

Weaver, CW.H. 1933. "Notes sur un Voyage en Inde, en Irak, en Perse, et en Turquie," *Revue Internationale du Travail* 28, 516–522.

Wilber, D. 1975. *Reza Shah Pahlavi*. Hicksville (NY): Exposition Press.

Williamson, J.W. 1927. *In a Persian Oil Field*. London: Benn.

Wilson. Arnold. 1942. *South West Persia. Letters and Diary of a Young Political Officer 1907–1*. London: Oxford UP.

Wirth, E. 1976. *Der Orienteppich und Europsa Ein Beitrag zu den vielfälltigen Aspekten west-ostlicher Kulturkontakte und Wirtschaftsbeziehungen*. Erlangen (Erlanger Geographischis Arbeiten 37).

Yanegani, E. 1935. "Recent Financial and Monetary History of Persia." Ph.D. diss. Columbia University, economics department.

Zabih, S. 1969. *The Communist Movement in Iran*. Berkeley : California UP.

Zahedi, `Ali. 1325/1947. *Sanaye`-ye Iran ba`d az jang*. Tehran.

INDEX

Ayn

'ababaf, 6
'Abbas Mirza, 3, 10, 11
'Abdorrahim Roshbilkov, 69
'Adalat, 38
'Ali Dashti, 43, 92
'Ali Qorban Niazochli, 69
'Ali Zhaleh, 47
'assar-e rowghan, 5
'Ata al-Molk, 123, 172
'Ata'ollah, 61

A

Abadeh, 78
Abdul Husain Dehqan, 82
Abo'l-Fazel Lesani, 43
Adib al-Saltaneh, 60
adult education, 48, 65
Agricultural Bank, 131, 132
Ahvaz, 56, 58, 68, 70, 71, 72, 73, 130, 131, 138, 171
a'inehsaz, 6
Akbar Mas'ud Saram ud-Dawla, 82
Ali Agha Hamadanian, 82
Ali Almasi, 82
Ali Muhammad Dehqan, 82
Amanollah, King of Afghanistan, 63
Amin al-Zarb, 14, 15, 17, 18, 20
Amol, 14, 17, 136
aniline, 17
Anjoman-e Asnifiyeh, 58
Anjoman-e Eslami, 19
Anjoman-e Ettehadiyeh-ye Telegrafi, 34
Anjoman-e Markazi-ye Asnaf, 58
Anjoman-e Sharqi, 19
anti-communist bill, 78
Apin, 44
Ardestan, 19
Armenian communist 'Workers Union', 53

Armenians, 32, 45, 54
Ata al Mulk, 82
Ayandeh, 125
Azad khvahan, 53
Azerbaijan, 10, 12, 36, 52, 66, 79, 87, 105, 107
Azizullah Maghen, 82
Azizullah Shekib, 82

B

Baharistan Nowbakht, 43
Baku, 32, 33, 38, 45, 57, 181
Bandar-e Khaz, 173
banna, 6
Banyor, 47
Barq press, 62
Basra, 16, 57, 69, 71
Belgian, 14, 18, 26, 27, 46
Belgians, 18, 27
Besharat al-Saltaneh, 34
Birikadeh, 14, 20, 119
Boital, 14
Bolshevik, 45, 47, 58, 65
Bolshevik-e Javan, 47, 65
broadcloth factory, 11

C

chakhmaqsaz, 6
chakmehduz, 5
Chalus, 99, 107, 108, 173
charmiduz, 5
children, 8, 22, 33, 64, 76, 78, 80, 85, 86, 88, 89, 90, 93, 98, 99, 101, 106
Chit, 82, 172
chitsaz, 5
Church Missionary Society, 88
Clive, 64, 72, 73, 74, 75
coal mining, 27, 126, 127, 128, 140
Comintern, 49, 58, 63, 66, 78

191

Communist Party, 29, 38, 42, 47, 59, 60, 61, 62, 66, 70, 72, 75
Comrade Reza, 73
Czechoslovakia, 157

D

dah-yakduz, 5
Dar al-Fonun, 12
Dashnakiyun, 32
Davar, 125, 157
davatgar, 6
Dehqan, Mirza Ahmad, 53
Dehqan, Mohammad Khan, 42, 43, 45, 46, 47, 50, 53, 79, 82, 132, 174
diet, 104, 106
Dutch, 7

E

Edareh-ye omur-e kheyriyeh-ye baladiyeh-ye Tehran, 86
Edareh-ye san'at va ma'aden, 128
ehrami, 6
Ejtema'iyun-e 'Amiyun, 32, 45
Eliahu Derlian, 82
Elkington, 68, 69, 70, 71, 72, 73, 74, 75
Enqelab-e sorkh, 43
Enzeli, 14, 20, 22, 27, 29, 32, 33, 34, 36, 38, 40, 42, 46, 48, 50, 51, 63, 64, 116, 126
Eqdam, 43, 170
Eqtesad-e Iran, 47
Ettefaq-e Kargaran, 36
Ettefaq-e Kargaran-e Markazi, 37
Ettehad-e Khorasan, 53
Ettehadiyeh Committee, 51
Ettehadiyeh-ye Kargaran-e Bikar-e Gilan, 51
Ettehadiyeh-ye 'Omumi-ye Asnaf, 59

F

fakhkhar, 5
Farahan, 8
Farhakht Club, 48
Farhang Club, 48
Farhangestan, 125
Fars Electric Comp, 82
Fars Manufacturing Company, 131, 132
Fath 'Ali Shah, 10
Fazlullah Dehesh Ata al-Mulk, 82
Fekr-e Azad, 53
Finch, 64
First Congress of Oil Workers, 66
Firuz Mohammadov, 69
Fletcher, 71, 72, 74, 75

football, 47, 65
French, 10, 14, 21, 125
Frenchmen, 13

G

Gajareh, 128
Ganjiev, 21
Gass, 72, 73
German, 15, 20, 72, 123, 126, 139, 140, 153, 154, 155, 157, 160
Germany, 78, 123, 135, 140, 152, 153, 154, 155, 156, 157, 160, 161, 188
Gholam Hoseyn Khan Nezam al-Dowleh, 62
Gilan, 12, 13, 20, 40, 42, 50, 51, 63, 64, 65, 187, 188
girls, 89, 90, 92, 98, 99, 101
glass factory, 13, 18, 25, 26
golabtunduz, 5
golchehduz, 5
gorji-banan, 63
gorjiduz, 5
Government borrowing, 145
guild, 5, 6, 7, 36, 41, 58, 59, 61, 121

H

Haft Kel, 70
Haidar Ali Immami, 82
hajjar, 6
Hajji Abbas Akbari, 82
Hajji 'Abdul Husain Akhavan Dehdashti, 82
Hajji Aghasi, 11
Hajji Hasan Ali Hamadani, 82
Hajji Mohammad Hoseyn Kazeruni, 19, 82, 164
Hajji Mohammad Taqi Shahrudi, 18
Hajji Muhammad 'Ali Sahaban, 82
Hajji Muhammad Hasan Bihbahani, 82
Hajji Muhammad Kazim Mithqali, 82
Hajji Rahim Aqa-ye Qazvini, 14
Hajji Rughani Rahimzada, 82
Hajji Sayyid Abdul Rahim Mahmudiya, 82
Hajji Sayyid Javad Kasai, 82
Hajji Sayyid Mustaffa Bunakdar, 82
Hajji Zainul Abodin Amin, 82
hakkak, 5
halabisaz, 6
Hamadan, 59, 90, 91, 97, 100, 123, 137, 167, 171
hammal, 63
Hanchak party, 48
Haqiqat, 13, 41, 42, 43, 44, 45, 46, 47, 48, 49, 52, 59
Hasan Kiadeh, 64
Hasan Sultani, 82

Hejazi, 61, 63
Hemmat, 32, 38
Herat, 11
Hey'at-e Asnaf, 58
Hezb-e Kargaran, 47, 52
Hezb-e Ranjbar, 52
Hezb-e Ranjbaran, 53
Hezb-e Tudeh, 33, 34, 36, 64, 65, 66, 79, 185, 186
Hiveh, 27
HMS Cyclamen, 57, 69, 71
Hotz & Zoon, 7
Howzeh-ye Taraqqi-ye Azadi, 53

I

ILO, 80, 81, 82, 84, 87, 88, 89, 90, 91, 92, 93, 94, 95, 96, 97, 100, 101, 104, 109, 110, 181, 185, 186
Imperial Bank, 146, 147, 148, 151, 152
Indians, 54, 55, 56, 58, 67, 69, 72
Iranshahr, 125
Iron, 118, 139
Isfahan, 5, 6, 7, 12, 14, 18, 19, 20, 32, 34, 54, 58, 75, 78, 79, 82, 102, 103, 104, 105, 107, 108, 120, 121, 123, 124, 126, 129, 130, 131, 132, 135, 138, 164, 181, 182, 186, 187, 189
Ishaq Sassoon, 82
Ishtamayun Party, 41
Ittihad Shahrez, 82

J

jahk, 5
Jalal Aryan, 82
Javad Kasai, 82

K

Kaghaz, 82
Kahrizak, 20, 119, 123, 136, 163, 174
kamansaz, 6
Kamsax, 94
Kanva, 82
Kar, 43, 47, 189
Karakahan, 63
kardgar, 6
Kavkaskaya Corporatsie, 50
Keredjivai Sorkhi, 64
Kerman, 4, 8, 16, 17, 34, 38, 58, 80, 84, 85, 86, 87, 88, 89, 90, 91, 92, 98, 99, 135, 138, 189
Kerosene, 14, 104
Keshavarz, 48, 51
Khalil Esmailov, 69
khatamsaz, 6

Khayyam Club, 68
khazduz, 5
Khorasan, 6, 53, 136
Khor Musa, 139
Khoshtaria, 20
Khoy'i brothers, 87
klub-e ejtema`iyun, 60
kolahduz, 5
kolah-e khod va chahar a'inehsaz, 6
kolichehduz, 5
Komunist, 47
Krupp, 140
Kucheki printing shop, 31
Kumiteh-e Kargaran, 53
Kushesh, 43

L

Labor Day, 48, 50, 51, 60, 62, 63, 64, 65, 66
Lalun, 128
Langerud, 34
Liazonov, 20, 32, 33, 34, 120
Linton, Bishop, 88, 89, 91, 99
londrehduz, 5
Lorimer, 85, 86
Lower Classes, 104

M

madraseh-ye san`ati, 124
Mahmudabad, 18, 136
Majma`-e ettefaq-e `omumi, 58
Majma`-ye Eqtesad, 125
Mard-e Azad, 125
Martin Essai, 82
Mashhad, xi, 14, 17, 20, 23, 27, 32, 43, 50, 53, 65, 119, 131, 132, 138, 166, 167
Mashhad-e Sar, 27, 167
Masjed-e Soleyman, 57, 68, 72
Masuleh, 12
May Day, 60, 75
Mazandaran, 11, 18, 64, 65, 79, 107, 108
Mehdi Kemaran, 59
Mehdi Namazi, 82
me`mar, 6
meshkibaf, 5
Michael Frunze, 69
migration, 31, 114, 159
Milan, 14
Miles Essai, 82
Ministry of Industry, 17, 128, 147
Mirza Abdul Samad, 53
Mirza Hoseyn Germani, 72

Mirza Hoseyn Khan Sepahsalar, 15
Mirza Hoseyn Movaqer, 72
Mirza Mehdi Khan Mirzaban, 69
Mirza Saleh, 11
Mirza Shehab Kermani, 60
Mirza Taqi Khan, 10, 11, 12, 15, 17
Mo'azzez al-Dowleh, 88
Modarres, 45, 87
Mohammad Ja'far, 64
Mohammad Shah, 3, 4, 10, 11
Mohammad Vothuq-e Homayun, 43
Mohammareh, 68, 70, 71, 74, 139, 165
Mohammed Aliov, 51
Mokhber al-Saltaneh, 52, 185
Molitor, 46
Moragent, 64
Mortazaqoli Khan Sani' al-Dowleh, 18
Mozaffar al-Din Shah, 85, 120
Mudliar, 55, 56, 57
Muhammad 'Ali Sahiban, 82
Muhammad Herati, 82
Muhammad Jafar Kaziruni, 82
Muhammad Javad Nilfurush, 82
Muhammad Shaikhzada, 82
Muhammad Taqi Shankal, 82
mutual assistance fund, 65

N

naddaf, 6
Nahzat-e Melli, 49
najjar, 6
Nakhtab, 82, 103
nanva, 41
naqdehduz, 5
naqqash-e zargar, 6
naqshduz, 5
Naser al-Din Shah, 11, 12, 16, 17
Nasihat, 43
Nassaji-ye Fars, 82
national bank, 113
Nerces Nercessian, 45
neypichaz-e qalyan, 6
Nezafat, 20, 119
Nishapur, 14, 165
Nosrat al-Dowleh, 45

O

OGPU, 49, 60, 62
orusiduz, 6
Ostad Mirza 'Ali Banna, 61
Ovanessiyan, 42, 47, 48, 50, 59, 60, 61, 63, 65, 66, 72, 188

P

Paper mill, 14, 20, 23, 119, 172
parcheh-ye eslami, 19
Parvaresh Club, 48
Pashm, 82
pashnehsaz, 6
Persaznaft, 51
Peykar, 43, 55, 101
pilgrimage, 151
Pishehvari, 45, 57, 62, 63
power plants, 18, 23
productivity, 26, 27, 101
Profintern, 29, 40, 58, 59, 61, 66, 101
pulakduz, 5
pustinduz, 5

Q

qannad, 5
Qara'at-Khaneh-ye Kargaran, 47
Qaracheh Dagh, 12
Qasim Rashti, 82
Qazvin, 15, 20, 38, 43, 48, 53, 117, 124, 164, 184
qollabduz, 5

R

Rabi'zadeh, 15, 120
rafugar, 6
Ramadan, 97
Rasht, 14, 15, 29, 32, 33, 34, 40, 43, 48, 50, 51, 52, 63, 64, 106, 116, 117, 119, 123, 126, 166
remittances, 55, 151, 152
Reza Khan, 31, 45, 48, 49, 50, 88, 122, 124, 125, 143
Reza Khan Saqaforush, 62
Rezaqoli 'Abdollahzadeh, 47, 61, 164
Ripken, 156
Risbaf, 82, 103, 172
Rogachef, Colonel, 43
Rokn al-Din Khan, 70
Romanovski, 44
Rudbar, 20, 119
Rughani & Cy, 82
Russian, 2, 3, 6, 13, 14, 15, 18, 21, 25, 26, 27, 28, 29, 31, 32, 33, 34, 36, 38, 39, 42, 43, 44, 45, 47, 48, 50, 51, 52, 53, 54, 58, 60, 63, 64, 67, 69, 72, 74, 78, 86, 115, 133, 137, 157, 166, 167
Russians, 13, 22, 27, 28, 36, 45, 50, 51, 63, 64, 68, 69, 70, 74, 100, 116, 166
Rusto, 64

S

sabbagh-e qadak, 5
Sabzevar, 14
Sagaev, 50
Sari, 12, 14, 167
sarkar, 54
Sayyed Asadollah Esfahani, 72
Sayyed Khalil, 70
Sayyed Mehdi Esfahani, 53
Sayyed Mohammad Taqi, 77
Sayyed Ya`qub, 45, 46
Sayyid Muhammad Atzal, 82
Schacht, 154, 156
Schaffter, 90, 91
Semnan, 15, 126, 139, 140
Sepahsalar, 15, 16, 181
Setareh-ye Sorkh, 43, 54, 63, 65, 66, 78, 101, 135, 188
Seyfi, 47, 61
Shafaq-e Sorkh, 43, 91, 92
Shahin, 43
Shahreza, 82, 103
Shamshak, 127, 128, 140
Shamshak mine, 127
shamshirsaz, 6
sha`rbaf, 5
Sharekat-e Eslami, 19
Sharekat-e Jadid, 62
Shareman Khan, 43
Shari`atmadari, 32
Sharikat-i sanayi`-yi dasti, 82
Shateran-e nanva, 41
Sheikh Khaz`al, 54, 57, 108
Sheikh Mohammad Sadr, 53
Shirinov, 64
Shokrollah Sofri, 43
Shumyatski, 44
Shurah-ye Mashaghel-e Kargaran, 86
silk weaving factory, 11
Siyasat, 43
Sohrab Zadeh Mudabber ol-Molk, 44
Soleyman Mirza, 40, 43, 45, 46, 49, 60
Soltanabad, 8, 91, 99, 166
Soviet, 30, 38, 41, 49, 51, 52, 53, 54, 62, 63, 64, 78, 153, 155, 161, 188
Spinning factory, 23, 118, 172
strike, 32, 33, 34, 35, 36, 37, 38, 39, 46, 47, 49, 50, 52, 53, 54, 55, 57, 64, 65, 66, 67, 68, 69, 71, 72, 73, 75, 76, 77, 78, 79, 101, 178
students, 10, 11, 12, 62, 114, 152, 157
Sugar mill, 13, 14, 20, 23, 119, 163, 173

T

Tabriz, 4, 6, 8, 11, 14, 20, 21, 29, 32, 33, 34, 40, 43, 47, 48, 50, 52, 58, 59, 64, 65, 66, 79, 90, 91, 98, 99, 101, 106, 107, 117, 118, 119, 120, 123, 124, 126, 130, 132, 136, 137
Tadayyon, 125
Tajrish, 123
Takammol, 47
Talesh, 20, 119
Tardov, 58
Tehran, 3, 6, 11, 12, 13, 14, 15, 16, 17, 18, 20, 23, 26, 29, 30, 31, 32, 33, 34, 36, 39, 40, 41, 42, 43, 45, 46, 48, 49, 58, 60, 61, 62, 63, 64, 67, 68, 70, 72, 73, 74, 75, 78, 79, 83, 86, 88, 91, 94, 96, 99, 100, 117, 119, 120, 121, 123, 124, 125, 126, 127, 132, 134, 135, 136, 138, 139, 140, 158, 159, 163, 181, 182, 183, 184, 185, 186, 187, 188, 189
Teymurtash, 72, 73, 92, 113, 125
tofangsaz, 6
Tombakov, 54
tramway workers, 33
Tufan, 41, 43

U

Uhlan Company, 71
Union of Bath Attendants, 41
Union of Bootmakers, 41
Union of Editors, 41
Union of Masons, 41
Union of Printers, 41, 49
Union of Tenants, 41
Union of Workmen, 41, 44, 49
Urmiyeh, 15, 20, 119, 120
USSR, 60, 152, 153, 154, 155, 156, 160, 161

V

Vatan, 75, 78, 82, 98, 101, 103, 108, 124, 172
Vazir-e Karma, 32
Vneshtorg, 45

W

wages, 33, 34, 35, 36, 37, 39, 46, 54, 55, 64, 65, 69, 72, 75, 76, 77, 79, 80, 83, 88, 89, 90, 91, 92, 93, 96, 97, 99, 100, 101, 102, 103, 104, 107, 108, 109, 110, 117, 137
women, 7, 8, 22, 71, 72, 74, 78, 80, 85, 88, 91, 93, 98, 99, 100, 101, 116, 125, 132

Z

Zainul Abidin Amin, 82
zargar, 6
zaribaf, 5
Zayandarud, 82
zerehsaz, 6
Ziegler & Co, 7, 8
Zirab, 140

www.ingramcontent.com/pod-product-compliance
Ingram Content Group UK Ltd.
Pitfield, Milton Keynes, MK11 3LW, UK
UKHW051300180426
11947UKWH00020B/1821